MAR 2 3 2017

D1476616

A Table Against Mine Enemies

[1] A Psalm of David.

The LORD is my shepherd; I shall not want.

[2] He maketh me to lie down in green pastures; He leadeth me beside the still waters.

[3] He restoreth my soul; He leadeth me in the paths of righteousness for His name's sake.

[4] Yea, though I walk through the valley of the shadow of death, I will fear no evil, for Thou art with me; Thy rod and Thy staff they comfort me.

[5] Thou shalt preparest before me **a table against mine enemies**; Thou anointest my head with oil; my cup runneth over.

[6] Surely goodness and mercy shall pursue me all the days of my life; and I will dwell in the house of the LORD forever.

¹ מזמור לדוד

ה׳ רעי לא אחסר.

² בנאות דשא ירביצני על מי מנחות ינהלני.

³ נפשי ישובב ינחני במעגלי־צדק למען שמו.

⁴ גם כי־אלך בגיא צלמות לא־אירא רע כי־אתה עמדי. שבטך ומשענתך המה ינחמני.

⁵ תערך לפני **שלחן נגד צררי** דשנת בשמן ראשי כוסי רויה.

⁶ אך טוב וחסד ירדפוני כל־ימי חיי ושבתי בבית־ה׳ לארך ימים.

A TABLE AGAINST MINE ENEMIES

Israel on the Lawfare Front

LARRY M. GOLDSTEIN

gefen publishing house בית הוצאה לאור גפן Est. 1981

JERUSALEM ◆ NEW YORK

Cover Design: Paz Corcos, StudioPaz
Typesetting: Raphaël Freeman, Renana Typesetting

ISBN: 978-965-229-896-6

1 3 5 7 9 8 6 4 2

Gefen Publishing House Ltd.
6 Hatzvi Street
Jerusalem 94386, Israel
972-2-538-0247
orders@gefenpublishing.com

Gefen Books
11 Edison Place
Springfield, NJ 07081
516-593-1234
orders@gefenpublishing.com

www.gefenpublishing.com

Printed in Israel

*   *   *

Library of Congress Cataloging-in-Publication Data

Names: Goldstein, Larry M., author.
Title: A table against mine enemies : Israel on the lawfare front / Larry M.
   Goldstein.
Description: Jerusalem, Israel ; Springfield, NJ : Gefen Publishing House
   Ltd., 2017. | Includes bibliographical references and index.
Identifiers: LCCN 2016035872 | ISBN 9789652298966
Subjects: LCSH: Arab-Israeli conflict--Law and legislation. | War on
   Terrorism, 2001-2009. | War (International law) | Government liability
   (International law) | Lawfare.
Classification: LCC KZ6795.A72 G658 2017 | DDC 341.6095694--
dc 3 LC record available at https://lccn.loc.gov/2016035872

I dedicate this book to the memory of my father, Sergeant Herbert Gold-stein, 347th Regiment, 87th Infantry Division, US 3rd Army under General George S. Patton, Jr. A combat veteran of World War II, he fought in the Battle of the Bulge and in the Assault Crossing of the Rhine River. Born 1925, died 1984. ‏ת.נ.צ.ב.ה.‎[1]

Sergeant Herbert Goldstein, Chicago, Illinois, 1943

---

[1] An acronym for Hebrew words translatable as, "May his soul be bound up in the source of eternal life." This is the traditional engraving on a Jewish headstone, and is derived from Abigail's blessing of David in 1 Samuel 25:29.

Summary Contents

Detailed Contents

Illustrations

Preface

During the twentieth century, warfare was characterized primarily by large armies fighting "conventional warfare," or perhaps more accurately "symmetric warfare" – typically uniformed combatants, with an artillery or air exchange followed by columns of tanks and combat infantrymen. The twenty-first century, on the other hand, has witnessed a transition to "asymmetric warfare" as the dominant form of military conflict. In asymmetric warfare, typically one of the combatants is a political state, with an organized army that uses standard or "conventional" weapons and that fights in a conventional manner, generally with soldiers in uniform. The other combatant is not a political state, but is rather a group of guerillas, or some kind of national movement that is not a state, in which the combatants are not organized into standard units, do not wear uniforms, and do not fight according to standard doctrine.[2]

In asymmetric warfare, the weapons are not limited to guns and bombs –

---

[2] Terms that are set off in quotation marks, and other terms or phrases that may not be known to the reader, are defined in the glossary at the end of the book. The two terms, "conventional warfare" and "symmetric warfare," are often used interchangeably, but they are not the same concept. Conventional warfare clearly includes what are considered to be "conventional weapons," and clearly excludes the ABC of weaponry – atomic, biological, and chemical. "Symmetric warfare" means conflict in which the sides are both regular armies, with uniforms, standard military equipment, command structures, etc. The two concepts overlap, since a war may be conventional and between symmetric forces. However, a conventional war, using conventional weapons, may also be fought between parties that are not equal, meaning that one side is a conventional army and the other side is an irregular or guerilla force. As used herein, "symmetric warfare" means

the new weapons include drones, robots, cyber tools, and the use of "lawfare" to embarrass traditional armies in the eyes of world opinion or to restrict the ability of a nation-state to defend itself. This book is primarily about "lawfare" – the use, or abuse, of law as a weapon of war.[3]

Asymmetric warfare will almost certainly be the main form of military conflict throughout this century. Lawfare will be one of the key weapons used in asymmetric warfare, and will become increasingly important to Israel, the United States, and other nations engaged in asymmetric warfare.[4]

This book focuses specifically on the use of law as a weapon in twenty-first century warfare. It encompasses all physical realms – the land, the sea, and the air. It includes the use of law in current fighting, and possible impacts of law on the forms of fighting that are likely to evolve over the next twenty to thirty years. The emphasis here is Israel, but lawfare is not limited to Israel, and examples are drawn also from the United States and the United Kingdom.

The book is composed of two parts. Part 1 introduces fundamental

---

war between armies or similar types of armed forces, and "asymmetric warfare" means war between parties that are not symmetric.

[3] Although there is not total agreement, the most commonly accepted definition of the term "lawfare" is "a method of warfare where the law is used as a means of realizing a military objective.... Rather than seeking battlefield victories, *per se*, challengers try to destroy the will to fight by undermining the public support that is indispensable ... [to] democracies," "Law and Military Interventions: Preserving Humanitarian Values in 21st Century Conflicts," Charles J. Dunlap, Jr., prepared for *Humanitarian Challenges in Military Intervention Conference,* and delivered at the *Carr Center for Human Rights Policy, Kennedy School of Government, Harvard University*, Washington, D.C., on November 29, 2001, available at http://people.duke.edu/~pfeaver/dunlap.pdf. A more specific and less formal definition might be "the use of law to inhibit or stymie military action, either by preventing the action beforehand, or by punishing the action after-the-fact and thereby inhibiting future action." All URL addresses for websites were valid and operational as of November 1, 2016, but changes may have occurred after that date.

[4] Lawfare will threaten countries that are engaged in battle, and who care about the laws of war. This will certainly include Israel, the United States, various European nations, and others. Lawfare will be of less importance to countries not intimately engaged in the laws of war, and will be perceived as an opportunity, rather than a threat, by guerilla groups seeking to use law against target countries.

concepts of lawfare. Chapter 1 explains the threat presented by lawfare against Western armies. Chapter 2 sets forth a defense against this threat by presenting specific cases brought by the Israel Law Center. Part II of the book presents three fronts of lawfare: the land (chapter 3), the sea (chapter 4), and the air (chapter 5). Chapters 3 and 4 present actions by activists, and cases brought by the Israel Law Center. Chapter 5 deals primarily with the future of warfare and discusses the legal issues expected to arise in future wars.

I was originally inspired to write *A Table Against Mine Enemies* by the activities of the Israel Law Center,[5] which is, to the best of my knowledge, the leading pro-Israel lawfare organization. Some of the activities of the Israel Law Center are highlighted here, but the book is not restricted to the activities of the Israel Law Center.

Excluded from this book are issues that might be important in the Israeli-Palestinian conflict,[6] but which are not specifically related to the laws of war. Lawsuits for damages against the PLO, the Palestinian Authority, and Iran for sponsoring or supporting terrorism are part of a general legal war, but they are more or less typical "civil actions" for damages (with some variations). Although these lawsuits often deal with acts of terror which might also violate the laws of war, the two concepts of warfare and terror are conceptually and legally distinct. Therefore, lawsuits involving terrorism are not included here. Similarly, if a plaintiff is awarded money damages as a result of such a lawsuit, the plaintiff must take action to collect the

---

[5] The Israel Law Center is called "Shurat HaDin" in Hebrew. The term is taken from the phrase *"lifnim mi'shurat hadin,"* translatable as "beyond the letter of the law." This is a legal principle of Jewish law which signifies that an ethical person should act beyond the strict law in specific cases – that is, in a manner more generous than the law would require, for the sake of peace between human beings. Throughout this book, I will refer to this organization only as "the Israel Law Center."

[6] I term the conflict "Israeli-Palestinian," not Arab-Israeli, since the description "Israeli-Palestinian" better reflects the current reality. The more general war between Arabs and Israeli Jews has been informally suspended, for duration unknown, by the rise of the Islamic civil war between the Shi'ites and the Sunnis. Intra-Islamic unrest has suspended, for now, the pan-Arab alliance against Israel. It is perhaps ironic that the two major enemies bordering Israel – Hamas in Gaza, and Hezbollah in Lebanon – are Sunni and Shi'ite, respectively.

damages. The struggle to collect civil judgments against terrorists, while certainly a critically important element of civil justice, is not included in this book about the laws of war.

A Table Against Mine Enemies is meant for readers who are not particularly knowledgeable in law, let alone international law or the laws of war, and who want to know more about this increasingly important topic. It is also for those who care about Israel, the United States, and the West, and most particularly about the members of the armed forces of these countries. The book is an interweaving of international law and personal stories; it may therefore also interest attorneys, academics, and others for whom the topics discussed herein form the web of their professional activities. They, too, are welcome to peruse herein, and take what benefit they can.

This is not intended to be a "political book," although people do not always agree on what that term means. However, I am a person, and I therefore have political views. My views are strongly pro-Israel, pro-America, and pro-Western. I do not apologize for these views, but I do not intend this book to be a personal manifesto. To the extent possible, I have presented the legal issues neutrally and dispassionately.

On a personal note, in writing this book I wish to thank those who have fought, and who continue to fight, for the values in which I believe. I thank my father, dead now these thirty years, who spent his late teenage years fighting in Western Europe against the Nazi cancer. I thank my children, who have served and who continue to serve, proudly, in the Israel Defense Forces. In my mind, my father and my children fight the same battle. This book is my gift to them.

Acknowledgments

Thank you to all the people at Shurat HaDin – Israel Law Center who provided me with material and advice. I note in particular Nitsana Darshan-Leitner and Avi Leitner. I also thank several Israel Law Center interns from the summer of 2014 and the winter of 2015, who provided me with background material: Sarah Behar, Christian Breitler, Carly Coleman, Rachel Fink, Matt Gerber, Kyle Kozak, Lani Lear, Dave Teitelbaum, and Seth Teleky. My special thanks go to Doron Almog, Liran Antebi, Robert Feldmeier, Yedidya Fraiman, and Gal Zuckerman, who reviewed drafts of the book and made many invaluable suggestions. I thank also Professor Orde F. Kittrie, of the Sandra Day O'Connor College of Law at Arizona State University, who kindly gave me a personal interview on the subject of lawfare.

Thanks also to Paz Corcos of StudioPaz, who did her excellent cover graphics, as always.

Finally, I must mention the team at Gefen Publishing House – publisher Ilan Greenfield, project manager Lynn Douek, and editors Tziporah Levine and Kezia Raffel Pride. A very professional crew, and a pleasure to work with. Thank you.

PART I

FUNDAMENTAL CONCEPTS

CHAPTER I

The Lawfare Attack

Introduction: The Testing Ground

> The conflict between Israel and the Palestinians is the world's nearest approximation to a lawfare laboratory. Just as the Spanish Civil War served as a testing and training ground for weapons, tactics, and strategies that would later be used in World War II, so does the Israeli-Palestinian conflict provide . . . a first look at the various cutting-edge lawfare weapons, tactics, and strategies that will soon be replicated in other conflicts.
>
> > – *Orde F. Kittrie, Professor of Law,*
> > *Arizona State University*[7]

The Israeli-Palestinian conflict is the testing ground for lawfare strategies, weapons, and tactics that will be used in wars throughout the world, and for decades to come. These wars will be fought using the same fundamental legal principles that are illustrated and explained in this chapter.

---

[7] Orde F. Kittrie, interview by the author, June 23, 2016. Professor Kittrie makes a similar point in his book *Lawfare: Law as a Weapon of War* (New York: Oxford University Press, 2016), 197.

I. Principles in the Laws of War

While there are a myriad of complex details pertaining to the laws of war, there are in essence only four basic principles. This section illustrates these principles through the case of General Doron Almog and Salah Shehade. It then provides examples of how the threat of criminal sanction based upon the laws of war can negatively impact the planning and execution of military operations. Finally, the section concludes by clarifying that the laws of war are incumbent upon both parties, regardless of each party's justification for engaging in war.

A. *The Story of Doron Almog and Salah Shehade*

This is a story of two men, Doron Almog and Salah Shehade.

Doron Almog, born in 1951, served for decades in the Israel Defense Forces and retired with the rank of major general. Almog fought in the War of Attrition (1967–1970), the Yom Kippur War (1973), and the First Lebanon War (1982–1985). He was the first commander on the ground in Uganda during the Entebbe Operation on July 4, 1976. He was one of the leaders of Operation Moses, which brought six thousand Ethiopian Jews to Israel in 1984–1985. He was the commanding general of the Southern Command, including the Gaza front, from December 8, 2000, until July 7, 2003.

Almog's life, while difficult in many ways, is also an example of triumph over sadness. His brother, Eran, was a tank commander during the Yom Kippur War whose tank suffered a direct hit – unable to climb out due to his injuries, Eran bled to death in his tank. Doron Almog had a son in 1984, whom he named Eran after his dead brother. The son Eran suffered from severe autism and intellectual disabilities – he never called Doron "father," and he died in 2007 at the age of twenty-three.[8]

---

[8] In addition, many members of Doron Almog's family – his uncle, aunt, and cousins – died in the suicide bombing of the Maxim Restaurant in Haifa on October 4, 2003. Killed were Zeev Almog (71), a retired admiral and former head of the naval officers' academy in Acre; Ruth Almog (70); their son Moshe (43); Moshe's son Tomer (9); and the son of Zeev and Ruth's daughter Galit, Assaf Shteier (10). Four other members of the

Toward the end of his military career, Almog worked with Aleh – Israel's foremost network of facilities for children with severe cognitive and intellectual disabilities – to found a rehabilitation village in the Negev Desert. This village, called "Aleh Negev – Nahalat Eran" after Almog's son, provides a sheltered environment for about 140 disabled children and young adults, including a mix of Jews and Bedouin. Doron Almog considers the founding of this village to be his greatest achievement in life. When Aleh Negev was named after his son in 2007, Doron Almog wrote a letter, in which he stated one of his main motivations for founding a home for severely disabled children: "We should never leave them behind, bleeding."[9]

Salah Shehade, born in Gaza two years after Doron Almog, was a member of Hamas. After the death of the master bomber Yahya Ayyash in 1996, Shehade became one of the three top leaders of Hamas. During the period 1996–2002, Shehade planned attacks against Israeli soldiers and civilians in both Gaza and Israel. He was personally responsible for planning some of the largest and highest profile suicide bombings of that period.[10] He was also heavily involved in the procurement of Qassam rockets and other weapons – both by smuggling and by local production. He was the head of the military wing of Hamas, known as Izz ad-Din al-Qassam Brigades ("the al-Qassam Brigades"), during the time when this group carried out suicide bombings inside Israel, killing hundreds of civilians. Shehade was

---

family were injured, including Oren Almog (10), son of Moshe and brother of Tomer, who was scarred and permanently blinded, but who nevertheless volunteered for IDF service in 2012.

[9] The last line of "Letter by Doron Almog," a eulogy delivered in March 2007 to mark the end of the thirty-day mourning period for Eran Almog, available at http://eng.nitzan-israel.org.il/home/get-involved/tell-your-story/letter-by-doron-almog.aspx.

[10] Of the hundreds of Hamas attacks for which Salah Shehade was responsible, I will note his specific planning and responsibility for (1) the Dolphinarium Discotheque suicide bombing, Tel Aviv, June 1, 2001, twenty-one dead, average age of the victims – seventeen; (2) the Sbarro Restaurant suicide bombing, Jerusalem, August 9, 2001, fifteen dead, including seven children and a pregnant woman; and (3) the Park Hotel suicide bombing at a Passover Seder, Netanya, March 27, 2002, thirty dead, including twenty-one retirees. Shehade could be described as the most murderous Hamas killer active in this time frame.

the chief of all Hamas military commanders and was actively involved in defining and implementing Hamas's policy of terror.

Shehade was a prime target of the Israel Defense Forces.[11] His movements were tracked. On July 22, 2002, at approximately eleven thirty at night, an Israeli F16 dropped a one-ton bomb on a house located in the Al Daraj neighborhood of Gaza City, in which, according to intelligence, Shehade was located. In fact, Shehade was indeed present, and he was killed, but the bomb also killed fourteen other people, including two members of Shehade's family and other civilians who had been in adjacent houses.

On September 11, 2005, two years after his retirement from the army, Doron Almog and his wife flew to London. Almog was scheduled to speak that evening at the Solihull Synagogue in Birmingham as part of his fund-raising efforts for Aleh Negev – Nahalat Eran. However, the day before Almog's arrival in London, Judge Timothy Workman of the Bow Street Magistrates' Court had issued an arrest warrant for Almog. Before Almog disembarked from the El Al flight, the Israeli military attaché boarded the plane and told Almog of the warrant. Almog then stayed on the plane until it refueled and returned to Israel. The British police did not board the plane to serve the warrant, because they knew the plane had armed sky marshals and possibly bodyguards, and they did not want to create either a diplomatic incident or a potentially dangerous situation. Later, the Israeli government objected to the warrant, and Jack Straw, the UK foreign minister at the time, apologized for the incident.

B. The Four Basic Principles of the Laws of War

Anyone who wishes to understand "lawfare" must understand the laws of war. There are literally hundreds of legal principles involving war, but ultimately there are only four basic principles: necessity (N), distinction (D), proportionality (P), and shielding (S). These four principles are referenced

---

[11] See, for example, "Shehade Was High on Israel Most-Wanted List," *CNN World*, July 23, 2002, available at http://edition.cnn.com/2002/WORLD/meast/07/23/shehade.profile/.

constantly, and anyone who follows media coverage of armed conflict will see these principles repeatedly in the coming years. All of these basic principles are illustrated in the case of Doron Almog and Salah Shehade.

1. NECESSITY (N)

"Necessity" (N) as a legal principle means that an attacker (whether an army or a less formal armed group) may attack only if achievement of the objective will create a direct military advantage or benefit for the attacker. There is no doubt whatsoever that the principle of necessity was observed here. Salah Shehade was the chief commander of the armed forces of a military enemy of Israel, personally responsible for the killing of hundreds of Israelis, and, of critical importance, actively involved in plans to kill additional civilians. It is unlawful for a state or army to kill someone as a matter of retribution or revenge; although legal steps might be taken against a person, lethal action would violate the principle of military necessity. Shehade was attacked not because he was a vicious killer who had murdered hundreds of children and elderly people, but rather because he planned to kill hundreds more. His elimination would therefore be of direct military benefit to Israel.[12]

2. DISTINCTION (D)

"Distinction" (D) means that an attacker must use reasonable efforts to distinguish between military objectives and possible non-military (civilian) harm. Often, such harm is euphemistically called "collateral damage." This principle, too, was observed here. Shehade's family, and other civilians living in the area, were not the target of the attack, and the IDF did not

---

[12] In particular, but only as one example among many, Shehade was planning a "mega-attack" to kill hundreds of civilians in one incident. The elimination of Shehade would put an end to such plans by preemptively terminating the mega-attack. See "Ethical Dilemmas in Fighting Terrorism" (2004) by Major General Amos Yadlin (formerly head of IDF Military Intelligence, Israeli military attaché in Washington, and head of the IDF team that outlined the principles of the war against terror), included in the compendium *What Israel Has Learned about Security: Nine IDF Officers Discuss Israel's Security Challenge* (Jerusalem: Jerusalem Center for Public Affairs, 2012), 130–31, available at http://jcpa.org/text/downloads/what-israel-has-learned-about-security.pdf.

indiscriminately attack an entire neighborhood because of Shehade's possible presence. After the attack, the IDF stated specifically that Shehade alone had been the sole target.[13] To the best of my knowledge, no one has ever claimed or argued that the IDF intentionally targeted civilians in the attack on Salah Shehade. Such a claim, if made, would be very weak, since the head of the military wing of Hamas was clearly a legitimate target.

3. PROPORTIONALITY (P)

"Proportionality" (P) means that prior to the action, an attacker must consider both the direct military benefit to be obtained, and the likelihood and severity of civilian casualties and civilian damage that could be caused by the attack. These two must be compared. If the likely damage to civilians is clearly greater than the direct military benefit to be obtained (that is, if D clearly exceeds N), then the attack is illegal and may not be made. The arguments between those supporting a specific military action, and those calling the same action a "war crime," often focus on whether the military advantage was "proportional" to the civilian harm. This judgment is made in reference to the attacker's actual knowledge at the time of planning and executing the attack, not in reference to what might have been learned after the attack.[14] Military intelligence is sometimes right, and sometimes

---

[13] "IDF Operation in Gaza Strip Last Night," Israel Defense Forces, July 23, 2002, available at https://web.archive.org/web/20030711164142/http://www.idf.il/english/announcements/2002/july/23.stm. See also an interesting article by the English lawyers who helped obtain the arrest warrant against Almog, and who have worked in the UK for the Palestinians and against Israel: Daniel Machover and Kate Maynard, "Prosecuting Alleged War Criminals in England and Wales," *Denning Law Journal* 18, no. 1 (2006): 109, available at http://ubplj.org/index.php/dlj/article/view/309. In 2006, Maynard was detained at Ben Gurion Airport and denied entry to Israel.

[14] In judging whether a military operation was "proportional," neither the actual results nor subsequently discovered information are relevant – these are both retrospective reviews. The question is rather whether the decision to act was proportional "from the point of view of... [the] commander [making the decision] *with the information available to him at the time* [of the decision]." Benjamin Wittes, "Israeli Targeting Procedures and the Concept of Proportionality," *Lawfare* (blog), December 15, 2015, available at https://www.lawfareblog.com/israeli-targeting-procedures-and-concept-proportionality. (Italics appear in the original article.)

wrong. Weapons are sometimes inaccurate, due to human error or the inherent limitations of weapons. The law, however, does not criminalize disproportionate *results*, but only disproportionate *intent*.[15]

As part of a proportionality analysis, the attacker must take reasonable actions to reduce the amount of civilian harm. Here, for example, the IDF stated that it attacked at night to avoid the civilians attendant on a daytime street, that it used only one bomb instead of two smaller bombs to reduce the risk of a miss, and that the chosen weaponry was appropriate both for its power (only sufficient to achieve the objective) and its accuracy.[16] The counterargument is that the civilian casualties, fourteen dead and tens of wounded, indicate that the attack was disproportionate, and hence a war crime. Of course, to be fair, those casualties must be weighed against the possible tens or hundreds of Israeli civilians that Shehade might have killed or wounded in the future, as he had done in the past.

As part of a proportionality analysis, the attacker should issue warnings to endangered civilians, but only if, and only to the degree, that such warn-

---

[15] Proportionality is a very difficult principle to apply in practice. In addition to the military target Shehade, fourteen civilians died in the attack. How does one weigh these civilians against the hundreds of Israeli civilian deaths that were being planned by Shehade? Might Shehade have been attacked at a different time, when he was not in the presence of civilians? Major General Yadlin, formerly cited, recounts that "Shehade was always surrounded by innocent people until one night in July, 2002, we found him almost alone. . . . [However, and unfortunately,] the intelligence about those in the surroundings buildings was wrong, and innocent people were killed," "Ethical Dilemmas in Fighting Terrorism," 131. There is no absolute immunity for civilians in a war, and without doubt military mistakes may be made. See, for example, Yonah Jeremy Bob, "Analysis: US Bombing of Afghan Hospital May Help Israel Face Its Own Demons" *Jerusalem Post*, November 28, 2015, http://www.jpost.com/Israel-News/Rule-of-Law-Investigation -fallout-435513, about the October 3, 2015, US bombing of a hospital in Kundaz, Afghanistan, that killed thirty civilians, including medical personnel from Doctors Without Borders. Would an attack on a military target, with a handful of civilians in proximity, be "proportional" to a potential saving of hundreds of Israeli civilians? Would the same attack be proportional if it was known that more than a dozen civilians might die? Proportionality is not judged by the results of the attack, but rather by the intent at the time of planning. Was the planning in this case legitimate? It is not possible to arrive at undisputed answers, but the questions nevertheless must be asked.

[16] Machover and Maynard, "Prosecuting Alleged War Criminals in England and Wales," 109–110.

ings are reasonably possible. Had the IDF issued a warning in the Shehade case, there would have been no chance to achieve the main objective – hence, in this case warnings were not "reasonably possible."

4. SHIELDING (S)

In addition to the three principles in planning an attack – necessity, distinction, and proportionality – there is a fourth principle that applies to the defender, not the attacker. This is the principle of "shielding" (S). There are three different forms of shielding, but they are all illegitimate, and they all constitute war crimes by a defender. In one form of shielding, the defender sets up a firing position – to fire a mortar or missile, to create a sniper's nest, etc. – in a civilian area (such as a school, hospital, prison, or house of worship) or in a location with many civilians present. In a second form of shielding, weapons and other military equipment are improperly stored in a civilian area. In a third form of shielding, symbols, vehicles, and other assets that should be devoted to protected purposes are instead used by combatants. For example, using a vehicle clearly marked with a Red Cross, or Red Crescent, or Red Star of David in order to transport combatants or military equipment is clearly a form of shielding, and therefore a war crime.

In this case, for example, Salah Shehade traveled and lived among civilians, rather than among fighters, and very likely part of that lifestyle was his attempt to create a "civilian shield" against attack, which is the first form of shielding. To the best of my knowledge, this case does not illustrate the use of the second or third forms of shielding.

C. Examples of the Effects of Lawfare on Soldiers in the Field

The laws of war, and the threat of criminal sanction based upon the laws of war, have a significant impact on both the planning and execution of specific military operations. Several examples are presented here from warfare in Iraq, Syria, Afghanistan, Gaza, and the Democratic Republic of Congo. In some cases, it is the action that causes a problem, but in other cases the problem is caused by the failure to act due to fear of legal consequences.

1. US EXAMPLE FROM IRAQ: THE PRICE OF HESITATION

This is an account of an American veteran of the Iraqi war who hesitated to act at a certain time, with tragic results.

> [H]is best friend and fellow soldier was killed in Iraq because he [the surviving veteran telling the story] hesitated when an insurgent presented a clear lethal threat to his unit. The hesitation... was not due to fear or inability to respond, but rather was a result of his haunting fear of legal reprisal [by his own side, not by lawfare activists].... Don't miss this point – at the moment of truth, rather than being focused on killing enemy combatants and keeping their soldiers alive, junior leaders [such as sergeants] are preoccupied with surviving the legal aftermath orchestrated by the senior leaders in their chain of command. This notion is reinforced by several young company commanders who told about improvements needed in the curriculum of our professional education courses – alarmingly, the number one recommendation was to add a course to teach leaders how to survive a Criminal Investigation Division (CID) post-incident review.[17]

In this example, it is not the threat of a lawsuit by legal activists, but rather the threat of legal consequences from his own side that caused the soldier to hesitate, resulting in the death of his comrade. There are legitimate reasons for, and also positive benefits from, the laws of war, but these laws are not intended to prevent soldiers from responding to hostile actions. When the laws of war act as a straitjacket and cause the death of one's own soldiers, something has gone awry.

2. US EXAMPLE FROM IRAQ: SNIPERS

The 2014 movie *American Sniper*, based on a book of the same name, opens in Nasiriya, in southern Iraq. The lead character, Chris Kyle, is positioned in a sniper's nest, and must decide whether to shoot a woman and child

---

[17] *Fighting Today's Wars: How America's Leaders Have Failed Our Warriors*, by US military advocates David G. Bolgiano (a former paratrooper) and James M. Patterson (a former Green Beret) (Mechanicsburg, PA: Stackpole Books, 2012), v.

who appear intent on attacking a convoy of US marines. The sniper reports this situation on the radio channel, and asks for visual confirmation of the target. He is told, "Negative [cannot confirm], your call." The sniper's spotting partner says to him, "They'd fry you if you're wrong." In short, if the sniper shoots and he is right, then he is a war hero. But if he shoots and he is wrong, he becomes a war criminal. In the end, he did shoot, and this was the correct decision, but had he erred – either way – he could have expected very little in the way of understanding or forgiveness.[18]

3. US EXAMPLE FROM IRAQ: AGAINST SNIPERS

In 2008, in the Baghdad suburb called Sadr City, a US army brigade is taking casualties from snipers located in an abandoned building. Countersniper fire proves ineffective, so the brigade commander calls in an Apache helicopter strike. Six Hellfire missiles destroy the abandoned building and terminate the sniper threat, but the brigade commander is investigated for use of excessive force. Although the brigade commander is exonerated in the formal investigation, the division commander sends a letter of reprimand, essentially ending the brigade commander's future in the army.[19]

4. US EXAMPLE FROM IRAQ: IMPROVISED EXPLOSIVE DEVICES

Also in Baghdad, in order to counteract improvised explosive devices (IEDs) and reduce casualties, SEAL snipers create a ruse whereby a bomb appears to detonate. When enemy insurgents come to follow-up the supposed IED,

---

[18] The relevant part of the movie may be seen at https://www.youtube.com/watch?v=99k3u9ay1gs. The book on which this movie incident is based tells a slightly different story. In the book, both the woman and child were there, but only the woman attacked and only she was shot. In the book, the sniper tried to call the Marines, but failed to make contact. Finally, in the book the sniper's spotting partner was the platoon chief, who did not reference the legal authorities, but rather, when the sniper hesitated, ordered the sniper to shoot. The book is called *American Sniper: The Autobiography of the Most Lethal Sniper in U.S. History*, by Chris Kyle, with Jim DeFelice and Scott McEwen (New York: Harper, 2014), 1–4. The specific details of this incident are not relevant here; the key is that people who are not ordinarily combatants – in this case a woman dressed in civilian clothes – may not be attacked unless their hostile intent is clear.

[19] Bolgiano and Patterson, *Fighting Today's Wars*, 54.

they are killed by the SEAL snipers. The Navy Judge Advocate General says the soldiers are killing people for mere "acts of civil disobedience," and causes the ruse to be shut down.[20]

5. US EXAMPLE FROM AFGHANISTAN: THE USE OF CIVILIANS FOR SHIELDING

US and NATO forces have been fighting in Afghanistan since 2001. During part of that period, specifically 2004–2010, the United States engaged Taliban forces in the Korengal Valley in the northeastern province of Kunar, on the Pakistani border. Here is one description of the rules under which the parties fought:

> [According to the] American rules of engagement...[US forces may] shoot people who are carrying a weapon or handheld radio. The Taliban know this, and...make children stand near them when they use their radios. The Americans don't dare shoot because, other than the obvious moral issues involved, killing civilians simple makes the war harder.[21]

We may describe this behavior by the Taliban in various ways – "shielding," "use of American rules of engagement against the US," "placing US forces in a moral dilemma," or, as discussed in this book, "using lawfare, or at least the threat of lawfare, to inhibit the enemy's freedom to act."

6. US EXAMPLE FROM SYRIA: THE REFUSAL TO BOMB ISIS HEADQUARTERS

The United States is aware of multiple possible ISIS targets in Syria, but will not bomb them for fear of causing civilian casualties. Raqqa, Syria, is the de facto capital city of ISIS. In Raqqa, a building that houses an ISIS administrative center is also a dormitory for tens of ISIS fighters. It is not targeted, however, because the building also houses a prison for civilians.[22]

---

[20] Ibid.

[21] Sebastian Junger, *War* (New York: Twelve, 2010), 46.

[22] Matthew Rosenberg and Eric Schmitt, "In ISIS Strategy, U.S. Weighs Risk to Civilians," *New York Times*, December 19, 2015, http://www.nytimes.com/2015/12/20/us/politics

In fact, this particular building, plus six other buildings that together are ISIS headquarters in Syria, will not be attacked for fear of causing civilian casualties.[23] The United States often refrains from attacking known and marked ISIS targets in Syria, Iraq, and Libya.[24]

7. ISRAELI EXAMPLE FROM GAZA: THE REFUSAL TO BOMB HAMAS HEADQUARTERS

Israel has fought wars with Hamas in 2008–2009, 2012, and 2014. Israel is fully aware of the location of Hamas facilities. In fact, in the Third Gaza War, in 2014, Hamas headquarters was located in the same building that houses Al-Shifa Hospital, in Gaza City.[25] Israel would derive great military benefit from destroying Hamas headquarters, but it did not do so during the war for fear of causing civilian casualties.

8. ISRAELI EXAMPLE FROM GAZA: DROPPING THE WRONG BOMB

The IDF bombed Salah Shehade on July 22, 2002. Israel received significant publicity as a result of the attack, most of it negative. As recounted by General Yadlin:

> In August, 2002 [that is, only a few days after the bombing of Salah Shehade], we had all the leadership of Hamas in one room, and we

---

/in-isis-strategy-us-weighs-risk-to-civilians.html. This is only one example of many. It has been estimated that 75 percent of allied air strikes launched against ISIS are aborted due to fear of striking civilians. Eric Schmitt, "U.S. Caution in Strikes Gives ISIS an Edge, Many Iraqis Say," *New York Times*, May 26, 2015, http://www.nytimes.com/2015/05/27/world/middleeast/with-isis-in-crosshairs-us-holds-back-to-protect-civilians.html.

[23] Schmitt, "U.S. Caution in Strike Gives ISIS an Edge."

[24] Guy Taylor, "U.S. Has Mapped ISIS Hiding Spots, but Won't Launch Strikes for Fear of Civilian Deaths," *Washington Times*, December 14, 2015, http://www.washingtontimes.com/news/2015/dec/14/us-has-mapped-isis-propaganda-centers-but-wont-lau/?page=all. See also "U.S. Does Not Want To Bomb ISIS Media Headquarters," *Washington Times*, December 17, 2015, http://fortruss.blogspot.co.il/2015/12/washington-times-us-does-not-want-to.html.

[25] "An Assessment of the 2014 Gaza Conflict," High Level Military Group, October 2015, http://www.high-level-military-group.org/, paragraphs 71, 103, 107, and 131. Al-Shifa is also known as the "Dar Al-Shifa" Hospital.

knew we needed a 2,000-pound bomb to eliminate them [like the 2,000-pound bomb used in the attack on Shehade]. Think about having Osama bin Laden and all the top leadership of al-Qaeda in one house. However, use of a 2,000-pound bomb was not approved – we used a much smaller bomb – and they all got up and ran away.[26]

This is exactly a case in which the threat of bad publicity and subsequent prosecution protected the top leadership of Hamas. In that sense, it might be said that the death of Shehade saved the other leaders of Hamas.

9. BRITISH EXAMPLE FROM AFGHANISTAN AND IRAQ: SOLDIERS ON TRIAL

As of the end of 2015, there were slightly more than one thousand compensation claims and lawsuits pending in the British courts against British veterans of the Afghani and Iraqi wars.[27] The claimants include suspected Taliban bomb makers, Iraqi prisoners, and the family of one Iraqi who was shot trying to grab the gun of a British soldier. These cases may continue for five years, ten years, or longer.[28] It is demoralizing to veterans, and a deterrent to those considering a military career in Britain, to know that they may be sued in British courts for doing their duty in foreign wars.[29]

---

[26] Yadlin, "Ethical Dilemmas in Fighting Terrorism," 127.

[27] Tim Ross, "£150m Legal Bill for Troops Just Doing Their Duty: Ministers Draw Up Plans to Pull Out of the European Convention on Human Rights Next Time the Armed Forces Are Sent into Combat," *The Telegraph*, October 17, 2015, http://www.telegraph.co .uk/news/uknews/defence/11938476/150m-legal-bill-for-troops-just-doing-their-duty.html.

[28] See, for example, Larissa Brown, "Betrayal of a Hero: Sgt. Kevin Williams Went Through 12 Years of Hell Before Being Cleared of Killing an Iraqi. Now He's Jobless and Broke … While the Dead Man's Family Are in Line for a Big Payout," *MailOnline*, March 26, 2015, at http://www.dailymail.co.uk/news/article-3008432/Betrayal-hero-Sgt-Kevin -Williams-went-12-years-hell-cleared-killing-Iraqi-s-jobless-broke-dead-man-s-family -line-big-payout.html; and see also Larisa Brown et al., "We Were Dragged through Five Years of Hell by the Government Say British Soldiers Taken to War Crimes Inquiry by 'Shameful' Lawyers," *MailOnline*, December 19, 2014, http://www.dailymail.co.uk/news /article-2878761/We-betrayed-government-say-British-soldiers-dragged-war-crimes -inquiry-cleared.html.

[29] On the toxic atmosphere for British soldiers created by these lawsuits, and on their negative impact on the US and Israel as well as on the UK, see the powerful comments

10. UN EXAMPLE FROM NORTH KIVU, CONGO: UNREALISTIC WARNINGS

North Kivu is a province located in the far east of the Democratic Republic of Congo, on the border with Uganda and Rwanda. It has been the scene of conflict since 2004, between forces of the government, Hutu militias, and Tutsi groups affiliated with the government of Rwanda. During all this time, the United Nations has been involved militarily through MONUSCO (short for "Mission de l'Organisation des Nations Unies pour la Stabilisation en RD Congo"). In 2008, the commander of the UN mission, General Bipin Rawat of India, stated that the UN could not defeat the rebels "unless... [the UN's] rules of engagement are rewritten." The UN's complete refusal to accept even the possibility of any civilian casualties makes its mission impossible. The rules of engagement required UN peacekeepers to drive in easily identifiable and clearly marked white trucks, to warn rebels of impending attacks, to fire warning shots before attacking, and to use helicopters solely for transportation and reconnaissance (but not for attack). With these kinds of rules, no offensive could win. "If I kill one civilian, there is no-one to hold my hand.... [T]he rules of engagement have to be rewritten, or... modified certainly," said General Rawat.[30]

These ten cases present the reality of the situation. The law does not forbid incidental harm to civilians or even the killing of civilians. It forbids the targeting of civilians, and also the acceptance of excessive risk to civilians in comparison to the benefit of a possible military benefit. Nevertheless, the law is sometimes distorted to inhibit, or to prevent entirely, military operations with a legitimate objective, that do not target civilians, and that are proportional in relation to reasonably anticipated civilian harm. These operations are legal, except when the application of the law is distorted.

---

by the former commander of British forces in Afghanistan, Colonel Richard Kemp, "Is Britain Destroying its Military to Appease Enemies?" Gatestone Institute, October 25, 2016, available at https://www.gatestoneinstitute.org/9181/british-military.

[30] David Blair in Goma (capital of North Kivu), "UN Commander Says Hands Are Tied in Congo," *The Telegraph*, November 17, 2008, http://www.telegraph.co.uk/news /worldnews/africaandindianocean/congo/3472724/UN-commander-says-hands-are -tied-in-Congo.html. See also Bolgiano and Patterson, *Fighting Today's Wars*, 105.

In operational planning, fear of collateral damage may cause attacks to be avoided or canceled, despite significant military benefit. That is true in the refusals to bomb ISIS or Hamas headquarters in cases 6 and 7, or in the cancellation of the very effective program against IEDs in case 4. In case 8, the attack occurred, but an ineffective weapon was chosen that both reduced the risk of civilian harm and failed to achieve the military objective.

In conducting operations, fear of legal consequences may cause fatal hesitation, as in case 1. In some instances, the rigid interpretation of laws may make almost all military action ineffective, which seemed to be true of UN intervention in DR Congo, case 10. In case 5, known enemies achieved temporary immunity by hiding behind civilians.

Perhaps worst of all, soldiers trying to do their best may find that they are subject to post-operation legal liability. In case 2, if Chris Kyle had killed the wrong civilian he could have been judged a war criminal – but if he had failed to shoot the right person, his comrades might have died. Legal concerns put an end to effective programs against snipers in case 3 and against IEDs in case 4. In a truly awful scenario, soldiers may find themselves civilly or criminally liable in the courts of their own countries, as per British veterans of the Afghan and Iraqi wars in case 9.[31]

The laws of war are critically important for maintaining civility and humanity, but legitimate warfare requires a balance between law and war.

---

[31] There have been discussions in the UK government since at least late 2015 to end the flood of lawsuits against British veterans by withdrawing from the European Human Rights Convention during wartime. Such a withdrawal would apparently follow precedents established by France, Turkey, and the Ukraine. Peter Walker and Owen Bowcott, "Plan for UK to Opt Out of European Convention on Human Rights," *Guardian*, October 4, 2016, available at https://www.theguardian.com/uk-news/2016/oct/03/plan-uk-military-opt-out-european-convention-human-rights. There is significant opposition to such a withdrawal from UK human rights activists, who believe that cases brought are valid and should be allowed in order to help eradicate "mistreatment on the battlefield." "UK to Opt Out of European Human Rights Convention in Wartime," *Times of Israel*, October 4, 2016, available at http://www.timesofisrael.com/uk-said-planning-to-opt-out-of-human-rights-convention-in-wartime/. Clearly there should be some kind of balance between protecting civilians in time of war and protecting soldiers from vexatious lawsuits. The UK government will presumably try to find the balance, but whatever the results of that effort, we can say that investigations and judicial proceedings that continue for five years, ten years, and even longer are absurd, are destructive of justice, and can only harm the morale of soldiers.

D. Jus ad Bellum vs. Jus in Bello: The Right of Self-Defense

The "laws of war" (also called "international humanitarian law") govern the way fighting must be conducted. These laws do *not* determine whether or not the war itself is just, or whether the reason for going to war is legal. As stated by Professor Michael Walzer, one of the leading scholars in the laws of war:

> The moral reality of war is divided into two parts. War is always judged twice, first with reference to the reasons states have for fighting, second with reference to the means they adopt.[32]

There is a fundamental distinction between the reasons for a particular war, and the conduct of that same war. In formal terminology, this is the distinction between what is known as *jus ad bellum* (literally, "right to war") versus *jus in bello* (literally, "right in war"). There are a limited number of legally recognized reasons for going to war, the chief of which is the right of self-defense, which is enshrined in Article 51 of the United Nations Charter. However, irrespective of whether the combatants are "just" in going to war, all combatants must adhere to the legal principles governing the manner in which a war is fought. These principles are known as *jus in bello*, and regulate the specific manner in which the war is conducted.[33]

People frequently err in discussing "morality in war." There is no legal concept called "morality in war," and people frequently confuse the legal issue by applying their own sense of the "justness of the war" (*jus ad bellum*) to the "fighting during war" (*jus in bello*).

The distinction between the reasons people fight and the way they fight is both logical and essential. To prove that, consider the opposite approach. Let us say that a party that is waging a "just war" (that is to say, the party that has a good and moral reason for going to war) is not bound by any

---

[32] Michael Walzer, *Just and Unjust Wars: A Moral Argument With Historical Illustrations,* 5th ed. (New York: Basic Books, 2015), 21. This book, first published in 1977, has become one of the standard reference texts for research in the laws of war.

[33] The concepts of "*jus in bello,*" "the laws of war," and "international humanitarian law" are all exactly the same. Scholars tend to use the first term, military people the second, and human rights experts the third, but they are all discussing the same thing.

rules in the conduct of war. This party, the "just party," may do anything – kill anyone associated with the opposition and by any means, destroy any building or facility under the physical control of the enemy, or anything else (provided only that the death and destruction is visited upon the enemy's combatants or civilians, but not upon some neutral third party). In contrast, the party that is not waging a "just war" (that is to say, the party that lacks a good and moral reason for going to war) is bound by a host of rules and restrictions that we call "laws of war."

What is the result – not the likely result, but rather the *certain* result – of this scheme for just and unjust parties? Each party will say, "I am the just party, the other side is the unjust party. I can do whatever I want to enemy combatants or enemy civilians, but the other side is subject to rules that do not apply to me." Each side will then feel free to do whatever it wants in the course of the war, without restriction. This is an impossibly unacceptable result. Therefore, to prevent a reality in which neither party feels bound to any rules, there must be a clear distinction between justness in going to war – *jus ad bellum* – and justness in the way the war is conducted – *jus in bello* (also called "laws of war" or "international humanitarian law"), such that the laws of war apply to all parties, in all wars, and all circumstances.

There are people who refuse to make this critical distinction between the laws of going to war and the laws of waging war. They are so emotionally bound up with one side or the other in a conflict that they say, "Our side is right, the other side is wrong, *and therefore our side can do whatever it wishes.*" This argument justifies atrocities by one party to the conflict and is simply wrong. Each party, whatever its reasons for going to war, must adhere to the principles of conducting the war.

Such people often make a corollary mistake, by saying, "Our side is right, the other side is wrong, and therefore every means of supposed 'self-defense' used by the other side is unjust and illegal, since the other side is unjust in going to war." This, too, is incorrect. Each party, whatever its reasons for going to war, may wage the war as long as it does so in accordance with the principles of conducting the war.

Both arguments, that is, "Our side went to war justly and may therefore do anything," and "Their side went to war unjustly and may therefore do nothing," are simply wrong. As Professor Walzer wrote, there are two entirely separate judgments, one as to the justness of the war (*jus ad bellum*) and the other as to the justness of the means of conducting the war (*jus in bello*). This is a critical distinction.

II. Changes in the External Environment

A paradigm shift is taking place in the laws of war.[34] In the twentieth century, during the age of symmetric warfare between armies, the laws of war were interpreted and applied to make sure that both sides adhered to a minimum level of conduct.[35] Combatants in symmetric wars may or may not have adhered rigidly to the laws of war, but generally they did not seek to exploit the laws cynically, attempting to use lawfare as a weapon against the other side. This cynical use of the laws of war is the paradigm shift that we are currently witnessing.

In recent years there has been an upheaval in the way the laws of war are understood and applied. There are at least two reasons for this paradigm shift. One reason is the creation of the International Criminal Court (ICC) in 2002. Although this court has had limited impact thus far, it is likely to rise in importance. The second reason is the increasing use of actions that are outside the prior legal framework. These two reasons for the paradigm shift in the laws of war – the rise of the ICC and the rise of extralegal attacks – are discussed below. I will use three interrelated charts to explain first, the

---

[34] The phrase "paradigm shift" was coined in 1962, by Professor Thomas Kuhn, in his book *The Structure of Scientific Revolutions* (Chicago: University of Chicago Press, 1962), ix. Professor Kuhn meant the phrase to apply to a fundamental change in the view of reality in a scientific field, such as evolution in the field of biology or atomic theory in the field of physics. However, in popular usage, the phrase has been extended to *all* fields, not just those in science. People sometimes use the phrase "game changer," which is the same thing as "paradigm shift," albeit less formal.

[35] It is of course the case that these laws were often "honored in breach," in the sense that a side would mouth the correct words but do whatever it wanted, even in breach of the laws of war. However, even in the dark days of the twentieth century, parties understood there was such a thing as "laws of war," and they generally did not defy the laws openly. In the twenty-first century's days of asymmetric law, that is no longer the case, as will be discussed below.

situation prior to the two major changes; second, the rise of the ICC; and third, the increasing use of actions outside the prior legal framework.

The three charts refer to the laws of war, otherwise known as "international humanitarian law" or "*jus in bello*." International humanitarian law, abbreviated "IHL," is the laws of war with an emphasis on protected parties – civilians, the wounded, the sick, chaplains, medical staff, and others – and on actions a combatant *must take or must not take* in order to protect such people. In contrast, *jus in bello* is the laws of war, but here with an emphasis on actions a combatant *may take* in the conduct of the war. In fact, IHL and *jus in bello* are exactly the same thing, with exactly the same results, albeit with different emphases.

A. The External Environment in the Twentieth Century

The first of the three interrelated charts illustrates the external environment prior to the major changes.

Chart 1.1: The External Environment in the Twentieth Century (Before Change)

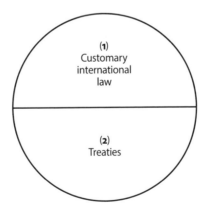

This model is relatively simple, yet it reflects well the legal environment of war in the twentieth century, prior to the two changes.

In this model, the laws of war are derived from two specific sources. One source is treaties between two or more countries, in which the obligations created are as agreed, and such obligations apply only to parties who have both accepted and ratified the treaty. The second is customary law, which is the way nations conduct armed combat. In most cases, the "customary law" intended is that which a party has accepted, either explicitly or by its conduct.[36] In a minority of cases, "customary law" is law that must be accepted by any civilized nation, and is therefore binding whether or not accepted by a country – in fact, in these few cases, a nation *must* accept the law, and is barred from disavowing the custom.[37]

B. First Change: The Rise of the International Criminal Court (ICC)

The second of the interrelated charts presents the first major change to the external legal environment – that it, the creation and rise of the International

---

[36] For example, almost every country in the world has adopted the Geneva Conventions I–IV of 1949, but many countries have not adopted the 1977 Additional Protocols I and II to the Geneva Conventions ("AP I" and "AP II"). Even though AP I and AP II may not be formally adopted, the non-adopters nevertheless have accepted, either through the public statements of their leaders or through their actions, specific sections of AP I and AP II as a matter of *binding customary international humanitarian law*. For example, the fundamental principle of "proportionality" is not defined in the Geneva Conventions, but is defined in Article 51 of Additional Protocol I. Although many countries have not adopted AP I or AP II, to the best of my knowledge all nations have accepted, as a matter of binding customary IHL, the concept of "proportionality." Indeed, proportionality is one of the most important principles in the laws of war.

[37] A prime example of law that may not be disavowed is the so-called "Martens Clause," in the preambles of the Hague Conventions of 1899 and 1907. The two formulations, of 1899 and 1907, are slightly different, but they are identical in general intent. As stated in the Hague Convention of 1907:

> Until a more complete code of the laws of war is issued, the High Contracting Parties think it right to declare that in cases not included in the Regulations adopted by them, populations and belligerents remain under the protection and empire of the principles of international law, as they result from the usages established between civilized nations, from the laws of humanity and the requirements of the public conscience.

Although more than a bit vague, the Martens Clause is still operative – it was one of the main supports of the decisions of the Nuremberg Military Trials of 1946–1949, and it is applied today in the evaluation of new weapons systems, such as robotics, UAVs, and cyber, discussed in chapter 5 below.

Criminal Court (ICC). The second chart includes all of the elements of the first chart, but also illustrates how the elements in the first chart are impacted by the rise of the ICC.

Chart 1.2: The Rise of the International Criminal Court (First Change)

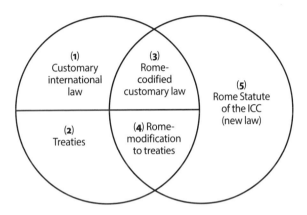

The International Criminal Court, based in The Hague, Netherlands, was created in 2002 by a treaty that is known as the Rome Statute.[38] The mandate of the ICC appears in Article 1 of the Rome Statute, which provides that the court "shall have the power to exercise its jurisdiction over persons for the most serious crimes of international concern, as referred to in this Statute, and shall be complementary to national criminal jurisdictions." That is to say, the court has jurisdiction over only those crimes listed in the statute, which are, according to Article 5, "(a) The crime of genocide; (b) Crimes against humanity; (c) War crimes; [and] (d) The crime of aggression."[39] Further, by Article 1, the Rome Statute does not override or conflict with national criminal laws, but merely "complements them." This is called the "principle of complementarity" and means that the court exercises jurisdiction only when national authorities are unable or unwilling to do so.

As shown in chart 1.2, the Rome Statute may codify customary interna-

---

[38] The "Rome Statute of the International Criminal Court," as currently amended, may be found at https://www.icc-cpi.int/nr/rdonlyres/add16852-aee9-4757-abe7-9cdc7cf02886 /283503/romestatuteng1.pdf.

[39] Genocide, crimes against humanity, war crimes, and crimes of aggression, are defined in, respectively, Articles 6, 7, 8, and 8 *bis* of the Rome Statute.

tional law,[40] modify a treaty,[41] or create entirely new law.[42] Modifications to treaties will apply only to nations that adopt the modifications (or that adopt the treaty after the modifications), and new law will apply only to nations that have adopted the Rome Statute, whereas changes to customary law may be applicable to all nations.

In the fourteen years of its existence (2002–2016), the court has tried nine defendants, all of whom were African. Five of these defendants were acquitted or had their charges dismissed, and four were convicted. In addition, the court has launched ten full investigations, of which nine concern possible crimes in Africa, and the tenth concerns possible crimes in Georgia. The court has also opened ten preliminary examinations (to see if a full investigation is warranted), of which four involve incidents in Africa, four involve incidents in the Middle East (including one of alleged crimes in Palestine, a second of alleged crimes involving the 2010 flotilla against the Gaza blockade, and a third of alleged crimes by British forces in Iraq), and the last two examinations involve alleged crimes in Colombia and the Ukraine, respectively.[43]

I have called the rise of the ICC a major change to the legal paradigm of war. Given such low numbers for level of activity (in terms of examinations, investigations, and final dispositions), and given the apparent emphasis, not to say bias, on activity focused in Africa, in what sense could the creation of the ICC be considered a "major change"?

---

[40] An example of changing customary law is the Rome Statute's definition of a war crime as launching an attack that will cause "widespread, long-term and severe damage to the natural environment" (Article 8(2)(b)(iv) of the Rome Statute). Prior to the Rome Statute, countries often considered harm to the environment, but the existence of a definition is new, as are the particular requirements – "widespread," "long-term," and "severe."

[41] For example, whereas Article 49 of Geneva Convention IV of 1949 prohibits "individual or mass forcible transfers," Article 8, section (2)(b)(iv)(viii) of the Rome Statute prohibits "transfer, directly or indirectly," which might include non-forcible transfers.

[42] The creation of a new international court, such as the ICC, to try war crimes is itself entirely new.

[43] These numbers are taken from the website of the International Criminal Court, "Situations under investigation," which may be viewed at https://www.icc-cpi.int/pages/situations.aspx.

1. Although the number of cases investigated, or tried, or brought to a successful conviction may seem low, the court was never intended to try hundreds of defendants, and cannot do so. ICC investigations and trials are major actions, extending over many years.

2. Every human endeavor will experience start-up problems, often severe start-up problems. That is true here.

3. The ICC has an additional burden in that it suffers severe political opposition in two respects. First, although more than one hundred countries have ratified the Rome Statute, approximately seventy-five countries have not, and this latter group includes countries such as Egypt, India, Iraq, Israel, the People's Republic of China, Russia, Saudi Arabia, and the United States. Countries representing more than 50 percent of the world's population have not adopted the Rome Statute.[44] There is significant opposition either to the very idea of the court, or at least to the court as it is instituted today. Second, there has been, is, and will be political opposition to every preliminary examination and every prosecution of the court, from the parties involved and from political allies of those parties.

4. As a result of its role and position, the ICC is justifiably sensitive to political considerations. On the one hand, the ICC must pursue its main goal, which, as stated in the preamble, paragraph 5 of the statute, is "to put an end to impunity for the perpetrators of these crimes and thus to contribute to the prevention of such crimes." Proponents of the ICC believe this can be done only through the legal actions defined in the statute. On the other hand, though it must pursue its main goal, the ICC must, to the extent possible, avoid antagonizing political interests. Even if the ICC were to become the greatest legal body in the history of humankind, if it excessively antagonizes powerful political interests, it will fail.

5. To judge the court solely on the number of indictments and convic-

---

[44] Very roughly, almost 40 percent of all countries have *not* adopted the Rome Statute, representing slightly more than 60 percent of the world's population. Compare "Countries in the World by Population (2016)," http://www.worldometers.info/world-population/population-by-country/ with "The States Parties to the Rome Statute," https://asp.icc-cpi.int/en_menus/asp/states%20parties/Pages/the%20states%20parties%20to%20the%20rome%20statute.aspx.

tions would be foolish. The main goal is not to put people in jail. Rather, the court's main goal is deterrence. Proponents of the ICC believe that its existence, and the possibility that it may act, will almost certainly have a deterrent effect against violations of the laws of war, notwithstanding any particular numbers of investigations, prosecutions, or convictions.

6. Asymmetric wars will dominate in the twenty-first century. Asymmetric wars have been with us throughout history, but they will now dominate the battlefield, and that is new. The legal norms have not caught up with this change. In addition, technological changes, to be discussed in chapter 5, will have tremendous impact on both war and the laws of war. In the field of the laws of war, and the use of lawfare, something must change. We do not know for certain whether the ICC will be part of the paradigm shift, but very likely some new international legal scheme will be instituted, which may be the ICC as it is exists today, or the ICC in a modified form, or something else.

7. The past focus on Africa might possibly be justified by the nature of the alleged crimes, because as mentioned, the ICC was created only to redress severe crimes, and only those crimes that would not be investigated or prosecuted by national courts. Further, in its preliminary examinations, the ICC appears to be trying to expand the geographic scope of its activities, although the ultimate success of such effort is currently unknown.[45]

Although the ICC has not had great impact in terms of the number of cases brought, prosecuted, or successfully completed, it has had a deterrent effect. Further, this deterrent effect is likely to increase over time. In that

---

[45] Very recently, Burundi, Gambia, and South Africa have all announced that they will withdraw from the ICC, while Kenya and Namibia have expressed interest in doing so (but have not announced final decisions). Whether or not any or all of these withdrawals will occur is not known at the date of this writing. Part of the alleged motivation for withdrawal appears to be a perception that the ICC focuses on crimes in Africa while ignoring crimes committed by citizens of Western nations. Some people feel, however, that these withdrawals are intended solely, or at least primarily, to give the withdrawing nations freedom to commit genocide without fear of legal consequences. See, "Gambia Joins South Africa and Burundi in Exodus from International Criminal Court", *Independent*, October 22, 2016, available at http://www.independent.co.uk/news /world/africa/gambia-international-criminal-court-hague-yahya-jammeh-south-africa -burundi-a7380516.html.

sense, the rise of the ICC is a major change in the legal environment leading to a new paradigm in the laws of war.[46]

C. Second Change: The Increase of Extralegal Attacks

The third of the interrelated charts presents the second major change in the external environment: the rise of what might be called "extralegal attacks," that is, new aspects and new means of attack based primarily on the increasing importance of asymmetric war. "Extralegal attacks" are not new in human history. However, during the era of symmetric warfare, through the end of the twentieth century, extralegal attacks either did not occur in war or they were of relatively limited impact. The past few years, however, have been different. Extralegal attacks have been particularly important in the context of the Israeli-Palestinian conflict, and they are likely to continue to be important, although perhaps in different forms. The chart below

---

[46] On the deterrent effect that the ICC has had, and that it may have in the future, see Professor Amichai Cohen and Legal Advocate Tal Mimran, "The Palestinian Authority and the International Court," Israel Democracy Institute, February 10, 2015, http://en .idi.org.il/analysis/articles/the-palestinian-authority-and-the-international-criminal -court/. The conclusion states:

> The way Israel investigates alleged violations of the laws of war during Operation Protective Edge [what I have called the "Third Gaza War," in 2014] is of the utmost importance.... The most effective shield against the intervention of external judicial entities, including the ICC, is a proper Israeli investigation that meets all of the requirements of international law [and in this way, to rely upon the principle of complementarity to forestall investigations or prosecutions by the ICC prosecutor].

The rise of the ICC has impacted internal Israeli investigations of alleged Israeli war crimes, and these internal investigations, *whatever their ultimate result*, deter future behavior that might be subject to investigation by the Israeli Military Advocate General, or by Israeli courts, or by special Israeli investigatory bodies, or by the ICC. I personally do not believe that the IDF has committed war crimes, but there will be investigations, and if necessary, prosecutions. This of course means that the mere existence of the ICC inhibits behavior that might be illegal, and that is the main purpose for which the ICC was created.

As a final note, I add that to the best of my knowledge, there is no legal structure or mechanism of any kind by Hamas or by the Palestinian Authority to investigate any of their own military activities.

includes all of the elements of the first and second charts, but also illustrates the placement and importance of extralegal attacks.

Chart 1.3: The Rise of the Extralegal Attacks (First and Second Changes)

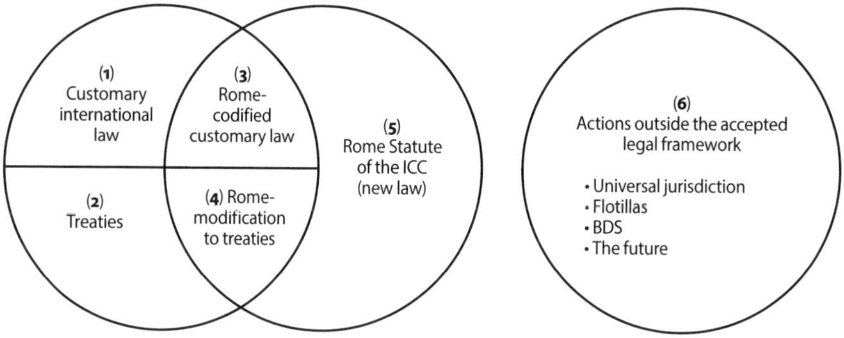

As can be seen, the attacks noted under category (6) in the chart are unconnected to the former legal network. Several examples are listed in category (6):

"Universal jurisdiction," the first example of an attack outside the prior framework, is a legal concept in which individual countries use their national laws to extend their jurisdiction to individuals involved in individual war crimes. An example is the case involving Javier Solana, which is discussed in chapter 2. Although non-territorial jurisdiction has been in existence for centuries, its current use – unrelated to the citizenship or residence of the victim or the aggressor, and all-encompassing even for single incidents with very limited casualties – is an unprecedented expansion of the concept of universal jurisdiction.

The three flotillas that attempted to break the Israeli naval blockade is a second example of extralegal attacks. A naval blockade to prevent enemy forces from rearming is not new. Attempts to "run" or "evade" a blockade are not new. The Gaza flotillas, however, did not attempt to import weapons or even to profiteer. The sole goal of the flotilla organizers was to embarrass the blockader in the eyes of international media and world opinion. This objective – to embarrass Israel in world opinion – is a function of the digital media age, and that is new. This new approach calls for new countertactics, which are discussed in chapter 4.

The third example of an extralegal attack is the anti-Israel BDS movement, short for "Boycott, Divestment, and Sanctions." The term "BDS" has been invented specifically to attack Israel, and has never been used against any other country.[47] BDS has no direct impact on the war or on the IDF, but it can create a hostile environment that may inhibit freedom of military action.

The fourth and last example of "extralegal attacks" concerns future issues relating to warfare, the laws of war, and lawfare. These issues will be used both by lawfare activists and by organizations opposing such activists. They are discussed in chapter 5.

III. The Internal Environment

The subtitle of this book is "Israel on the Lawfare Front." No one approaching this topic can have any idea of its meaning without understanding the internal environment of this battlefront, that is, the mindset of the Jews living in the Land of Israel. In this section, I will present what I consider to be the main thoughts shaping this mindset, and I will explain why they

---

[47] The closest precedent to BDS is perhaps the anti-apartheid boycott of the Republic of South Africa, but that is a very inexact precedent. In an article entitled "On Israel-Palestine and BDS," published in *The Nation*, July 2, 2014, http://www.thenation.com /article/israel-palestine-and-bds/, Noam Chomsky, well known as both a leading leftist and a severe critic of Israel, lists five reasons why BDS against Israel is different from the boycott against South Africa: (1) The movement against South Africa included each of the three actions implied in BDS, but there is no activity for sanction of Israel by Western governments, so the anti-Israel movement is more properly "BD"; (2) Among other things, BDS calls for the right of return of millions of Palestinians to pre-1967 Israel, but there is "no meaningful [international] support" for this according to Chomsky, and it is not "dictated by international law"; (3) Foreign investments had dried up in South Africa decades before the boycott took hold, while today "US investment is flowing into Israel" (as well as from Europe and Asia, although these sources of investment are not noted by Chomsky); (4) A compromise was possible in South Africa which called for the mixing of populations without changing the structure of society, but no such compromise is apparent in the case of Israel; and (5) the opponents of South Africa had a great ally – both military and in civilian aid – in Cuba, but there is no comparable ally for the Palestinians.

are relevant to this topic. The section concludes with a brief discussion of the internal environment's relevance to the laws of war.

A. The Three Thoughts Ever Present

Every country is unique, and is fundamentally different from all others. This is reflected obviously in its natural geography and in its architecture, but external manifestations are of secondary importance. The true distinction between nations is in the character of the people – the way they hear and see, how they filter sensation, the way they interpret, and their understanding of their place in the world.

Anyone who spends significant time in Israel comes to understand that there are three thoughts ever present in the minds of the Jews of Israel. These thoughts run like internal rivers, flowing underground throughout the length and breadth of the land. From time to time these rivers break forth to the surface, sometimes as a gentle brook, other times as a blasting geyser. It is impossible to predict when the breakouts will come, or with what force, but they will come. These thoughts are not always conscious, and they are not always discussed, but they are ever present.

I. JUDAISM AND RELIGION

The first of the three thoughts is religion, and specifically Judaism. The importance of Judaism to Israel is reflected in the basic statistics. As of May 2016, there were about 6.38 million Jews in Israel, representing about 75 percent of the total population of 8.52 million.[48] The breakdown of the Jewish population of Israel among religious and nonreligious is more fluid than the absolute numbers of Jews, because categories of religiosity are often a bit blurred. Generally, poll after poll shows that Jews in Israel fall into three categories: 20–30 percent "religious," 30–40 percent "traditional" or "traditional-religious," and 40–50 percent "secular."[49]

---

[48] "Latest Population Statistics for Israel (Updated May, 2016)," Jewish Virtual Library, http://www.jewishvirtuallibrary.org/jsource/Society_&_Culture/newpop.html.

[49] See, for example, Gil Ronen, "58 Percent of Jewish Israelis are Religious or 'Tradition-alists,'" *Arutz Sheva* (*Israel National News*), September 26, 2011 – about 20 percent of

Are the numbers of self-defined religious and religious-traditional "high" or "low," and by what standard? Some people believe they are relatively low,[50] but consider two other factors. First, primarily due to higher birth rates, the Jews in Israel who define themselves as "religious" are increasing both in absolute numbers and as a percentage of the total Jewish population.[51] Second, terms like "nonreligious" and "secular" have a different

Israeli Jews are "religious," 13 percent are "religious traditionalists," 25 percent are "traditionalists who are not so religious," and 42 percent are secular, available at http://www.israelnationalnews.com/News/News.aspx/148286#.Vu-wN3197RY. See also the recent report of the Pew Research Center, "Israel's Religiously Divided Society," Washington, D.C., March 8, 2016, available at http://www.pewforum.org/files/2016/03/Israel-Survey-Full-Report.pdf, shows, at p. 5, self-definition of Israeli Jews as 22 percent religious, 29 percent traditional, and 49 percent secular. The numbers will change slightly from poll to poll, but the basic allocation remains the same.

[50] For example, "Israel Among the Least Religious Countries in the World," *Haaretz*, April 14, 2015, http://www.haaretz.com/world-news/1.651616, refers to a WIN/Gallup Poll in which 30 percent of Israelis described themselves as "religious," which is lower than the self-reporting in every single region of the world. Although this is on a par with the relatively secular England and Sweden, it is much below the self-reports of "religious" in Western Europe (43 percent), Australia (44 percent), and North America (55 percent), and far below self-reports in Africa (86 percent) and the Middle East (81 percent). This is a bit deceptive, however, because if we were asking only, "Do you believe in God?" or "Do you take part in some religious activities?" the number of "religious" Jews would almost certainly include the traditionalists, placing the total in Israel at about 55–60 percent.

[51] Jewish Virtual Library, ibid., attributes the growth in the overall Jewish population specifically to the relatively high Orthodox Jewish birthrate. See, for example, Michael Lipka, "Controversy over New Israeli Law Highlights Growing Ultra-Orthodox Population," Pew Research Center, March 13, 2014, http://www.pewresearch.org/fact-tank/2014/03/13/controversy-over-new-israeli-law-highlights-growing-ultra-orthodox-population/, showing growth of the ultra-Orthodox (also known as "Haredi") alone at 0.36 percent per year in the period 2011–2030, and this would surely be in the range of 0.40–0.50 percent for the entire religious sector if the modern Orthodox (also known as "non-Haredi Orthodox") were included. To put this in proper perspective, a groundbreaking study by Israel's Central Bureau of Statistics indicates that the number of ultra-Orthodox in Israel comprised about 12 percent of all Israeli Jews in 2009, but this will rise, primarily due to differentials in birthrates, to about 22 percent in 2034, and about 34 percent in 2059. Ari Paltiel, Michel Sepulchre, Irene Kornilenko, and Martin Maldonado, "Long-Range Population Projections for Israel: 2009–2059," Israel Government Central Bureau of Statistics, Demography and Census Department, March 21, 2012, available at http://www.cbs.gov.il/publications/tec27.pdf, tables on pages 70, 71, and 72. The ultimate impact of this demographic shift is unclear, because the ultra-Orthodox appear to be integrating gradually into Israeli society. See Jeremy Sharon, "Haredi

meaning in Israel. The vast majority of Jews in Israel, even the so-called "secular," observe the major holidays and other Jewish events.[52]

Beyond the numbers are the stories – the times and places in which the underground river of religion breaks through to the surface. In the city of Modi'in, while walking through a park I came upon a group of people doing traditional Israeli folk dancing. By the dress of the group, the absence of any kippot, and the gender-mixed dancing, it was clear beyond any doubt that this was an entirely secular group, but the music to which they were dancing was "Adon Olam" (Master of the world), one of the most religious songs in the Jewish liturgy, sung on every Sabbath and on the evening of the Day of Atonement. On Ibn Gvirol Street in Tel Aviv, one might see a young girl, provocatively dressed, go into a pharmacy and reach up to touch the mezuzah[53] with her hand. A visitor to Israel will find cab drivers

---

Employment, Military Service, Higher Education, All On the Rise," *Jerusalem Post*, August 15, 2016, at http://www.jpost.com/Israel-News/Haredi-employment-military-service-higher-education-all-on-the-rise-464168. This integrating trend appears to be caused by pressure from the ultra-Orthodox public for more secular education and better employment, rather than by political pressure from the government or threat of legal sanction. Yedidia Stern, "A New Approach To Dealing with Israel's Ultra-Orthodox," *The Jewish Week*, August 11, 2016, available at http://www.thejewishweek.com/editorial-opinion/opinion/new-approach-dealing-israels-ultra-orthodox. In whatever way this trend develops, and whatever the cause, there is no doubt but that Israeli Jewish society is becoming more religious year by year.

[52] For example, according to one report, 90 percent of Israeli Jews celebrate the Passover Seder, 85 percent say it is important to celebrate the Jewish holidays, 68 percent fast on the Day of Atonement, and 67 percent do not eat bread during Passover. Yoni Dayan and Jeremy Sharon, "Israeli Jews Becoming More Religious, Poll Finds," *Jerusalem Post*, January 26, 2012, citing a survey from the Israel Democracy Institute from 2009, http://www.jpost.com/National-News/Israeli-Jews-becoming-more-religious-poll-finds. The Pew research study of 2016 also suggests that 93 percent of Israeli Jews celebrate the Passover Seder, 60 percent fast on the Day of Atonement, and 63 percent keep kosher in their homes. "Israel's Religiously Divided Society," 51.

[53] The "mezuzah" is a piece of parchment that includes the verses 6:4–9 and 11:13–21 from the book of Deuteronomy, expressing the central Jewish belief in the unity of God, the duty to teach this belief to children and to place the declaration on the doorpost of one's house, and the consequences of fulfilling or failing to fulfill these duties. No one actually "touches" or kisses the mezuzah, but rather the case in which the mezuzah is located. Nevertheless, colloquial language refers to "touching the mezuzah."

throughout the country eager to discuss the conditions under which the Messiah will come. Stories like these are so common and so well known that they are not worthy of comment to people who have lived in Israel.

Although there is no formally "established" religion in Israel, and freedom of worship is guaranteed, nevertheless Orthodox Judaism has a major impact on the status – including rights of marriage and divorce – of Israeli Jews. Many countries have an arrangement in which a particular religion is "preferred" or "official." We could cite, for example, Orthodox Christianity in Greece, Catholicism in Ireland, Lutheranism in the Nordic countries (Denmark, Finland, Iceland, Norway, and Sweden),[54] Anglicanism in England, and Islam in many Arab countries (Sunni Islam in Saudi Arabia, UAE, and a dozen other countries). In this regard, Judaism in Israel is not unique.

However, there are three things that are unique about Israel and religion. Anyone who wishes to understand Israel's motivations or actions in the military sphere should understand these three things. First:

> Judaism is the only religion [in the world] that is linked to a particular geographic area, and the complex tension between land and people has been a continuous motif in religious Jewish identity.[55]

No other country (including those countries with an established or formal religion) links its geographic area with a religion. We could say, "Argentina is overwhelmingly Roman Catholic" or "Saudi Arabia does not permit the permanent settlement of non-Muslims," but no country, except Israel, says, "Our land is the one and only place where our religion was born and must continue."[56] This linkage creates a complex and sometimes tense relationship between the Land of Israel, the people of Israel, and the religion of Israel. This relationship is always in the mind of Israeli Jews, whether they

---

[54] These examples – Greece, Ireland, and Scandinavia – are taken from Ruth Shamir Popkin, *Jewish Identity: The Challenge of Peoplehood Today* (Jerusalem: Gefen Publishing House, 2015), 168–69.

[55] Ibid., 216.

[56] Of course, this does not say that Jews are unable or barred from living in any country, nor should they be, but there is a linkage between Judaism and Israel that does not exist between Judaism and any other country.

are religious or not. It has a direct and substantial impact on the motivation of the Jews living in Israel and particularly on the Jews serving in the Israel Defense Forces.

Second, "across the generations [the Jewish] religion was unquestionably the single most important factor in the survival of Jewish identity."[57] The Jews were scattered across the globe for two thousand years, from the destruction of the Second Temple to the rise of the State of Israel. Without Judaism, there is no possibility that the Jews would have survived that period of exile.

Third, in large part due to the first two considerations – the very close connection between the religion and the land, and the critical role played by Judaism in the survival of the Jews – many attitudes and actions prevalent among the Jews of Israel are motivated, either consciously or subconsciously, by religion. I will mention only two here.

In Judaism, there is great emphasis on the sanctity of life. In particular, almost all other religious laws are suspended when there is a threat to life, even if the threat is relatively minor. This Jewish value, the sanctity of life, impacts the way soldiers of the IDF engage in warfare.

In Judaism, great value is placed on the freedom and liberty of the person. The biblical emphasis on liberty is well known. As an example we can cite Leviticus 25:10, "Proclaim liberty throughout all the land unto all inhabitants thereof" – the verse engraved on the Liberty Bell.[58] The reason liberty is so important is that we are servants of God, not of people. We must be free in order to accept God and worship only Him. The Jewish emphasis on individual liberty has had and continues to have a tremendous impact on Israeli society.

2. THE ISRAEL DEFENSE FORCES (IDF)

The IDF is a vital component of Israeli society, in many ways. Most obviously, it is responsible for the defense of the country. In the Middle East, that is a major responsibility.

---

[57] Popkin, *Jewish Identity*, 216.

[58] For non-American readers, the "Liberty Bell" is a symbol of the American Revolution (1775–1783) and of American independence. It is currently housed and on public display in the Liberty Bell Center at Independence Mall, in Philadelphia, Pennsylvania.

The IDF is a conscription army, which means that the IDF may call upon all men and women reaching the age of service. The percentage of those serving has dropped somewhat in recent years, but large numbers of young men and women still serve, estimated at 50 percent of each age cohort.[59] The result is that a significant number of Jewish families, almost surely the great majority, have a blood connection to one or more soldiers in the army. Common army terms – service, danger, duty, etc. – are not theoretical, because for most families these terms are attached to specific people.[60]

The army is an integrator of multiple cultures. Jews came to Israel from all parts of the world, bringing very different cultures and attitudes. In older days, the army was one of the few points at which these different cultures would interact and begin to assume a common national culture.[61]

---

[59] Currently about 50 percent of eligible persons serve in the army, and due to demographic changes the number is likely to fall to 40 percent in years to come. Yaakov Katz, "60 Percent of Israelis Won't Serve in IDF by 2020," November 18, 2011, *Jerusalem Post*, http://www.jpost.com/Defense/60-percent-of-Israelis-wont-serve-in-IDF-by-2020. The decline in the percentage of youth serving in the army is likely to have no impact on the fighting ability of the army, partly because of some of the changes that are discussed in chapter 5 below. The IDF has been an integrating force in Israel, so this decline in the percentage of those serving might have other impacts on Israeli society, but that remains to be seen.

[60] It is of course the case that not every soldier is actually in harm's way, but on a relative basis, Israeli soldiers are heavily oriented to combat. The ratio of combat to non-combat soldiers is generally called the "tooth-to-tail ratio" or the "T3R." A 2010 study by the international consulting firm McKinsey compared the armed forces of thirty-three countries, representing over 90 percent of global defense spending. Many countries of Western Europe, the Middle East, and East Asia are included, as well as the United States, Brazil, Russia, China, India, and many others. The average percentage of combat soldiers (defined as "armor, infantry, reconnaissance, and combat aviation") to all soldiers was 26 percent, whereas Israel, with a combat percentage of 38 percent, was ranked fourth highest of the thirty-three countries. Scott Gebicke and Samuel Magid, "Lessons from around the World: Benchmarking Performance in Defense" (McKinsey and Company, 2010), exhibit 3, p. 4. These statistics in no way detract from the great contributions of those in combat support (defined by McKinsey as artillery, engineers, and the signal corps), or in military intelligence, the cyber corps, the Military Advocate General, military medical personnel, the navy, and many others. Nevertheless, these ground troops, plus combat aviators, generally stand at the greatest risk of harm. Again, the defense contribution of the IDF, and the risk of injury or death borne by IDF soldiers, is one of the three thoughts which I have called "ever present in the Israeli mentality."

[61] This occurs today also. As one of my sons, a soldier in the Givati Brigade, told me,

The army is also a very strong binder of individuals to the collective welfare. While that is true of all armies, it is especially true of the Israeli army because of the two roles discussed above. In addition, the current situation in the world is dangerous for the West in general, and for Israel in particular. Israelis know their enemy and his genocidal intent. That knowledge generates respect for, and loyalty to, the army. Finally, there is a very strong feeling in Israel that fundamentally, when all is done, the Jews must rely on themselves alone. Allies can help, but cannot bear the main burden.

The presence of danger and the comforting existence of the IDF are ever present in the mentality of Israeli Jews. Danger is always ready to make an appearance on the news, or on the street. Even if it is not a constant topic of discussion, the army is an ever-present thought. People in Israel take great pride in the IDF, with good reason.

3. THE DESTRUCTION OF THE EUROPEAN JEWS

The third thought ever present in the mentality of the Israelis is the destruction of the European Jews. We must be clear here. The main thing is not the fact that a genocidal maniac sought to kill a certain people. That, unfortunately, has been a constant of history. It is rather that so many people knew for so long and did nothing – it is this lack of action that made the Holocaust as deadly as it was for the Jews. This is the third ever-present thought, permanently burned into the memory of the Israelis – not the fact that Iranians have stated repeatedly that they will kill us, but that in the end, we can depend on ourselves alone.

In the western part of Jerusalem, there is a memorial museum to the victims of the Holocaust. The museum is called "Yad Vashem," literally "Place and Name." The museum's name is taken from Isaiah 56:5:

> I shall give to them, in My house and within My walls, a place and a name better than sons and daughters. An eternal name shall I give them, that they not be cut off.[62]

"You meet everyone in the army." Indeed. He meant that different cultures, social classes, and character types all mix together.

[62] This is my translation from the Hebrew. Other translations I have seen are slightly

In the museum, there is one place that has been reconstructed to look like a street in the Warsaw Ghetto, with a cobblestone floor, tramway tracks, and lampposts from the early twentieth century. On one of the walls of this place is a video screen that shows a short movie, a bit over two minutes, in a continuous loop.

One of the objectives of the Germans in their management of the Warsaw Ghetto was to weaken the population prior to its expulsion for mass extermination. To that end, the Germans decreed that the amount of food that would be allowed into the ghetto would be sufficient to provide each person with 184 calories per day. A diet of this kind is not sufficient to sustain any human being for any significant period of time.[63] In circumstances such as these, where the certain fate of those obeying the law is death, the inevitable result is the rise of smuggling and a black market, which indeed happened in the Warsaw Ghetto. But a world dominated by the black market is a brutal world – it is a world in which the weak simply cannot compete with the strong. In this case, "the weak" means orphaned children, who were simply unable to protect themselves.

The two-minute movie shows, in a continuous loop, scenes of small children, sometimes brother and sister, begging and starving to death on the streets of the Warsaw Ghetto. These are difficult scenes to view, but there is no replacement or substitute. If you go to Yad Vashem in Jerusalem, see the movie and watch it from the beginning to the end. You will then understand the Israelis, and what they will do to defend their country.[64]

---

different, but the general concept – to give a memorial so that the dead may not be forgotten – is unchanged.

[63] By contrast, the official ration for Poles was 699 per day, which is also insufficient to sustain life, while the ration for Germans in Poland was 2,613 calories per day. Charles G. Roland's *Courage Under Siege: Disease, Starvation and Death in the Warsaw Ghetto* (New York: Oxford University Press, 1992), chapter 6, pp. 99–104, available at http://remember.org/courage/chapter6.

[64] I am not entirely sure that the Allies refused to act because they hated the Jews. In the case of Roosevelt, for example, he had political considerations, and his attitude was probably due more to indifference than hostility – although in the end, the result was the same for the Jews of Europe. The thought that is most concerning now, more than seventy years after the end of World War II, is whether or not anything would be different

B. The Relevance of the Three Thoughts to the Laws of War

Is any of this material on the internal environment of combatants relevant to the laws of war? In other words, are the standards in the laws of war the same for everyone in all situations, or can they change depending on the parties involved and their internal environments?

This is a very difficult question. The Jews might say, "We have had a very painful history, full of persecution and bloodshed. This will impact the way we view things, and must be considered when we stand to judgment for the commission of war crimes. We are able to act only in accordance with our feelings and our historical memory." There is much to admire in this argument, but then every country has its history and its unique view. Have not Asian peoples suffered? Have not African peoples suffered? Have not European Catholics and European Protestants caused each other great suffering? Have not the Muslims suffered? Most particularly, will not the Palestinians say, "We, too, have suffered. We have been dispossessed and persecuted, like the Jews." Many, many peoples have tales of woe, sometimes terrible tales. Does this mean that each people must have its own standard for conduct in time of war? If every country, due to its history, will define for itself what is "legal in war," then what remains of the laws of war for all?

There is no perfect answer, but in my mind, the following must be considered:

To take the extreme view, "each nation must decide for itself," would lead immediately to chaos and the end of the laws of war. This cannot happen, and therefore it will not happen.

To take the opposite extreme, "the internal environment is irrelevant," is simply not realistic. Jews will not act the same as Eskimos, who will not

---

today. If genocide were being committed, particularly over a long period of time, would the world do anything about it? Biafra, 1967–1970, 1,000,000 dead. Uganda, 1969–1979, 300,000 dead. Ethiopia, 1975–1978, 1,500,000 dead. Cambodia, 1975–1979, 2,000,000 dead. Rwanda, 1994, 800,000 dead. Darfur, February 2003 and ongoing, 400,000 dead. Syrian civil war, March 2011 and ongoing, 500,000 dead. I do not know if the world will do anything about the next genocide, but the Jews do well to rely only on themselves.

act the same as Brazilians, who will not act the same as Arabs. People will be different and will act differently.

The laws of war are criminal laws, not civil. For criminal liability to attach, there must be both a criminal action and criminal intent.[65] In criminal law, there is a single definition of each "crime," applicable to every person, but this describes only the action. The actor's intent cannot be known for certain, but it is inferred from the circumstances of the case. The actor is totally excused from liability only if he or she is clearly insane or otherwise mentally incompetent. Mental incompetence cannot be assumed for nations. However, the actor's degree of guilt, and hence also the degree of punishment, depend, at least to some degree, on the actor's subjective or "internal" reality. In my mind, this moderation, based on the internal reality of combatants, must apply also in the laws of war – not to excuse or justify, but to mitigate liability in appropriate cases. This must be done because, as I have said, to ignore the internal reality of the Jews, or the internal reality of the Arabs, is simply to ignore reality completely.

The relevance of the internal reality is one of the most important debates of our time regarding the laws of war and lawfare. This debate was conducted in some detail by Professors Schmitt, Merriam, Cohen, and Shany, as presented in the appendix at the end of this book.

IV. A Summary of Chapter 1

Chapter 1 sets forth the most fundamental concepts in the laws of war. The topic of this book – Israel on the lawfare front – cannot be grasped without an understanding of these fundamental concepts.

There is a critical distinction between reasons and justifications for going to war, called *jus ad bellum*, and the manner in which a war is waged, called *jus in bello*. This book is about the laws related to waging war, the *jus in bello*. There are four main principles that always apply in the waging of war, and these are necessity (N), distinction (D), proportionality (P), and

---

[65] The formal legal terms are "*actus reus*" for criminal action and "*mens rea*" for criminal intent.

shielding (S). There are other principles as well, although a strong argument can be made that every other principle must relate to one of these four main principles.

The old legal environment for waging war was valid through the end of the twentieth century, in the age in which symmetric wars were the dominant mode of fighting. The dominant mode of fighting now, and very probably for the rest of the twenty-first century, will be asymmetric war. The old legal environment is not suited for the new type of war, and a paradigm shift is required. We are in the midst of such a shift now. It will certainly include elements from the old environment, but it will also include new elements.

One major change to the legal environment is the creation of the International Criminal Court. The ICC has thus far had a minor impact in numbers of cases and defendants, but it has nevertheless had a deterrent effect. The court is subject to very serious political pressures, but if it can manage those pressures then it is likely to become increasingly important over the next few decades in the interpretation and application of the laws of war. A second change to the legal environment is the rise of attacks outside of the old framework, which have been called here "extralegal attacks." Examples of such attacks, discussed herein, are universal jurisdiction (to be discussed further in chapter 2), flotillas (to be discussed further in chapter 3), boycott/divestment/sanctions (BDS), and future developments (to be discussed further in chapter 5).

Whereas the legal environment of war may be called the "external environment," the "internal environment" is the mentality and identity of the combatants. There are three major thoughts that are always present in the minds of Israeli Jews. These three thoughts are (1) religion and the core values of Judaism, (2) security concerns and the Israel Defense Forces, and (3) the destruction of European Jews, particularly the refusal of the non-murderers to take action to prevent the murders. There is an important discussion as to whether the internal environment can have an impact on the laws of war. In the end, the laws of war do not change, but war is an interaction of two living bodies, and that interaction will of necessity impact the ways in which the combatants understand and apply the laws of war.

CHAPTER 2

The Fight against Lawfare

Introduction: The Logical End to Defensive Warfare

> The only logical end to defensive warfare is surrender.
>
> – *Napoleon Bonaparte*[66]

There have been many successful defensive battles throughout history. Within only the past hundred years, one might think of the French defense on the Western Front in WWI, the Russian defense at Stalingrad in WWII, the American defense at the Battle of the Bulge in WWII, and the UN forces defense of the Pusan Perimeter in the Korean War. But no matter how great these defensive actions, they do not ultimately win the war. A general offensive, or at least a specific attack of some kind, is typically required to achieve a decisive victory.

We might classify attacks into one of three types. The first is the opening of hostilities – that is, an attack that is not in response to actual or anticipated military action of the other side, but rather is the first act of fighting. The

---

[66] Many people report this quotation, but in different forms, and never with attribution by date, place, or source. It is doubtful that Napoleon ever said this, and in that sense the quotation is apocryphal. Nevertheless, it does seem to reflect Napoleon's general attitude about warfare, which was aggressive in the extreme, and perhaps for that reason the quotation is attributed to him.

second is counterattack, which is often combined with a defense against the first attack by an enemy. The third is known as "anticipatory self-defense," also known as "preemption," which shares features of the other types in that it is the initial military action, but it is taken in response to what is perceived to be a clear military threat of the enemy.

The Israel Law Center, known in Hebrew as Shurat HaDin, is an organization devoted to fighting on the lawfare front. It is the chief pro-Israel lawfare NGO active today. The actions of an organization such as the Israel Law Center are without doubt aggressive, and can be termed "attacks," but they are only of the second and third type. The Israel Law Center has not begun hostilities, but is rather responding to the attacks of Israel's enemies. In some cases, its actions are in the form of a counterattack against a specific action of the enemy, and in other cases it is a type of "anticipatory self-defense" – again in response to an enemy, but this time in anticipation of a hostile action expected from the enemy. In this chapter, examples of both actions – counterattack and anticipatory self-defense – are presented.

I. An Example of Counterattack: The Case of Javier Solana

Javier Solana is one of the great Spanish political figures of modern times. Initially a professor of physics, he became first a representative in the Spanish Parliament, then the Spanish minister of foreign affairs in the period 1992–1995. In December 1995, he became the secretary general of NATO, a position he held until October 6, 1999. He later became the secretary general of the Council of the European Union (the highest official in the European Parliament) in the period October 1999–December 2009.

In late 2008, Judge Fernando Andreu, of the Central Magistrates' Court Number Four of the High Court in Madrid, opened a preliminary investigation into the death of Salah Shehade in 2002 (previously discussed in chapter 1).[67] This investigation was based on a doctrine called "universal

---

[67] The preliminary investigation came in response to a complaint that was filed on June 24, 2008, by certain Gazans injured in the attack on Shehade.

jurisdiction," according to which any court in any location, or any international organization, may try for criminal responsibility any person alleged to have committed crimes against humanity, genocide, extrajudicial executions, or war crimes. According to this doctrine, jurisdiction may be asserted irrespective of the place of the alleged crime, the nationality or residence of the accused, the nationality or residence of the alleged victim, or any other particular relation with the state or organization seeking to assert jurisdiction.

On January 29, 2009, Judge Andreu issued an order that a full investigation, possibly leading to indictment, trial, and conviction, must be opened against Doron Almog (chief of the Southern Command of the IDF), Benjamin Ben-Eliezer (Israeli minister of defense), Abraham Dichter (director of the Israeli General Security Service, also known as Shabak or Shin Bet), Giora Elan (chairman of the Israeli National Security Council), Dan Halutz (commander of the Israeli Air Force), Michael Herzog (military secretary of the Israeli Ministry of Defense), Ariel Sharon (former Israeli prime minister, totally disabled by a stroke three years before the Spanish case), and Moshe Ya'alon (IDF chief of staff). On May 4, 2009, Judge Andreu issued his opinion that Spanish courts are competent to judge Israeli defendants in the matter of Salah Shehade.

Spanish prosecutors immediately appealed this decision, seeking to overrule Judge Andreu's exercise of jurisdiction. On June 30, 2009, the Spanish National Court of Appeals accepted the appeal, overruled Judge Andreu, and dismissed the criminal investigation. The Spanish Supreme Court affirmed the decision of the Court of Appeals on March 4, 2010, and published its decision on April 13, 2010.[68]

---

[68] This account is taken from four sources: (1) Ido Rosenzweig and Yuval Shany, "Update on Universal Jurisdiction: Spanish Supreme Court Affirms Decision to Close Inquiry into Targeted Killing of Salah Shehadeh" (Israel Democracy Institute, April 5, 2010), available at http://en.idi.org.il/analysis/terrorism-and-democracy/issue-no-17/update-on-universal-jurisdiction-spanish-supreme-court-affirms-decision-to-close-inquiry-into-targeted-killing-of-salah-shehadeh; (2) Claudia Jiménez Cortés, "Combating Impunity for International Crimes in Spain: From the Prosecution of Pinochet to the Indictment of Garzón" (Institut Català Internacional per la Pau, May 2011), 33–34, http://icip.gencat.cat/web/.content/continguts/publicacions/workingpapers/2011/arxius/2._01-80_wp

Universal jurisdiction by its appellation may apply worldwide, but it is implemented according to the specific legislation of a particular country. The relevant statute here, Article 23.4 of Spain's Judicial Power Organization Act, was passed in 1985, and applied to "Spaniards or foreigners outside the national territory [of Spain]" who allegedly committed any of the listed crimes. On November 3, 2009, after the rejection of Judge Andreu's ruling by the Court of Appeals, the Spanish legislature amended Article 23.4 to require first, "that the alleged perpetrators are present in Spain, that there are victims of Spanish nationality or that there is some relevant link with Spain," and second, "that no other competent country or international court has initiated proceedings, of such crimes [in which case the exercise of universal jurisdiction will be suspended during the course of such proceedings]."[69]

What caused the reversal of Judge Andreu's decision, as well as the basic change in the statute applying universal jurisdiction in Spain? Diplomatic discussions, presumably involving Israel, the United States, and possibly others, must have played a role. In addition, however, shortly after Judge Andreu's ruling in late January 2009, the Israel Law Center began preparation of a criminal indictment, *based specifically on Article 23.4 of Spain's Judicial Power Organization Act*, against Javier Solana, at that time the highest executive in the European Union.

While Solana was the head of NATO, the Kosovo War occurred, during February 28, 1998–June 11, 1999. Between March 24, 1999, and June 10, 1999, NATO bombed Yugoslavia in an attempt to end the war. Although the bombing was said to be "strategic" and directed solely at "military infra-

---

_2011-1_ing.pdf; (3) Tribunal Supremo (supreme court) of Spain, Criminal Division, Appeal no. 1979/2009, March 4, 2010 (unofficial translation from the original Spanish to English), http://ccrjustice.org/sites/default/files/assets/files/AlDaraj_SupremeCourt _Decision_03.04.2010_ENG.pdf; and (4) Anne Herzberg, NGO "Lawfare": Exploitation of Courts in the Arab-Israeli Conflict, 2nd ed., NGO Monitor Monograph Series (Jerusalem: NGO Monitor, December 2010), 45–52, http://www.ngo-monitor.org. il/data/images/File/lawfare-monograph.pdf.

[69] "The Scope and Application of the Principle of Universal Jurisdiction: Information Provided by Spain" in response to resolution 64/117 of the UN General Assembly, United Nations, December 19, 2009, http://www.un.org/en/ga/sixth/66/ScopeAppUniJuri _StatesComments/Spain%20(S%20to%20E).pdf, at p. 9.

structure," it also killed about five hundred civilians and destroyed civilian factories, buildings, and businesses. In one particularly tragic instance, NATO bombed a civilian train while it was passing over the Grdelica gorge, killing fourteen civilians including children and a pregnant woman, and injuring at least sixteen others. There was no intent to kill or harm civilians, and the entire attack appeared to be a mistake, but the casualties occurred nevertheless. If one may say that the top Israeli military and political officials are guilty of war crimes for unintentionally killing fourteen civilians while eliminating a master terrorist responsible for the murder of hundreds, should not Javier Solana also be a war criminal for heading an organization that killed, albeit unintentionally, fourteen civilians in this one incident and another five hundred during a seventy-eight-day bombing campaign?

This was the complaint against Solana, based on the violation of Article 23.4, that was about to be filed by the Israel Law Center. The preparation of the complaint was communicated to Spanish authorities, who asked the Israel Law Center to delay filing. The ultimate result was the overruling of Judge Andreu's decision, and a change in Article 23.4.

This was not an attack by the Israel Law Center, since the attack was initiated by those who filed a criminal complaint against Israeli military and political leaders. This is rather an example of a counterattack – not against the lawfare activists, but rather against the Spanish legal system that initially permitted the criminal complaint against the Israelis to be filed and reviewed. Had the Spaniards continued with their case, the Israel Law Center would have filed the complaint against one of the most famous Spanish political figures of current times. Thus, the Spaniards would have been forced to either prosecute their own leader for criminal liability or expose their entire system as a hypocritical sham – claiming moral superiority for pursuing universal justice but in fact picking and choosing which defendants to prosecute. The Spaniards did not want to face that choice, and so in the end they chose a third way by quashing the complaint against multiple Israeli officials, and by amending their law.

Although this was the end of Judge Andreu's decision, it was not the end of universal jurisdiction asserted against Israeli leaders in Spain. The amendment to Article 23.4 was not airtight, since it still permitted the exercise of jurisdiction if (1) a non-Spaniard alleged criminal happened to be present in Spain for any reason, and (2) if no court had initiated proceedings in relation to the alleged war crimes. On the basis of the amended statute, Judge Jose de la Mata of the Spanish National Court ordered, in November 2015, that Prime Minister Netanyahu and Israeli ministers Ehud Barak, Benny Begin, Avigdor Lieberman, Eliezer Marom, Moshe Ya'alon, and Eli Yishai be placed on a police registry, so that any of them who came to Spain could be detained, arrested, or charged. This order was based upon the events that occurred in 2010 on the ship *Mavi Marmara*, when several people were killed as they tried to break the weapons blockade of Gaza.[70] However, Judge de la Mata's order was clearly a jurisdictional error, and was found so by a Spanish court.

Article 23.4 had been amended further on March 13, 2015, prior to Judge de la Mata's order. By this second amendment, genocide, crimes against humanity, and war crimes may be brought in Spanish courts only against "a Spanish citizen or a foreign citizen who is habitually resident in Spain or a foreigner who is found in Spain and whose extradition had been denied by Spanish authorities."[71] None of these categories applied to the Israeli citizens who were the subject of Judge de la Mata's order. Hence Judge de la Mata's order was overruled, and registration of Israelis as possible war criminals was canceled.[72]

How successful were the Israel Law Center's efforts in the battle against universal jurisdiction in Spain? In the short run, the efforts clearly suc-

---

[70] This incident occurred on May 31, 2010, during Flotilla 1. All three of the flotillas against the weapons blockade are discussed in chapter 4. It may be noted that none of the persons killed on the *Mavi Marmara* were Spanish citizens, although there were three Spaniards on the ship at the time of the incident.

[71] See "Boletín Oficial del Estado, Núm. 63, Sec.1, Pág. 23027, section 4(a)," available at https://www.boe.es/boe/dias/2014/03/14/pdfs/BOE-A-2014-2709.pdf.

[72] There are many articles discussing Judge de la Mata's order against Netanyahu and other Israelis. See, for example, "Spanish Judge Seeks to Prosecute PM over 2010 Flotilla Raid," *Times of Israel*, November 17, 2015, http://www.timesofisrael.com/spanish-judge -seeks-to-prosecute-pm-over-2010-flotilla-raid, and "Spain Lifts War Crime Listing for Netanyahu, 6 Others," *Jewish Telegraphic Agency*, December 27, 2015, reprinted in *Times of Israel*, http://www.timesofisrael.com/spain-lifts-war-crime-listing-for-netanyahu -6-others.

ceeded, since the original decision of Judge Andreu was overruled, and the statute was amended. In the long run, even more successful, because the Spanish statute, Article 23.4, was amended a second time to permit allegations of war crimes only against Spanish citizens or people who have a close and abiding connection to Spain, a definition that does not apply to Israel's military or political leaders. Whether due to the Israel Law Center's threat to sue Javier Solana in 2009, or to continuing diplomatic pressure, or more probably to both, the counterattack against Spain's broad exercise of universal jurisdiction was very successful.[73]

The experience of the Spanish cases against Doron Almog, Benjamin Netanyahu, Ariel Sharon, and many other Israeli officials, as recounted here, is not unique. In fact, over the past few years, more than a dozen cases have been filed against Israeli military and political officials in countries such as Belgium, Canada, Denmark, the Netherlands, New Zealand, Norway, Spain, Switzerland, Turkey, the United Kingdom, and the United States. These cases have been filed by Palestinian NGOs, especially the Palestinian Centre for Human Rights (PCHR), the Center for Constitutional Rights (CCR), and their allies.[74] Almost certainly the leading cases are those

---

[73] The combination of diplomatic pressure and lawsuits is extremely potent. Why did Spain amend Article 23.4 in 2009, and again in 2014? Political pressure came not only from the United States and Israel, but also from China, after a Spanish judge issued arrest orders against both the former Chinese prime minister and the former Chinese president for alleged war crimes committed in Tibet. Also, Spain learned that "universal jurisdiction" cuts both ways when, in addition to the threat against Javier Solana, Argentine judge María Romilda Servini de Cubría issued arrest warrants against four Spanish police officials who allegedly engaged in the torture of innocent civilians during the Franco regime of the mid-twentieth century. See Ralph Minder, "Argentine Judge Seeks to Put Spanish Officials on Trial," *New York Times*, September 13, 2013, http://www.nytimes.com/2013/10/01/world/europe/argentine-judge-seeks-to-put-franco-officials-on-trial.html?_r=0. A major problem with "universal jurisdiction" is that once it starts to apply, it seems to have no end.

[74] See, for example, Anne Herzberg, "Lawfare Against Israel," *Wall Street Journal*, November 5, 2008, www.wsj.com/articles/SB122583394143998285, which cites the PCHR, the CCR, and Al-Haq as the three leading Palestinian NGOs fighting against Israel. Herzberg is the legal advisor for NGO Monitor, which monitors and reports on anti-Israel NGOs. Additional anti-Israel NGOs are listed at "Lawfare, International Law, and Human Rights" on NGO Monitor's website, http://www.ngo-monitor.org/key-issues/lawfare-international-law-and-human-rights/about/.

filed in Belgium, Spain, and the UK. In each of these three countries, the suits against the Israeli officials were overplayed. Not only were the cases dismissed without a finding of liability, but in each of these countries – Belgium, Spain, and the UK – severe restrictions were placed on the exercise of universal jurisdiction. Universal jurisdiction is permissive; it is not mandatory. Countries exercise such jurisdiction to punish notorious crimes, and to deter the repeat of such crimes in the future. When the system is abused, however, when a decent legal concept such as universal jurisdiction is misused to advance political ends unrelated to the concept, the result, as happened here, is that the system rejects the concept and limits its scope for future action.[75]

II. Examples of Anticipatory Self-Defense: Filings at the International Criminal Court

Since at least 2009, the Palestinian Authority tried to adopt the Rome Statute and join the International Criminal Court. However, this treaty (the

---

[75] The failed lawsuits against Israeli officials in Belgium, Spain, and the UK are discussed at length in Dr. Raphael Ben-Ari's "Universal Jurisdiction: Learning the Costs of Political Manipulation," in *The Palestinian Manipulation of the International Community*, ed. Alan Baker (Jerusalem: Jerusalem Center for Public Affairs, 2014), 23–45, http://jcpa.org /wp-content/uploads/2014/04/Palestinian_Manipulation.pdf. It was a combination of law and politics that led to the defeat of the complaints and the severe narrowing of the statutes. In Belgium, a 1999 statute with sweeping scope was used to file a complaint against Ariel Sharon, then prime minister of Israel. Subsequent Belgian complaints filed against President Bush and other Americans for conduct in the Iraq War led to American threats to close the NATO headquarters located in Brussels. The Belgian statute was then quickly amended, and under the new law the complaint against Sharon was dismissed. In Spain, as noted, the legal threat against Javier Solana and the Chinese threat of retaliation against Spain were enough to lead to a severe narrowing of the law and the dismissal of the complaint against many Israeli military and political figures. In the UK, a string of arrest warrants and cases were launched against Israelis in the period 2002–2009, including against Minister of Defense Shaul Mofaz in 2002 and 2004, Doron Almog in 2005, and Foreign Minister Tzipi Livni in 2009. The sheer volume of these complaints, the brazenness of the abuse of British jurisdiction, and a British fear that American officials would also be sued induced a procedural change in September 2011 – henceforth, no arrest warrant could be issued without prior notification to and consultation with the UK attorney general and the British Cabinet. In essence, this was the end of unbridled and unprincipled universal jurisdiction in the UK.

Rome Statute) may be adopted only by nation states, and therefore there was considerable doubt as to whether a nation called "Palestine" could join. In December 2014, the ICC decided that Palestine would be allowed to join the treaty, which it did on January 7, 2015, effective April 1, 2015. In June 2015, the Palestinian Authority submitted its first complaint to the ICC, related to Israel's conduct of the Gaza War of 2014. On August 3, 2015, the PA filed its second ICC complaint against Israel, this one related to the Duma arson incident. It is likely that the PA is contemplating additional complaints to be filed against Israel at the ICC.

For its part, the Israel Law Center is preparing a "tsunami of its own war crimes complaints against Palestinian leaders including the senior ranks of Hamas and the PLO."[76] In fact, during 2014–2015, the Israel Law Center filed complaints at the ICC against Khaled Mashal (political head of Hamas), Mahmoud Abbas (head of Fatah and president of the Palestinian Authority), Jibril Rajoub (head of the Palestinian football association), Majid Faraj (head of the Palestinian General Intelligence Agency), and Rami Hamdallah (simultaneously prime minister and minister of the interior for the Palestinian Authority), as well as against Turkey for its conquest and occupation of northern Cyprus. The complaints against Mashal and Abbas were both filed in 2014, before the PA's adoption of the Rome Statute; they are a form of "anticipatory self-defense" and will be considered below. The complaint against Turkey will be considered in chapter 3.

A. The Case of Khaled Mashal

Khaled Mashal is the political head (but not the military head) of Hamas. Born in 1956, he started life humbly, received a BS in physics from Kuwait University, and worked as a teacher in the period 1978–1984. During college, he became active in Palestinian politics. He eventually joined Hamas, and became chairman of the Hamas Political Bureau in 1996. Mashal has stated publicly, and repeatedly, that Hamas will end its fighting if Israel will return to the 1967 borders and accept the "right of return" of every Palestinian

---

[76] "Defending Israeli Soldiers in the ICC," website of the Israel Law Center, http://israellawcenter.org/activities/defending-israeli-soldiers-in-the-icc/.

living outside of Israel (currently about 7 million), conditions that would effectively mean the end of the State of Israel.

Although Mashal is the head of Hamas, which rules the Gaza Strip, he has never lived in Gaza, and has not lived in any part of Palestine at any time over the past fifty years. He did, however, visit Gaza in late 2012, after a complete absence of thirty-seven years from any part of Palestine. Today he lives in a luxury hotel in Doha, the capital city of Qatar, and he was in that hotel during the Third Gaza War of 2014. He has been able to afford the lifestyle of a luxury hotel because despite his humble start, he has amassed a fortune estimated at $3 billion, through a business whose exact nature is not clear.[77]

The Israel Law Center filed a complaint at the International Criminal Court on September 2, 2014, charging Khaled Mashal with "war crimes" as defined by international humanitarian law.[78] Although the complaint was filed one week after the end of the Third Gaza War of 2014, nevertheless its does not focus on war crimes against Israeli civilians, such as targeting civilians (a violation of both the necessity and distinction principles), or firing weapons without guidance systems toward civilian settlements (a violation of the distinction principle), or storing military hardware in UN refugee centers or placing Hamas headquarters within the largest hospital in Gaza or firing rockets from schools (all of which are violations of the shielding principle). Rather, the complaint charges Hamas, and Mashal

---

[77] Some of Mashal's money apparently came from charitable donations to Hamas, particularly the so-called "Syrian Fund" amassed during the period 2001–2011, when Mashal headed the Hamas office in Damascus. See, for example, Doron Peskin, "Hamas Got Rich as Gaza Was Plunged into Poverty," *Ynet News*, July 15, 2014, http://www.ynetnews .com/articles/0,7340,L-4543634,00.html; Roi Kais, "Private Jets, Restaurants, Luxury Hotels: The Good Life of Senior Hamas Officials," *Ynet News*, July 22, 2014, http:// www.ynetnews.com/articles/0,7340,L-4548202,00.html; and Ella Levy-Weinrib, "Meet the Hamas Billionaires," *Globes*, July 24, 2014, http://www.globes.co.il/en/article-the -phenomenal-wealth-of-hamas-leaders-1000957953.

[78] The legal complaint is entitled "Shurat Ha-Din Israel Law Center, *The complainant v. Khaled Mashal, Accused of War Crimes*, Communication to the Prosecutor of the International Criminal Court regarding war crimes committed by Khaled Mashal," September 2, 2014, and may be found at http://israellawcenter.org/wp-content/uploads/2014/11 /ICC-Khaled-Mashal.pdf. It will be called here "Complaint against Mashal."

as the political head of Hamas, with extrajudicial killings. Under Article 8, section 2(c)(iv) of the Rome Statute, it is a crime of war to pass sentence of and carry out "executions without previous judgment pronounced by a regularly constituted court, affording all judicial guarantees which are generally recognized as indispensable." The complaint alleges that Mashal knew of the circumstances of the executions and controlled Hamas, but failed to take any steps to stop these illegal and extrajudicial killings.[79] Thus, Mashal was charged with the war crime of "execution without due process."[80] Two groups of civilians were executed. None of the victims were Jews or Israelis, but rather they were all Arabs living in Gaza. In the first group, eighteen Arab civilians were accused of being "collaborators" with Israel. All of these eighteen civilians had been imprisoned by Hamas for at least two years prior to the war, so it is not clear how they could have "collaborated" with Israel during the war. There were no formal charges; there was no trial, no court, and no judicial decision. These eighteen persons were executed on August 22, 2014, seven executed publicly and eleven executed in a Gaza City police station.[81]

The second group of Arab civilians, twenty persons in all, was not charged with "collaboration," but rather with engaging in antiwar protests against the Hamas government in Gaza. These twenty civilians were executed, again without any formal charges or trial, on July 28, 2014.[82]

This complaint has been pending at the ICC from the time it was filed in September 2014.

Why did the Israel Law Center choose to focus its complaint on the extrajudicial killings of Arab civilians, rather than on war crimes against Israeli civilians? There are several reasons. First, there is something intrinsically horrific about persons in wartime who execute their own people. Hamas and Mashal should be shown for what they are; the complaint highlights the nature of the Hamas regime. Second, there appears to be

---

[79] Complaint against Mashal, 4, 11.

[80] Complaint against Mashal, 2–4, 13.

[81] Complaint against Mashal, 4–5.

[82] Complaint against Mashal, 5.

universal condemnation of this behavior. Even the Palestinian Authority condemned Hamas for these "random executions" that were "not...in accordance with the law."[83] And third, the charge of extrajudicial executions is unique to Mashal, at least in reference to the Third Gaza War. The Palestinian Authority, which is not based in and does not control Gaza, could not be responsible for war crimes committed in Gaza during the war.

The fact that this particular complaint focuses on extrajudicial executions does not preclude future complaints against Mashal or Hamas for violations of the traditional legal principles of necessity, distinction, proportionality, and, especially, in the case of Hamas, shielding.

B. The Case of Mahmoud Abbas

Mahmoud Abbas, also known as Abu Mazen, is chairman of the Palestine Liberation Organization and president of the Palestinian Authority. Born in 1935, he graduated in law from the University of Damascus, then earned a PhD in 1982 from the People's Friendship University of Russia. His doctorate thesis, entitled "The Secret Connection between the Nazis and the Leaders of the Zionist Movement, 1933–1945," claimed that the Nazis and Zionists collaborated to kill the Jews of Europe. The thesis was later published as an Arabic-language book. Abbas became involved in Palestinian politics in the 1950s, joined the PLO in 1961, and in 1972 provided the funds needed for terrorists to carry out the Munich massacre of Israeli Olympic athletes. After Yasser Arafat's death, Abbas was elected president of the PA in 2005, and although his term of office ended in 2009, he has continued to hold that position, without any other election, to the present day.

Like Khaled Mashal, Mahmoud Abbas and the Abbas family also seem to have done very well in business, amassing perhaps $100 million, apparently through monopolies on American cigarettes sold in the territories controlled by the Palestinian Authority, USAID funding for infrastructure projects in the territories, and special preferences for retail business.[84]

---

[83] Complaint against Mashal, 6.

[84] Jonathan Schanzer, "The Brothers Abbas: Are the Sons of the Palestinian President

The Israel Law Center filed a complaint at the International Criminal Court on November 11, 2014, charging Mahmoud Abbas with "war crimes" as defined by international humanitarian law.[85] The complaint alleges that during the Third Gaza War, July–August 2014, armed groups of the PLO (called "Fatah" in the complaint) fired from Gaza into Israel more than two thousand rockets and mortars. Further, although these projectiles lacked guidance systems (and hence, their firing is a violation of the distinction principle of warfare), the PLO deliberately aimed these projectiles at civilian targets (which allegations, if true, are clear violations of both the necessity and distinction principles of warfare). Under Article 8, section 2(c)(i) of the Rome Statute, it is a crime of war to commit "violence to life and person, in particular murder of all kinds, mutilation, cruel treatment and torture." The deliberate targeting of civilians in warfare is "violence to life and person," equivalent to "murder." The complaint alleges that Abbas knew of the civilian targeting and controlled the PLO, but failed to take any steps to stop what was essentially murder.[86]

In particular, the Al-Aksa Martyrs' Brigade fired 620 rockets, the Abu Nidal Brigade 532 rockets, and the Abdul Kader Husseini Brigade 864 rockets and mortars. Specific civilian targets included the cities and towns of Ashdod, Ashkelon, Netivot, and Sderot, and the kibbutzim (mixed agricultural/factory settlements, entirely civilian) of Ein Shlosha, Kfar Aza, Nirim, and Nir Oz.[87] The firings were specifically intended, according to public

---

Growing Rich off Their Father's System?" Foreign Policy Group, June 5, 2012, http://foreignpolicy.com/2012/06/05/the-brothers-abbas/. This article was used as the basis of a defamation lawsuit brought by Yasser Abbas, son of Mahmoud Abbas, against both the Foreign Policy Group and the author Schanzer. The lawsuit was dismissed by the US District Court in September 2013, and the dismissal was affirmed in April 2015 by the US Appellate Court for the District of Columbia.

[85] The legal complaint is entitled "Shurat HaDin – Israel Law Center, *The complainant* v. Mahmoud Abbas (also known as Abu Mazen), *Accused of War Crimes*, Communication to the Prosecutor of the International Criminal Court regarding war crimes committed by Mahmoud Abbas (also known as Abu Mazen)," November 11, 2014, and may be found at http://israellawcenter.org/wp-content/uploads/2014/11/ICC-Complaint-Mahmoud-Abbas.pdf. It will be called here, "Complaint against Abbas."

[86] Complaint against Abbas, 4, 10–13.

[87] Complaint against Abbas, 5–7.

statements of the PLO and in particular of the Al-Aksa Martyrs' Brigade, to terrorize and kill Israeli civilians.[88] Mahmoud Abbas was aware of these firings, in fact discussed them on Palestinian television while they were happening, but failed to do anything to stop them.[89] Since the complaint against Abbas was filed in November 2014, it has been pending at the ICC.

How successful have been the Israel Law Center's filings of complaints at the International Criminal Court? If the sole goal were to stop the Palestinian Authority's membership in the ICC, then the efforts failed. The Palestinian Authority pursued national membership, the ICC permitted membership even though there is no "state of Palestine," the PA adopted the Rome Statute and became a member of the ICC, the PA has filed multiple complaints against Israel at the ICC, and the future seems to hold more PA complaints to be filed against Israel.

That is not the end of the matter, however. The Israel Law Center has filed, thus far, five complaints at the ICC against top Palestinian officials, and is prepared to file a storm of additional complaints. The ICC, and most particularly Chief Prosecutor Bensouda, are fully aware that the filings of the PA, based on allegations of Israeli war crimes during the Third Gaza War of 2014, are not isolated incidents, but rather part of a legal war that is now going on between the PA and Israel on multiple fronts. In an article entitled "The Future of the Hague May Hinge on the War in Gaza,"[90] journalist Benny Avni has emphasized a negative perception of the ICC, calling the court "toothless," having "failed to score any high-profile convictions," and having an "abysmal record." He states, I think correctly, that the ICC's entry into the Israeli-Palestinian debate may have fateful consequences for the court. Neither the Israel Law Center nor the State of Israel has the power to prevent the ICC's review of complaints filed by the PA, but the ICC will be aware of the stakes at all times, and will be subject to diplomatic and legal pressures counteracting the pressure created by the complaints of

---

[88] Complaint against Abbas, 7–8.

[89] Complaint against Abbas, 10.

[90] Newsweek, January 13, 2015, available at http://europe.newsweek.com/israel-palestine-hague-international-criminal-court-mahmoud-abbas-298891?rm=eu.

the Palestinian Authority. We may say that the Israel Law Center's filings of complaints have failed as a matter of anticipatory self-defense, since they did not prevent the PA's attack on Israel at the ICC. Nevertheless, these filings now constitute a counterattack – they ensure that the court cannot act with impunity against the interests of Israel, and their ultimate success or failure as a counterattack will be determined by the proceedings at the ICC over the next few years.

III. A Summary of Chapter 2

The battle against lawfare activists cannot be won by purely defensive measures, by merely acting as defendants in cases filed either at the International Criminal Court or at national courts in their exercise of universal jurisdiction. Victory requires that aggressive actions be taken against the activists.

Chapter 2 has presented examples of two kinds of such aggressive action. In the first example, instead of merely defending Israeli officials in a Spanish court, a complaint was prepared against one of the most well-known and widely admired Spanish diplomats. Based on the same Spanish statute used against the Israelis, and presenting similar arguments of unintended civilian deaths in an otherwise clearly justified military operation, the Israel Law Center's complaint against Javier Solana would have created havoc in the Spanish legal system, forcing that system either to prosecute its honored native son or to admit the hypocrisy of a law that is enforced only against foreigners. In the end, Spain avoided this Hobbesian choice by quashing the case against the Israeli leaders and amending the statute so that a similar embarrassment would not occur in the future. This was an example of a successful counterattack.

The next two examples, complaints against Mashal and Abbas, demonstrate "anticipatory self-defense," as they constitute an attempt to dissuade the Palestinians from joining the International Criminal Court and from subsequently filing complaints at the court. The anticipation was not successful, since the Palestinians ultimately joined and became active at the ICC, but the examples were effective as a kind of counterattack – not against the Palestinian Authority, but rather against the ICC itself. The ICC was launched in 2002 with excellent intentions and high hopes, but thus far it has not realized these hopes. It is now involved in the Israeli-Palestinian conflict, one of the major struggles of modern times, and almost certainly fated to continue into the coming decades. The way the ICC handles these complaints may determine ultimately whether the ICC succeeds or fails. The Israel Law Center will be on hand to make sure that Israel's interests are fully presented and protected in this struggle at the ICC.

PART II

THREE FIELDS OF LAWFARE: LAND, SEA, AND AIR

CHAPTER 3

The Land: On Rejection and Walls

Introduction: Can the Israeli–Palestinian Dispute Be Resolved?

[T]here is only one thing holding up peace right now – a peace agreement between Israel and the Palestinian people – and this is that the Palestinian people will not forcefully and forthrightly announce that they do not have a right to return to the pre-1967 borders of Israel ... millions of [Palestinian] people ... to inundate that country [Israel], which would mean that country [Israel] wouldn't exist anymore.... [T]he other issues, the settlements, all these other things are solvable.... But until the Palestinians step forward and make that agreement [to renounce a right of return], ... there won't be peace and there won't be agreements....

– United States Congressman Dana Rohrabacher,
California, 48th Congressional District[91]

---

[91] "Threats to Israel: Terrorist Funding and Trade Boycotts," Hearing before the Subcommittee on Terrorism, Nonproliferation, and Trade of the Committee on Foreign Affairs House of Representatives, One Hundred Thirteenth Congress, Second Session, March 5, 2014, Serial no. 113–128, Statement by Congressman Rohrabacher, at p. 4 of the transcript. Both the transcript and an audiovisual recording of the hearing are available at

Despite many efforts to achieve peace over the past eighty years, peace has not been achieved. The Palestinians have rejected at least five peace offers, including the proposal of the Peel Commission in 1937, the UN Partition Plan in 1947, Israel's offer of peace in 1968 shortly after the Six-Day War, Ehud Barak's offer at Camp David in 2000, and Ehud Olmert's offer in 2008.[92] Instead of accepting an offer of peace, the Palestinians have demanded, continue to demand, and have never renounced the right of millions of Palestinians to move from various locations in the Middle East, and in truth from locations around the world, to Tel Aviv, Haifa, Ramle, Lod, and dozens of other primarily Jewish cities that are located in the State of Israel. As Congressman Rohrabacher said, the "return" of millions of Palestinians to Israel – *not* to any of the so-called "territories" but rather to pre-1967 Israel – would mean the end of the State of Israel. This is something that Israeli Jews will never accept, no matter what inducements may be offered and no matter what punishments may be threatened or applied.

That, however, is not the end of the matter. Despite what may be considered at times to be a placid appearance, no states and no groups of people are static. Change is *always* occurring, perhaps not to the eye, but in the hearts and minds of the people involved. What are the prospects for change in the Israeli-Palestinian dispute? How do these prospects affect lawfare? These questions are at the core of chapter 3.

I. Palestinian Rejectionism: The Essence of the Dispute

The percentage of Judea and Samaria, also called the "West Bank," which is inhabited or owned by Jews is less than 7 percent of the total area. In

---

http://foreignaffairs.house.gov/hearing/subcommittee-hearing-threats-israel-terrorist-funding-and-trade-boycotts.

[92] The peace offers of 1937, 1947, 2000, and 2008, are listed at Lewis Rosen, "Shlomo Avineri and the Two-State Solution," *Times of Israel*, October 12, 2005, http://blogs.timesofisrael.com/shlomo-avineri-and-the-two-state-solution/. The 1968 peace offer is discussed by William Fulton at "Israel Gives U.N. Mid-East Peace Plan," *Chicago Tribune*, Wednesday, October 9, 1968, p. 1, available at http://archives.chicagotribune.com/1968/10/09/page/1/article/israel-gives-u-n-mid-east-peace-plan.

numerical terms, this is about 146 square miles, the equivalent of about 12 miles by 12 miles. Visually, think of this as being a bit less than one-third the size of New York City, or a bit less than one-fourth the size of London. It is this area that is said by the Palestinians to be "occupied."[93] The dispute, however, is not about this miniscule drop of land, nor is it about the entire area of Judea and Samaria / the West Bank. Rather, it is about the "occupation" of any part of the Land of Israel by any Jews, and the alleged "right" to dispossess the Jews by flooding the land with millions of children and grandchildren and great-grandchildren of people who left Israel in the 1940s. This is what the Palestinians say, this is what they teach their children, and this is what they honor by financial compensation and encouragement. The problem is not Jewish "occupation" of anything, but rather Palestinian "rejectionism" of any Jewish presence in the Land of Israel.[94]

A. Statements of Rejection

The Palestinians are currently split between Hamas in Gaza and the Palestinian Authority ("PA") in Judea and Samaria / the West Bank.

As to Hamas, very little needs to be said. The governing document of Hamas, alternatively called the "Hamas Covenant of 1988" or "The Covenant

---

[93] According to *B'Tselem*, one of the most left-wing NGOs active in Israel today and a vigorous opponent of Jewish settlement in Judea and Samaria / West Bank, the total percentage of land either inhabited by Jews or not inhabited but within the municipal boundaries of Jewish settlements, is about 6.8 percent. Yehezkel Lein and Eyal Weizman, "Land Grab: Israel's Settlement Policy in the West Bank", *B'Tselem*, May, 2002, Table 9, page 116, available at https://www.btselem.org/download/200205_land_grab_eng.pdf. To state this in a way that is perhaps more palatable to the Palestinians, more than 93 percent of the disputed land is not inhabited or owned by Jews.

[94] The concept of Jewish "control" of land is nebulous in comparison to "inhabitation" or "ownership". Although Israeli Jews inhabit or own about 7% of the disputed territories, most people would agree that the percentage of the disputed area "controlled" by Jews is significantly greater than the area of inhabitation or ownership. However, for purposes of reaching and implementing a resolution of the Israeli-Palestinian dispute, the most contentious area is that of "inhabitation and ownership", not that of "control." Moreover, if it is true, as contended in this book, that the Palestinians reject any presence of any Jews in any part of Judea and Samaria/West Bank under any circumstances, then the distinctions between "inhabitation", "ownership", and "control", are in any case irrelevant, since no compromise agreement can be reached.

of the Islamic Resistance Movement," states that Israel will continue to exist "until Islam will obliterate it" (preface – paragraph 2). Repeated reference is made in the covenant to the "struggle against the Jews" (introduction – paragraph 5), "the Jews' usurpation of Palestine" (Article 15), the "Nazi treatment" of the Jews against "women and children" (Article 20), etc. Repeated reference is made to the "Zionist invaders" (Article 7), "the Zionist invasion" (Articles 28 and 35), "the Zionist enemy" (Article 36), etc. Many, many similar statements could be cited from this document, which both founded and now directs Hamas.[95]

The political leader of Hamas, Khaled Mashal, has stated that "Palestine" is from the Jordan River to the Mediterranean Sea, that there will be "no relinquishing or forsaking even an inch or small part of it," and that Hamas will triumph "through resistance and blood" or through "implement[ing] the Right of Return, and ... [putting] an end to the loathsome Zionist occupation...."[96] No objective observer could arrive at any conclusion but that Hamas refuses any accommodation or compromise with the Jews, in any part of what the Jews call the Land of Israel west of the Jordan River.

The founding document and guiding force of the PA is called "The Palestinian National Charter: Resolutions of the Palestine National Council, July 1–17, 1968." The charter shares the same content, and the same tone, as the Hamas Covenant of 1988. For example: "Palestine, with the boundaries it had during the British Mandate, is an indivisible unit" (Article 2 of the PA charter). Zionism is an "occupation" (Article 4), an "invasion" (Article 5), "imperialism" (Article 8), "imperialistic aggression" (Article 15), etc. The Balfour Declaration of 1917 is "deemed null and void," the Jews have no historical or religious tie to Palestine, and they are not a nation (all in

---

[95] All quotes taken from "Hamas Covenant 1988," the Avalon Project: Documents in Law, History and Diplomacy, Lillian Goldman Law Library, Yale Law School, http://avalon .law.yale.edu/20th_century/hamas.asp. The Avalon Project is an outstanding collection of documents in legal and political history from 4000 BCE to the twenty-first century, all of which are freely available online.

[96] "Hamas Leader Khaled Mash'al: We Will Not Relinquish an Inch of Palestine, from the River to the Sea," MEMRI – The Middle East Media Research Institute, Clip no. 3761, December 7, 2012, available at http://www.memritv.org/clip_transcript/en/3671.html.

Article 20). The Palestinians have a "right to return" to Israel (Articles 9 and 26).[97]

These statements in the Palestinian National Charter are neither happenstance nor outdated. They are the essence of the Palestinian movement today.[98] In an article from 2015,[99] the Israeli Arab journalist Khaled Abu Toameh[100] wrote the following:

> There are two main reasons why Palestinians will not sign a real and meaningful peace agreement with Israel...in the foreseeable future.
>
> The first is a total lack of education for peace. The second is related to the absence of a leader who is authorized – or has the guts – to embark on such a risky mission....
>
> [T]he Palestinian leadership has long been inciting its people against Israel to a point where it has become almost impossible to talk about any form of compromise between Israelis and Palestinians.
>
> Since its inception in 1994, the Palestinian Authority (PA) has devoted most of its energies and propaganda to delegitimizing

---

[97] All quotes in this paragraph are from "The Palestinian National Charter: Resolutions of the Palestine National Council July 1–17, 1968," the Avalon Project: Documents in Law, History and Diplomacy, Lillian Goldman Law Library, Yale Law School, http:// avalon.law.yale.edu/20th_century/plocov.asp.

[98] See, for example, the televised interview with Saeb Erekat, the Palestinians' "chief negotiator" with Israel, entitled "Have Palestinian Leaders Failed Their People?" The interview aired in the UK television program *Head to Head* on February 28, 2014. In the interview, at time 9:14, Erekat demands for each Palestinian, "number one, the right of return to Palestine [presumably the West Bank and Gaza], return to Israel with compensation [which is the "right of return" and would mean the death of Israel], or remaining where he is with compensation." Erekat states specifically, several times, "I will never recognize Israel as a Jewish state." The interview is available at https://www.youtube .com/watch?v=-7x0121TzKU, and the transcript, published April 2, 2014, is available at http://www.aljazeera.com/programmes/headtohead/2014/03/transcript-dr-saeb -erekat-201432611433441126.html. Many references could be made to relatively recent statements from some of the most senior political and religious leaders of the Palestinians.

[99] Khaled Abu Toameh, "Why Palestinians Cannot Make Peace with Israel," Gatestone Institute, July 13, 2015, available at http://www.gatestoneinstitute.org/6142/palestinians -peace-israel.

[100] Producer and consultant for *NBC News* since 1989, writer for the *Jerusalem Post*, and commentator for the conservative think tank Gatestone Institute.

and isolating Israel... [and] this incitement continued even as the PA was negotiating with Israel in an attempt to reach a peace agreement.

If you want to make peace with Israel, you do not tell your people every now and then that the Western Wall has no religious significance to Jews and is, in fact, holy Muslim property [as stated by the former chief justice of the Palestinian religious court Tayseer Al-Tamimi and also by the Palestinian Authority minister of religious affairs Mahmoud Al-Habbash]....

You cannot make peace with Israel if you continue to deny Jewish history or links to the land [as Hanan Ashrawi did]....

It will be impossible to make peace with Israel at a time when the Palestinian Authority is telling its people that Jews use wild pigs to drive Palestinian farmers out of their fields and homes in the West Bank [as PA president Mahmoud Abbas did]....

This is in addition to the PA's worldwide campaign to isolate, delegitimize and demonize Israel and Israelis. PA leaders and representatives who continue to accuse Israel of "war crimes" and "genocide" are certainly not preparing their people for peace with Israel. On the contrary, such allegations serve to further agitate Palestinians against Israel.

Yet this is not only about the lack of education for peace or anti-Israel incitement....

[N]o Palestinian leader has a mandate to reach an everlasting peace agreement with Israel. That is because no leader in Ramallah or the Gaza Strip is authorized to end the conflict with Israel.

If Yasser Arafat was not able to accept the generous offer made by former Prime Minister Ehud Barak at the 2000 Camp David summit, who is Mahmoud Abbas to make any form of concession to Israel? Arafat was quoted back then as saying that he rejected the offer because he did not want to end up drinking tea with assassinated Egyptian President Anwar Sadat, the first Arab leader to sign a peace agreement with Israel.

In many ways, Abbas can only blame himself for the situation he faces today. If you are telling your people that you will never make concessions, how can you ever sign a peace agreement with Israel?

This is the essence of the problem, as stated by Abu Toameh. There is no education for peace. Public statements by the main Palestinian leaders – the president, the head of the religious court, the minister of religious affairs – stress that the Jews have no connection to the land, to Jerusalem, to the Temple, or to the Western Wall. These statements stress that all of the land, especially the parts most holy to the Jews, are exclusive Muslim property, and the Palestinians will make no concession or compromise whatsoever. This is what is meant by "Palestinian rejectionism," and it is the core reason for the lack of peace – not the alleged "occupation" of less than two hundred square miles. Worse, the Palestinians in authority teach this rejectionism to their children.

B. The Education of the Young Palestinians

There are very many statements and articles by non-Palestinians, both Israelis and other persons, emphasizing the circle of hate propagated by the Palestinians against Israel, Jews, Judaism, and Zionism. For example, in December 2015, the Palestinian authority tried to import, through Haifa port, four thousand toy dolls. Each doll was hooded, and had a raised arm with a hand capable of holding a toy rock that was to be thrown at Jews (presumably at toy Jews). Andrew Percy, a member of the British Parliament, wrote thus:

> The dolls encourage Palestinian children to throw rocks at Israelis. Incitement to violence is commonplace in the Palestinian Territories and amounts to psychological abuse of children. The doll is just the latest example of the hate and abuse directed at Israel, or rather Jews, which routinely appears in Palestinian textbooks and official PA TV children's programmes. As many as 25 schools have been reportedly named after Palestinian terrorists who targeted and murdered Israeli civilians.... [T]he PA nurtures an environment where children learn that attacking Israelis is somehow a noble cause. Palestinian youths grow up in streets bearing the names of Palestinian killers, and attend football stadia named after terrorist murderers.... This is an ideology that teaches children that if they die trying to kill

innocent Israelis then they will be heroes, and possibly honoured with a school in their name![101]

Is the Palestinian hatred and rejectionism really as bad as portrayed by MP Percy? Consider that in early 2016, the Palestinians and the Palestinian Authority celebrated the founding of Fatah (an acronym for the Palestinian National Liberation Movement, the largest faction of the various groups that comprise the PLO). The celebrations included a parade in Bethlehem, which featured, according to the official newspaper of the Palestinian Authority,

> children…carrying models of RPGs (rocket-propelled grenades) and explosive [suicide] belts, and they all walked through the [Dheisheh] refugee camp in the procession, during which the sound of songs of the national revolution were heard.[102]

The toy suicide belts had toy sticks of dynamite, and the toy RPG launchers were accompanied by plastic grenades, all of these worn by small boys. A member of the Central Committee of the Palestinian Authority, the minister of tourism and antiquities, and the head of the Palestinian General Intelligence Agency were all present at the celebrations.[103] In other words,

---

[101] Andrew Percy, "How Not to Help the Palestinian Children," *Times of Israel*, January 7, 2016, available at http://blogs.timesofisrael.com/how-not-to-help-palestinian-children/.

[102] Appearing in "Fatah Marked the Anniversary of the Launch in Bethlehem," *Al-Hayat Al-Jadida Newspaper*, January 8, 2016. The original article was in Arabic, which was translated and cited in an article by Itamar Marcus and Nan Jacques Zilberdik, "Palestinian Children Wear 'Suicide Belts' to Celebrate Fatah's 51 Years of Violence," Palestinian Media Watch, January 11, 2016, available at http://www.palwatch.org/main.aspx?fi=157&doc_id=16869.

[103] The General Intelligence Agency (often abbreviated as the "GIA"), in Arabic the Mukhabbarat al-Amma, is the main intelligence arm of the Palestinian Authority, with over three thousand officers engaged in intelligence and counter-espionage operations. "Palestine Security and Intelligence Agencies," GlobalSecurity.org, available at http://www.globalsecurity.org/intell/world/palestine/. The head of the GIA, Majid Faraj, was present at the celebration in Bethlehem. On January 5, 2015, the Israel Law Center filed a complaint with the International Criminal Court, alleging that in the period July 2012–November 2014, Faraj, as head of the GIA, committed "crimes against humanity" by the extralegal seizure and torture of innocent civilians in fifty-four specific cases. That case is pending. The complaint, entitled "Shurat HaDin – Israel Law Center, *The complainant v.*

a parade in which young boys are used to laud and encourage suicide bombing is attended by some of the highest officials in the Palestinian Authority.

As a second example, a Jordanian-Palestinian schoolteacher posted on Facebook a video of his young daughter holding a large knife. The video shows a conversation between the daughter and her father, the teacher.

> DAUGHTER: "I want to stab a Jew."
>
> FATHER: "Why do you want to stab the Jew?"
>
> DAUGHTER: "Because he stole our land."
>
> FATHER: "They stole our land. With what do you want to stab them?"
>
> DAUGHTER: "With a knife."
>
> FATHER: "Oh, you're so strong! Allah willing, my dear."[104]

This is the legacy that a professional teacher wishes to leave his daughter.[105]

The third and last example noted here is a video, entitled "Camp Jihad," filmed in the summer of 2013 at two summer camps sponsored and financed by the UNRWA (the UN Relief and Works Agency). The video, widely available on the Internet,[106] was filmed at the Balata refugee camp north of

---

Majid Faraj, *Accused of Crimes Against Humanity*, Communication to the Prosecutor of the International Criminal Court regarding The Crimes Against Humanity committed by Majid Faraj," is available at http://israellawcenter.org/wp-content/uploads/2015/01/ICC-Communication-Faraj.pdf.

[104] "Palestinian Preschool Girl Holds Knife, Says, 'I Want to Stab a Jew.'" The video, in Arabic, was originally posted to Facebook by the father on October 16, 2015. English subtitles were added by MEMRI, which posted the translated version on October 20, 2015. The video is available at https://www.youtube.com/watch?v=hy-S3hcahZo. An article about this video appears at "Watch: 'I Want to Stab a Jew,' Young Girl Tells Her Teacher Father," *Times of Israel*, October 20, 2015, available at http://www.timesofisrael.com/watch-i-want-to-stab-a-jew-young-girl-tells-her-teacher-father/.

[105] The attitude of the father displayed in this story is not atypical or unusual. In an interview on January 19, 2016, Tawfik Tirawi, member of the Fatah Central Committee, expressed delight that his two-year-old son sang, "Daddy, buy me a machine gun and a rifle, so that I will defeat Israel and the Zionists!" "Fatah Official: Palestine alongside Israel Is Just 'a Phase,'" *Times of Israel*, January 22, 2016, available at http://www.timesofisrael.com/fatah-official-palestine-alongside-israel-is-just-a-phase/. Similar stories could be referenced.

[106] For example, at https://www.youtube.com/watch?v=aC1FR5VeuOk, and at https://

Nablus and in the Gaza Strip. It is difficult to convey in words what is shown in a hate-filled twenty-minute video, but the essence is that the children are taught to yearn intensively for their return to cities and towns in Israel (such as Haifa, Jaffa, and Acre), places which they themselves have never been but which they have been told were the home locales of their families. The children are quoted extensively in the video. For example, about three-quarters into the video, one little girl says, "I will defeat the Jews. They are a gang of infidels and Christians. They don't like Allah and they do not worship Allah. And they hate us." Toward the end of the video, one teacher shouts, "Palestine is an Arab land from the river to the sea," after which small children repeat the phrase. They repeat this back and forth, shouting from teacher to children, three times, with the children waving their fists and pounding on a table.

We can say that societies are never static, because beliefs and attitudes are changing every day in the hearts and minds of their people. Among the Palestinians, hatred and rejection of Israel, and of a Jewish presence anywhere "from the river to the sea," grows stronger every day – financed by the UN, the EU, England, Germany, Norway, and the United States.[107]

---

www.youtube.com/watch?v=kbrafPTe_LQ.

[107] These six organizations and countries appear to be the main financers of the jihad-supporting summer camps. See Elisa Greenberg, "UNRWA Summer: Camp Jihad?" *inFocus*, November 3, 2014, available at http://www.cameraoncampus.org/blog/unrwa-summer -camp-jihad/#.Vp-zPk9bLCM. See also Lazar Berman, "Palestinian Kids Taught to Hate Israel in UN-Funded Camps, Clip Shows," *Times of Israel*, August 14, 2013, available at http://www.timesofisrael.com/palestinian-kids-taught-to-hate-israel-in-un-funded -camps-clip-shows/. The funding of jihad-supporting camps is not atypical for these entities. Europeans in particular are heavily involved in funding lawfare attacks on Israel. For example, the government of Norway provides substantial funds, indirectly, to Al-Haq, one of the leading Palestinian NGOs active in launching lawfare attacks against Israel. See, e.g., Lahav Harkov, "Report Finds Norwegian Government Funds Organization Supporting BDS Campaigns," *Jerusalem Post*, August 29, 2016, available at http://www.jpost.com/Arab-Israeli-Conflict/Report-finds-Norwegian-government -funds-organization-supporting-BDS-campaigns-466346. On the general issue of Western funding for anti-Israel activities – especially by the United States, Germany, and the UN, and particularly for the production of anti-Israel documentaries – see Tuvia Tenenbom, *Catch the Jew!* (Jerusalem: Gefen Publishing House, 2015), throughout the book, and in particular at 391–94, 429, and 433–34.

C. The Murder Compensation Table of the Palestinian Authority

In addition to rejectionist statements and rejectionist education of its children, the Palestinian Authority extends and deepens hatred of Israel in a more immediate and possibly more deadly form.

The Palestinian Authority creates legislation in areas under its control, and publishes such legislation in the PA Registry. On April 13, 2011, the PA Registry published PA Government Resolution of 2010, numbers 19–23.[108] According to this law, every Arab, whether Palestinian or Israeli, who is imprisoned in an Israeli jail for terror activity of any kind, is entitled to monthly financial compensation. The law does not refer to a prisoner's terror activity, but rather to "his struggle against the occupation." The crimes for which compensation is paid are not limited to those that occur in the "occupied territories," or in the "West Bank," but include also the kidnapping and murder of Jews in pre-1967 Israel. The crimes for which compensation is paid are not limited to attacks against soldiers or police, but include also the killing of old people, pregnant women, children, babies, and other civilians. In short, killing of all kinds is compensated, provided that the prisoner is sentenced to jail. The amount of compensation depends, however, on how many people are murdered, how gruesome the crimes, the criminal intent of the murderers, and all other factors that are taken into account in the sentencing, because the level of compensation, as legislated by the Palestinian Authority, depends on the length of the sentence meted out to the killer by the Israeli courts.

Here is the table by which monthly compensation is paid, according to Government Resolution No. 23 of the statute.

---

[108] Information about the law is taken from two articles by Palestinian Media Watch: "PA to Pay Salaries to All Terrorists in Israeli Prisons," May 20, 2011, available at http://palwatch.org/main.aspx?fi=157&doc_id=5001, and the more general article "PA Salaries to Terrorists," which includes a compendium of more than one hundred sixty articles on this topic from the years 2000–2016, available at http://www.palwatch.org/main.aspx?fi=1005.

Table 3.1: The Murder Compensation Table of the Palestinian Authority

Length of Sentence by the Israeli Court	Monthly Compensation Paid by the Palestinian Authority (in New Israel Shekels)
0–3 years	1,400 shekels/month
3–5 years	2,000 shekels/month
5–10 years	4,000 shekels/month
10–15 years	6,000 shekels/month
15–20 years	7,000 shekels/month
20–25 years	8,000 shekels/month
25–30 years	10,000 shekels/month
Over 30 years	12,000 shekels/month

In addition, there is a supplement of three hundred shekels per month for every married prisoner, and a further supplement of fifty shekels per month for each child of the prisoner. The emphasis on family is admirable, but the law provides that the prisoner has full discretion to direct payment to a closed bank account of the prisoner, to the prisoner's family, or to anyone else selected by the prisoner. A special supplement of three hundred shekels per month is paid to any prisoner from Jerusalem, and another supplement of five hundred shekels per month is paid to any Israeli Arab (as opposed to a Palestinian), thereby providing extra incentives for natives of Jerusalem and Israeli Arabs. The law has been in effect, and payments are being made, from January 1, 2011.

Let us put these numbers into an American context. The shekel-to-dollar exchange rate is about 4 to 1. The average Palestinian income per capita in 2015 has been estimated as $2,866.80 per year, whereas the average per capita income of a United States citizen in 2015 has been estimated as $55,836.80 per year.[109] Let us now restate the numbers in a way that is clearer.

---

[109] These numbers are GDP (gross domestic product) per capita, estimated by the World Bank in a multi-country comparison. World Bank, "GDP Per Capita (Current US$)," 2016, comparing the results in 1960 with those in 2015, available at http://data.worldbank.org/indicator/NY.GDP.PCAP.CD. It is important to note that the Palestinian number includes both the West Bank and Gaza.

Table 3.2: The Murder Compensation Table of the Palestinian Authority in American Equivalent Purchasing Power

Length of Sentence by the Israeli Court	Monthly Compensation Paid by the PA (in USD equivalent)	Annual Compensation Paid by the PA (in USD equivalent)	Annual Purchasing Power in the PA Territories Based on Per Capita Income
0–3 years	$350/month	$4,200	$82,000
3–5 years	$500/month	$6,000	$117,000
5–10 years	$1,000/month	$12,000	$234,000
10–15 years	$1,500/month	$18,000	$351,000
15–20 years	$1,750/month	$21,000	$409,000
20–25 years	$2,000/month	$24,000	$467,000
25–30 years	$2,500/month	$30,000	$584,000
Over 30 years	$3,000/month	$36,000	$701,000

Let's be clear with two examples. Perhaps a prisoner is convicted of possession of firearms with intent to sell for a planned terror attack. A typical sentence might be two years. During that time, a prisoner will receive compensation with equivalent spending power of $82,000 per year, a total of $164,000 of spending power for sitting two years in jail. This is not a very lucrative crime. But compare, for example, Abdullah Barghouti, serving sixty-seven life sentences for the murder of sixty-six Israeli civilians in the Sbarro Restaurant bombing (August 9, 2001), the Café Moment bombing (March 9, 2002), and others. Mr. Barghouti is receiving, as of January 1, 2011, the spending power equivalent of $701,000 per year, a total of $4.2 million in spending power in the period 2011–2016, which he can enjoy if he is ever released, or which he may bestow on anyone of his choosing.

Think of these payments as an incentive to commit murder. What would happen if Anglo-Texans published, as a matter of state law, that anyone who killed a Mexican-American in Texas and was imprisoned for life would receive $700,000 during every year of imprisonment? Or for that matter, if Mexican-Americans published the same financial deal for the murder of Anglos? Or if the federal government offered the same reward for the murder of homosexuals? Of if a different state offered these inducements for killing

Jews, or Catholics, or Asian-Americans, or blacks, or anyone else? That is the equivalent of what the Palestinian Authority is doing.

Let there be no doubt – this money is being paid to terrorists and their families at the rate of about $137.8 million per year, which is equal to about 3.2 percent of the entire budget of the Palestinian Authority.[110] Again in American terms, the budget of the US federal government in 2016 is approximately $4 trillion, and 3.2 percent of that would be $130 billion – that sum is the equivalent of what the Palestinian Authority pays to terrorists and their families every year. This money is paid as the highest priority of the PA, before funding of the police, welfare, infrastructure, or any other payment.[111] *An entity that pays this kind of money to prisoners who have murdered civilian men, women, children, and babies is not interested in peace, and has rejected the presence of Jews in any part of the Land of Israel.* That is the burden that must be borne by the Jews of Israel, and that is the reality through which all Israeli-Palestinian lawfare issues must be seen.

"[T]he core problem is not about land or the situations of the Palestinians but rather hatred of Jews in general. . . . Jewish hatred is at the core of the issue."[112] The sole obstacle to peace in the Israeli-Palestinian conflict is the Palestinians' rejection of the Jews.[113]

---

[110] The $137.8M payment for prisoners is from Michael Wilner and Ariel Ben Solomon, "Congressmen Voice Concern over Palestinian Stipend Program for Convicts," *Jerusalem Post*, July 6, 2016, http://www.jpost.com/International/Congressman-voice-concern-over-Palestinian-stipend-program-for-convicts-459700. The PA's budget for 2016, $4.25 billion, is reported by Ahmad Melhem, "Who's Going to Pay for Palestinian Budget Gap?" *Al-Monitor*, February 4, 2016, http://www.al-monitor.com/pulse/originals/2016/02/abbas-approve-palestinian-budget-deficit.html. The $137.8M sum includes only terrorists tried, convicted, and imprisoned. An additional sum of about $165 million per year is paid to the families of dead terrorists who were not tried in court. The additional sum is not included in the discussion here.

[111] Although the Palestinian Authority has hundreds of millions of dollars to pay to people who have murdered Jews, the Palestinian Authority has not managed to build one hospital or one university in more than twenty years. Evelyn Gordon, "Where Providing Water Is a Crime," *Commentary Magazine*, January 29, 2016, January 29, 2016, available at https://www.commentarymagazine.com/foreign-policy/middle-east/israel/rawabi-palestine-providing-water-crime/. This is what "priority of payment" means – full payment to murderers, and no payment for health or higher education.

[112] Sinem Tezyapar, "The Abuse of Islam as Part of the Demonization of Israel," in Baker, *Palestinian Manipulation*, 99, available at http://jcpa.org/overview_palestinian_manipulation/.

[113] The concept of murder compensation caused distress to donor nations, which insisted

II. The Struggle over Land

The current charge of the Palestinians is the "occupation" of what they call "the West Bank," and what the Jews call "Biblical Judea and Samaria." What is the source for this charge against the Israelis? What is the defense against the charge? How has the Israel Law Center counterattacked against this charge, and what is the likely future of lawfare related to "occupation"?

that the Palestinian Authority stop funding terrorist prisoners. In order to protect its donations, the PA claimed in 2014 that funding would no longer come from the PA, but only from the PLO (which did not receive international donations). There are, however, two problems with this transfer of responsibility from the PA to the PLO. First, whether it is distributed by the PA or by the PLO, funding for jailed terrorists creates the same motivation, and it is indeed an incentive to murder. See Evelyn C. Gordon, "Stop Subsidizing Terror Murder," *Commentary Magazine*, June 30, 2016, available at https://www.commentarymagazine.com/terrorism/us-terror-subsidizing-murder/; alternative source *Analysis from Israel*, July 2, 2016, http://evelyncgordon.com/stop-subsidizing-terror-murder/. Second, the supposed transfer is a complete sham. In reality, the money continues to come from donations to the PA, being routed first from the PA to the PLO, and then distributed by the PLO to the terrorists and their families. The PA, not the PLO, continues to decide who to pay and at what levels. In fact, the former PA minister of prisoners' affairs became the PLO commissioner of prisoners' affairs, and continues to distribute the money under the direction of PA head Mahmoud Abbas. Itamar Marcus, "The PA's Billion Dollar Fraud," Palestinian Media Watch, April 27, 2016, available at http://www.palwatch.org/main.aspx?fi=157&doc_id=17807.

To their credit, some US legislators, such as Senator Dan Coats (R-Indiana), are outraged by this sham transfer, and by the entire concept of subsidizing murder. These legislators are seeking to cut funding to the PA by an amount equal to the sum paid by the PA, through the PLO, to terrorists. See Michael Wilner, "Senator Questions Palestinian Aid Directed to Stipends for Convicted Murders," *Times of Israel*, June 24, 2016, available at http://www.jpost.com/International/Senator-questions-Palestinian-aid-directed-to-stipends-for-convicted-murderers-457641; and see also Wilner and Ben Solomon, "Congressmen Voice Concern over Palestinian Stipend for Convicts," ibid. The UK also is investigating whether its annual aid to the Palestinian Authority had been used to fund convicted terrorists, and has frozen part of that aid. "UK Freezes $30M in Aid Over Salaries for Terrorists," *Times of Israel*, October 7, 2016, available at http://www.timesofisrael.com/uk-freezes-30m-in-aid-to-palestinians-over-payments-to-terrorists/; and *Jewish Telegraphic Agency*, "Britain Freezes Aid Payments to Palestinians Over Terrorists' Salaries," *Jerusalem Post*, October 7, 2016, available at http://www.jpost.com/Arab-Israeli-Conflict/Britain-freezes-aid-payments-to-Palestinians-over-terrorists-salaries-469659.

A. The Charge: Population Transfer in Violation of the Rome Statute

Forced expulsion of civilians is a war crime under Article 49 the Geneva Convention IV of 1949. This is the specific language:

> Individual or mass forcible transfers, as well as deportations of protected persons from occupied territory to the territory of the Occupying Power or to that of any other country, occupied or not, are prohibited, regardless of their motive. *The Occupying Power shall not deport or transfer parts of its own civilian population into the territory it occupies.* [Italics mine.]

The main charge against Israel is not that it has forcibly transferred Palestinians out, and if such a charge would be made, it would be easily defeated in a legal forum. Rather, the charge is that Israelis have moved into Judea and Samaria / the West Bank. The great difficulty for Israel's accusers is that they must allege and prove that Israel "deported or transferred" its own population into the territory, and that is a very difficult proposition to prove.

However, the language of the Rome Statute, which created the International Criminal Court, is entirely different from the Geneva Convention. Under Article 8 of the Rome Statute, entitled "War crimes," section 2(b)(viii) defines as a war crime

> [t]he transfer, directly or indirectly, by the Occupying Power of parts of its own civilian population into the territory it occupies, or the deportation or transfer of all or parts of the population of the occupied territory within or outside this territory. [Italics mine.]

This clause, "transfer, directly or indirectly," does not appear anywhere in the Geneva Conventions, and is completely unprecedented in international humanitarian law. Here the charge is not action by the Israeli government (which would be "direct transfer"), but rather enablement (which might be "indirect transfer"). Indeed, since there is no definition in law for the term used here – "indirect transfer" – one might argue that mere inaction, or a failure to uproot, could itself be some kind of "indirect transfer." Although the entire section is unclear, as well as many of its individual parameters, nevertheless the Palestinians have alleged that Israel, by allowing Jews to move into the territory (or possibly by failing to uproot them) is guilty of war crimes under section 2(b)(viii) of Article 8 of the Rome Statute.[114]

This section of the Rome Statute was created at the explicit behest of the Arab League, and for the specific purpose of creating a new "war crime" to cover the movement of Jews into Judea and Samaria / the West Bank,[115] irrespective of whether or not such movement is sanctioned by the government of Israel, whether the government of Israel actually took any action at all, whether or not the movement of persons occurred to previously uninhabited land, and whether or not the movement had any explicit impact on any persons formerly living in the territory. This section of the Rome Statute is the basis of the charge against Israel for "occupying" the Land of Israel.

B. The Defense: Bill of Attainder and Other Legal Arguments

There is a clear and obvious problem with section 2(b)(viii) of Article 8 – it is aimed only at Israel. A statute or other legal command that is aimed at a specific entity is called a "bill of attainder." In such a bill, the targeted

---

[114] "15 December 2014 – Statement by Ambassador Riyad Mansour [Permanent Observer of Palestine to the United Nations] before the Assembly of States Parties to the Rome Statute of the International Criminal Court (thirteenth session), General Debate, New York," Palestine at the UN, December 16, 2014, available at http://palestineun.org/15-december-2014-statement-by-ambassador-riyad-mansour-before-the-assembly-of-states-parties-to-the-rome-statute-of-the-international-criminal-court-thirteenth-session-general-debate-new-york/, quoted from Kittrie, Lawfare, 223 and 421 at n.239.

[115] Kittrie, Lawfare, 13, and Eugene Kontorovich, "Palestinians Seek to Take Advantage of ICC's Unique 'Israel' Provision," Washington Post, January 5, 2015, available at https://www.washingtonpost.com/news/volokh-conspiracy/wp/2015/01/05/palestinians-seek-to-take-advantage-of-iccs-unique-israel-provision/. I should note, however, that according to another source it is not the entirety of the Arab League that proposed this law, but specifically Egypt and Syria, although again the law was targeted specifically at Israel. See Raphael Ahren, "Ex-ICC Prosecutor Hails Israeli Report on Settlements' Legality," Times of Israel, December 17, 2015, available at http://www.timesofisrael.com/former-icc-prosecutor-hails-israeli-report-on-settlements-legality/.

person or persons may be called by name, but more typically the statute is written such that the target's name is not stated but the identity is clear beyond any doubt.[116] That is the case here. The bill of attainder that is section 2(b)(viii) might incidentally capture other countries, but its clear intent is to condemn Israel.

The bill of attainder is at the very heart of dictatorial government. If the government can pass and implement a law criminalizing, penalizing, seizing assets from, imprisoning, and ultimately executing anyone it wants, typically without trial, and often by outlawing an action after the fact,[117] then in the most brutal fashion no one is safe from the government.[118] It is for this reason that the US constitution prohibits the federal government from passing such a bill (Article 1, section 9, clause 3), and also prohibits the individual states from passing such a bill (Article 1, section 10, clause 1).

---

[116] For example, British readers may understand that Catherine Howard, the fifth wife of King Henry VIII, was condemned and executed upon such a bill – her name was not mentioned, but the terms of the bill left no doubt as to Parliament's target.

[117] A law that criminalizes an action after the action has occurred is called an *"ex post facto"* law. Bills of attainder often have retroactive application, in which case they are also *ex post facto*, but that is not essential to the definition of "bill of attainder." Such a bill may also have only future effect, but still be targeted at a single person or a clearly identified group of people.

[118] One of the best examples in modern times for the use of bills of attainder is the Nuremberg Race Laws of 1935. These laws, originally directed only at Jews and later extended to cover Gypsies and blacks, denied German citizenship to persons in the targeted groups, and outlawed marriage or family relations between Germans and members of the targeted groups. See, for example, summary by the US Holocaust Memorial Museum, http://www.ushmm.org/outreach/en/article.php?ModuleId=10007695. In their initial actions, and certainly before the beginning of WWII, the Germans sought to act "legally," first in stripping Jews of citizenship and property rights by "statutes" – in fact, bills of attainder – and only then taking action against the Jews, always in accordance with the properly passed statutes. It was only later, and specifically in fulfillment of the program to exterminate the Jews, that the Germans abandoned all pretense of legality. When a dictatorship begins to pass bills of attainder against a specific group, the logical end is the extermination of that group. A pointed contrast to the Nuremberg Laws, with the intent of immediate extermination, was the planned murder of the Jews of Persia, as related in the book of Esther 3:13–15. The ultimate intention, whether in Germany or in Persia, was the same, and in both cases bills of attainder were used, although the speed of the process varied.

There is unanimity of opinion about this in the United States, and in fact all of the state constitutions of the fifty individual states prohibit bills of attainder. Nevertheless, it is the bill of attainder, created in section 2(b)(viii) of Article 8 of the Rome Statute, that the Palestinians seek to apply against Israel in Judea and Samaria / the West Bank.[119]

Even if we momentarily put aside the fact that section 2(b)(viii) of Article 8 of the Rome Statute is an outrageously discriminatory bill of attainder, Israel can legitimately make the following arguments:[120]

1. Since the time of the Bible, when the Jews ruled in Judea and Samaria, there has never been any sovereign power in the area. The Ottoman Empire, which ruled in the period 1517–1917, never claimed sovereignty, nor did Britain thereafter (1917–1948), nor did Jordan (1948–1967), nor did Israel (1967–2016), nor did the Palestinians at any time. Neither the Geneva Convention nor the Rome Statute applies to a location that does not have a sovereign power.

2. Almost all of the settlement activity occurred before the time that "Palestine" was admitted as a signatory to the Rome Statute. By its own terms, the Rome Statute applies only to activity that occurs after a complainant has become a member of the statute. Even if the Rome Statute applies in substance (which is in dispute), it does not apply to activity that occurred

---

[119] "The essence of any legal system … is that the law applies equally to all." Robbie Sabel, "Manipulating International Law as part of Anti-Israel 'Lawfare,'" in Baker, *Palestinian Manipulation*, 20. This essential principle – "equality before the law" – is subverted by the "bill of attainder" and by its close relative, "the double standard." These two terms are related, but distinct. In the bill of attainder, two different standards are created, one against the targeted group, and the other for everyone else. With a "double standard," there is only one law for everyone, but the law is interpreted and enforced harshly against a targeted group, and leniently (often much more leniently) against everyone else. In general, a bill of attainder is very much worse than a double standard, because the passage of such a bill is a sure sign of the cynicism and hypocrisy of the bill's proponents – they no longer care enough to preserve even the form of fairness or legality.

Double standards have certainly been applied against Israel, but also against all Western countries and all Western armies engaged in asymmetric warfare. The bill of attainder, however, is unique against Israel.

[120] Adapted from Kittrie, *Lawfare*, 228–29.

before Palestine joined the ICC, and hence the settlements cannot be the basis of a crime.[121]

3. For the ICC to become involved in the dispute between the Israelis and Palestinians would be completely unprecedented. As of the beginning of 2016, the ICC had received almost twelve thousand requests (called "communications") to investigate possible violations of the Rome Statute. Nevertheless, despite these thousands of requests to investigate, Professor Eugene Kontorovich, one of the leading legal scholars in this field, points out that the ICC has

- never accepted a referral by one state against another;
- never accepted a referral by a state that is a member of the Rome Statute against a state that is not a member;
- never decided any issues about the status of disputed territory, nor prosecuted any alleged crimes arising in a disputed territory;
- never pursued crimes that do not involve large-scale murder and extreme brutality; and
- never prosecuted anyone for "settlement activity" or anything similar.[122]

If the ICC agrees to hear a complaint by the Palestinians against Israeli settlement activity, the ICC would necessarily set a precedent in all five of these areas. Such precedents would likely create a tremendous, a truly massive expansion in the scope of cases that could, and almost certainly

---

[121] Timing is a critical element of any alleged crime under the Rome Statute. If timing were not an issue, then, for example, parties might complain to the ICC about the United States' settlement of America, or about the UK's settlement of Australia.

[122] This list is based on Eugene Kontorovich's "Politicizing the International Criminal Court," Jerusalem Center for Public Affairs, April 2014, available at http://jcpa.org /politicizing_the_international_criminal_court/. Professor Kontorovich has also pointed out that the ICC is not alone. No court of any nation, and no international body, has ever prosecuted a charge of "settlement activity." It is odd, not to say anomalous, that Nazi Germany can annex large parts of Poland and resettle more than five hundred thousand Germans in such annexed territory, and not face any charge of "settlement" or "settlement activity" at the Nuremberg Military Trials, whereas Israel may be prosecuted for allowing (not for settling) Jews into its biblical homeland.

would, be brought to the ICC. The ICC would be required to hear and decide these cases, or admit (either openly or implicitly) that it takes cases only when they are directed against Israel.

4. Even if all the other arguments were ignored, still the ICC only pursues cases that it considers of sufficient "gravity," and this is necessary in order to justify the tremendous commitment of time, resources, and attention each case requires.[123] The ICC was created explicitly to prosecute and convict persons responsible for "unimaginable atrocities that deeply shock the conscience of humanity," "grave crimes [that] threaten the peace, security and well-being of the world," and "the most serious crimes of international concern to the international community,"[124] such as the specific crimes of "genocide," "crimes against humanity," "war crimes," and the "crime of aggression."[125] In this way, the ICC will both "put an end to impunity" for such criminals, and also "contribute to the prevention of such crimes" in the future.[126]

Could it be said that the voluntary movement of Jews into Judea and Samaria / the West Bank, a land they believe to be theirs, constitutes "an unimaginable atrocity that deeply shocks the conscience of humanity"? Would this movement "threaten the peace, security and well-being of the world"? Is this movement of Jews the kind of "genocide" or large-scale murder that would justify a criminal prosecution at the ICC? Not only would such a prosecution be unprecedented, as discussed above, but in addition it would make a mockery of the "gravity" requirement for a crime under the Rome Statute.

5. Finally, to prosecute Israel alone for "occupation," when other countries which might be "occupiers" are not even investigated, would be the

---

[123] Article 17(1)(d) limits prosecution to alleged crimes considered by the chief prosecutor of the ICC to be of "sufficient gravity." The term "gravity" is used eleven times in the Rome Statute, and the phrase "sufficient gravity" appears twice, but neither "gravity" nor "sufficient gravity" is defined anywhere in the Rome Statute.

[124] These categories are stated explicitly in the preamble to the Rome Statute at paragraphs 3 and 9, and in Article 5.

[125] These specific crimes are listed in the Rome Statute at Article 5, section 1.

[126] Rome Statute, preamble, paragraph 5.

rankest kind of hypocrisy, and is unworthy of the International Criminal Court. This argument was the basis of the complaint filed by the Israel Law Center, as discussed below.

C. The Anticipatory Self-Defense: The Complaint against Turkey at the ICC

In anticipation of possible action by the Palestinians at the ICC, the Israel Law Center worked with several Greek Cypriots to prepare a complaint at the ICC against Turkey for its illegal occupation of northern Cyprus.[127] The complaint, filed on July 14, 2014, states that on July 20, 1974, Turkey invaded the northeastern part of Cyprus, and since that time has exercised exclusive control over 36 percent of the island. Further, Turkey has engaged in certain activities in northeastern Cyprus that appear to be illegal and that merit full investigation by the ICC. This complaint is still under advisement by the ICC, and the court has not yet taken any substantive action.

The Israel Law Center's purpose in helping to file this complaint is to make clear to the ICC, the Palestinians, and indeed the world that any ICC complaint against the alleged "occupation" by Israel of Judea and Samaria / the West Bank will require the ICC to either investigate and prosecute cases around the world that are similar to that of Israel, or to admit (openly or by implication) that the ICC investigates complaints only if they are against Israel.

Are the allegations in the complaint against Turkey similar to the Palestinian charges against Israel? In some ways, yes: Turkey occupies northeastern Cyprus, and the Palestinians allege Israeli occupation of Judea and Samaria / the West Bank. Persons from the Turkish mainland have moved into northeastern Cyprus, and the Palestinians say Israeli Jews have moved into Judea and Samaria / the West Bank. And Turkey has built

---

[127] The complaint is entitled "Mep Costas Mavrides & Cypriots Against Turkish War Crimes, *The complainants v.* The Republic of Turkey, *Accused of War Crimes*, Communication to the Prosecutor of International Criminal Court regarding the situation in Occupied Cyprus," July 14, 2014, and may be found at http://israellawcenter.org/wp-content/uploads/2014/11/ICC-Turkey.pdf.

and continues to build waterworks, electric resources, and human infra-structure (particularly universities and hotels) in northeastern Cyprus; the Palestinians allege that Israel has built roads, waterworks, and electric resources in the disputed territory.

It would seem, therefore, that any complaint against Turkey should be prosecuted with the same vigor by the ICC as a complaint against Israel. However, several reasons make the complaint against Turkey even more serious, and demand more immediate attention, than any future complaint against Israel. In particular:

- Priority in time: The complaint against Turkey is two years old, and no complaint has yet been filed against Israel for settlement activity.
- Declaration of statehood: Turkey had declared the Turkish Republic of Northern Cyprus, or TRNC. Although Turkey is the only country in the world that has recognized the TRNC, this recognition clearly reflects Turkey's intent of *permanent* control of the disputed territory. Israel has not declared a state in the disputed territory, has not stated an intent to annex the territory, and has never stated an intent to *permanently* control the disputed territory.[128]
- Massive transfer of population into the disputed territory, with apparent intent to turn the original population into a minority in the disputed territory: The Turkish component of northeastern Cyprus has grown from about 28 percent in 1996 to over 45 percent today, with an apparent intention to make Greek Cypriots a minority in the Turkish Republic of Northern Cyprus.[129] Much of the Turkish population growth has been since 2002, the year that Cyprus became a member of the Rome Statute, and all of this growth is, according to

---

[128] Statements exist of Israeli intent to retain control of some parts of the disputed terri-tory, specifically in exchange for other land of equal area to be given to the Palestinians. Whatever one may think about these statements, they are not nearly as serious as what Turkey has actually done in Cyprus.

[129] According to some opinions, the Turks are already above 50 percent in northeastern Cyprus. See Kontorovich, "Politicizing the International Criminal Court," Introduction, first paragraph.

the Israel Law Center's complaint, a violation of section 2(b)(viii) of Article 8 of the Rome Statute. In comparison, Jews comprise about 15 percent of the population of Judea and Samaria / the West Bank, there is no realistic possibility (and no stated intent) to turn the Arabs of the territory into a minority, and almost 100 percent of the Jewish population growth occurred before the Palestinian Authority was admitted into membership in the ICC, meaning such growth cannot serve as the basis of any complaint.

- Massive government support: The Turkish government has given active and massive support to the Turkish population of northeastern Cyprus, including transferring Greek homes to Turks, providing special jobs for Turkish settlers, and exempting Turkish settlers from the Turkish military draft. There is nothing comparable in Israel – Arab homes have not been given to Jews, there are no special employment prospects for Jews in Judea and Samaria / the West Bank, and most definitely such Jews have no exemption from the Israeli military draft.
- Human Rights Decisions: Both the European Humans Rights Commission and the European Court of Human Rights have found a violation of international law in the transfer of Turkish settlers into northeastern Cyprus. There has been no equivalent decision regarding Israel.[130]

Whether a legitimate complaint could be made by the Palestinians against Israel is a moot point. The Palestinians would undoubtedly argue that Israeli "occupation" must be investigated by the ICC, and the Israelis would oppose the investigation. However, what is not in doubt is the severity of allegations against Turkey for its activities in northern Cyprus. In some specific areas, the activities of Turkey are comparable to those of Israel, but in several other areas, the activities of Turkey in northeastern Cyprus are much worse (at least according to the allegations) than the activities of Israel in Judea and Samaria / the West Bank.

---

[130] There has been a legal decision regarding Israel's security barrier, which is discussed below, but that decision relates to the barrier rather than to the transfer of population into the disputed territory.

So far the ICC has not investigated Turkey, despite the complaint. If the ICC were to choose to investigate Israel on some future complaint, but decline to investigate the significantly worse activities of Turkey, the ICC would be seen as a sham and a hypocrite that chooses to act according to political pressures rather than in accordance with the ICC mission stated in the Rome Statute.

Would it be possible, then, for the ICC to say, "We will investigate both Turkey and Israel"? Yes, that would indeed be possible, and pursuant to such a decision the ICC should also investigate all the other cases around the world in which a country controls or "occupies" disputed territory and allegedly transfers its population into the disputed territory. Here is a partial list of such occupying powers as of 2016:

1. China in Tibet
2. Hezbollah in Lebanon
3. India in Kashmir, although some people claim that Pakistan occupies Indian parts of Kashmir, and it may be that both India and Pakistan occupy parts of Kashmir belonging to the other country.
4. Iran in Kurdistan. Also, Iran in Iraq unless Iran withdraws from Iraq after the war with ISIS.
5. Morocco in the Western Sahara
6. Russia in Abkhazia, Chechnya, the Crimea, Georgia, South Ossetia, and the Ukraine
7. Spain in the Basque country and in Catalonia. France also is occupying part of the Basque country.
8. Turkey in Kurdistan
9. The UK in the Falkland Islands, and also in Gibraltar
10. All of the countries that have made territorial claims to parts of Antarctica, including Argentina, Australia, Chile, France, New Zealand, Norway, and the United Kingdom. These seven countries recognize each other's claims, but no one else does. There are no indigenous populations in Antarctica, hence no dispossession of native populations, but section 2(b)(viii) of Article 8 outlaws transfers *into* a territory, and that has been done by some or all of these countries into Antarctica.

This is not a complete list, and indeed there will be many other occupations arising in the future, all of which the ICC must investigate once it has opened the Pandora's box of Israeli settlement in Judea and Samaria / the West Bank. Either the ICC will investigate impartially, or it will be shown up as a fraud of so-called international "law."

III. The Security Barrier

As a result of dozens of suicide-bomb attacks by terrorists, killing hundreds of Israeli civilians and injuring hundreds more, in 2002 Israel began to build a "security barrier" between Israel and parts of the territories in dispute (Judea and Samaria / the West Bank) from which the bombers had come into Israel. To be clear, there were at least eighty bombing attacks in the period 2000–June 2002 alone, before construction began. The sole purpose of the barrier was to reduce the number of suicide attacks, and it has been extremely effective in achieving this purpose.[131] This section focuses on the International Court of Justice's advisory opinion regarding the security barrier, and on Israel's response to that opinion.

A. The 2004 Advisory Opinion of the International Court of Justice

On behalf of the Palestinians, the Arab states lobbied the UN General Assembly to ask the International Court of Justice ("ICJ") for an advisory ruling about the barrier.[132] This was the exact question submitted to the court on December 8, 2003:

---

[131] As stated by Major General Amos Yadlin, former head of Israel's Military Intelligence, "Everyone can see that where the anti-terror fence was built, the number of terror attacks in the area facing it dropped almost to zero. One of the reasons ... is [that] the fence ... closes off the ease of getting into Israel's cities. In addition, closing the border ... freezes the situation and it becomes easier ... to trace the movement of operational members of Hamas and Islamic Jihad." Yadlin, "Ethical Dilemmas in Fighting Terrorism," 132.

[132] Unlike the International Criminal Court, which deals solely with criminal charges

What are the legal consequences arising from the construction of the wall being built by Israel, the occupying Power, in the Occupied Palestinian Territory, including in and around East Jerusalem, as described in the report of the Secretary-General, considering the rules and principles of international law, including the Fourth Geneva Convention of 1949, and relevant Security Council and General Assembly resolutions?

This question was hardly impartial, although that is probably to be expected of the General Assembly.[133] The barrier is not a "wall" – 90–95 percent is wire fence. Furthermore, Israel does not consider itself to be "occupying" the territories, although that term is used twice in the question. And finally, the question focuses specifically on the "wall," or what Israel calls, more accurately, the "security fence." There is no specific reference to "settlements" or, more generally, to land.

---

against individuals, the International Court of Justice deals only with civil charges between nations, and with "advisory opinions" requested by the UN Security Council, or the UN General Assembly, or other organs and agencies of the UN. Resolutions of the UN General Assembly have no legally binding force; similarly, advisory opinions of the ICJ that are related to such resolutions are not binding on anyone. Resolutions of the UN Security Council do have legally binding force, but only when the Security Council finds a "threat to the peace, breach of the peace, or act of aggression," under Article 39 of the UN charter. There was no Security Council resolution regarding the referral of the matter to the ICJ, and no finding that the security barrier was a "threat to peace," "breach of peace" or "act of aggression." Therefore, the opinion of the court was advisory only. The decision of the ICJ, entitled *Advisory Opinion Concerning Legal Consequences of the Construction of a Wall in the Occupied Palestinian Territory* (July 9, 2004), is available at http://www.icj-cij.org/docket/files/131/1671.pdf.

[133] In fact, although the vote to request a judicial decision was 90–8, an additional seventy-four countries explicitly abstained and sixteen did not vote at all. Thus, those who requested the decision were a minority of the total number of UN members. The weakness of the referral undoubtedly reflects the outrageous bias of the question submitted – "wall" (which it is not, since over 90 percent is a fence), "occupying Power" (which is in dispute), and inclusion of east Jerusalem (which includes the holiest Jewish sites, existing for thousands of years). On the weakness of the vote, see Gerald M. Steinberg, "The UN, the ICJ, and the Separation Barrier: War by Other Means," NGO Monitor, *Israel Law Review* 38 (2005): 340, http://www.ngo-monitor.org/academic-publications/_the _un_the_icj_and_the_separation_barrier_war_by_other_means_/. See also Gerald M. Steinberg, "The Role of the NGOs in the Palestinian Political War Against Israel," in Baker, *Palestinian Manipulation*, 68.

The ICJ issued its decision on July 9, 2004. The decision included, among other things:

- A finding of the court that the barrier is illegal under the Fourth Geneva Convention of 1949, because most of the barrier was in the disputed territories. The court explicitly refrained from comment on parts of the barrier in pre-1967 Israel.
- A conclusion of the court – not related to the specific findings, not requested by the General Assembly, and not required for decision on the main question – that the establishment of settlements in the disputed territories (including east Jerusalem) is in breach of international law.
- A rejection of the argument that the barrier was necessary or justified by Israel's right of self-defense. This rejection was not part of the findings of the court, but it was stated specifically, and it was necessary to the finding on the illegality of the barrier. According to the ICJ, whether or not the barrier has effectively reduced attacks, Israel as an occupying power has no right of self-defense to construct such a barrier.[134]

What could be said about this advisory opinion of the ICJ?

First, the advisory opinion was based upon a biased General Assembly that crafted a question designed to incriminate Israel even before any evidence was heard.

Second, despite various exhortations by the court, the opinion is advisory only and has no binding effect on anyone.

Third, Israel rejected the court's authority to resolve this aspect or other

---

[134] About this very limited view of self-defense, one commentator opined, "It is safe to say that the Court's treatment of the matter has caused more confusion than clarification." Heather Harrison Dinniss, *Cyber Warfare and the Laws of War* (New York: Cambridge University Press, 2014), 96. The court's decision on this issue has also been called "startling in its brevity," "unsatisfactory," and "unclear." Sean D. Murphy, "Ipse Dixit at the I.C.J." (Public Law and Legal Theory Working Paper no. 120, George Washington Law School, December 4, 2004), pp. 3, 12, available at http://ssrn.com/abstract=488125, later published in the *American Journal of International Law* 99, no. 1, 2005.

aspects of the Israeli-Palestinian dispute. Israel had a right to do so, and hence Israel was not before the court.

Fourth, the court failed to consider Israel's stated intentions. In written comments, Israel stated that the barrier was intended only to stop or reduce terrorist suicide attacks ("effectively to combat terror attacks launched from the West Bank"), that the barrier was temporary only, that Israel had not annexed or stated any intention to annex any part of the territories, and that Israel would, at whatever trouble and expense, remove the barrier pursuant to a political resolution between Israel and the Palestinians. The court ignored most of these points. As to the argument of self-defense (to reduce attacks), the court's entire opinion was:

> Article 51 of the Charter [that created the United Nations] thus recognizes the existence of an inherent right of self-defence in the case of armed attack by one State against another State. However, Israel does not claim that the attacks against it are imputable to a foreign state.... Consequently, the Court concludes that Article 51 of the Charter has no relevance in this case.[135]

Article 51, the right of any state to act in its self-defense, was the main argument against a finding of illegality. The quoted passage is all the court said about the Article 51 right of self-defense. It ignored the fact that suicide bombings decreased dramatically, almost coincident with the construction of the barrier, from forty-seven in 2002, to twenty-three in 2003, to seventeen in 2004, and continuing downward. Israeli civilian deaths from suicide bombings were 220 in 2002, dropping by half in 2003, and half again in 2004 – yet this too went unnoticed by the court.[136]

---

[135] Paragraph 139 of the decision of the ICJ, p. 194.

[136] Lance David LeClaire, "10 Grim Separation Walls from Around the World," *Listverse*, September 27, 2014, available at http://listverse.com/2014/09/27/10-grim-separation -walls-from-around-the-world/. All of these facts were apparent even at the time the decision was rendered, but they were not discussed or noted in any way by the International Court of Justice.

B. The Response to the Advisory Opinion of the ICJ

What has been the response of Israel to the advisory opinion of the International Court of Justice? Effectively, nothing at all. There have been, of course, diplomatic words, but specific action was neither required nor taken. The advisory opinion of the ICJ was clearly a lawfare action by the Arab states against Israel. What was the reaction of the Israel Law Center, the premier Israeli organization in the lawfare struggle? Again, nothing at all.

Why has no action been taken? Why have Israel and the Israel Law Center chosen to do essentially nothing?

When the Berlin Wall was torn down in 1989, there were sixteen fences or walls between countries in the world. As of August 2015, sixty-five such barriers exist.[137] A very partial list includes the following:

1. Wall in Baghdad separating Shi'ites and Sunnis
2. Electrified fence between Botswana and Zimbabwe
3. Brunei's fence against Malaysia to keep out refugees
4. Bulgaria's fence against Turkey to keep out refugees
5. Egypt's wall against southern Gaza to keep out Hamas and Muslim Brotherhood terrorists
6. Greece's fence against Turkey to keep out refugees
7. Hungary's fence against Serbia to keep out refugees
8. India's fence against Bangladesh to keep out migrants
9. India's fence against Pakistan to keep out terrorists
10. Iran's wall against Iraq to keep out terrorists
11. Israel's fence against Gaza to keep out Hamas terrorists
12. Israel's fence against Lebanon to keep out Hezbollah terrorists
13. Israel's fence against the territories to keep out West Bank terrorists

---

[137] Simon Tomlinson, "World of Walls: How 65 Countries Have Erected Fences on Their Borders – Four Times As Many As When the Berlin Wall Was Toppled – as Governments Try to Hold Back the Tide of Migrants," *MailOnline*, August 21, 2015, citing Elisabeth Vallet, scientific director at the Raoul Dandurand Chair of Strategic and Diplomatic Studies of the University of Quebec, Montreal, Canada, available at http://www.dailymail.co.uk/news/article-3205724/How-65-countries-erected-security-walls-borders.html#ixzz3yCE4EZgU.

14. Kenya's fence against Somalia to keep out terrorists
15. Kuwait's barrier against Iraq to prevent infiltration
16. Macedonia's fence against Greece to keep out refugees
17. Malaysia's wall against Thailand
18. Morocco's sand berm in the Western Sahara to keep out Polisario rebels
19. Fence separating North and South Korea
20. Northern Ireland's barrier in Belfast to separate Catholics and Protestants. In fact, there are about one hundred barriers in Belfast, plus additional walls in Derry.
21. Russia's wall against Georgia to maintain Russian control of South Ossetia
22. Saudi Arabia's fence against Iraq to keep out ISIS terrorists
23. Saudi Arabia's wall against Yemen to keep out provocateurs
24. Slovenia's fence against Croatia to keep out refugees
25. Spain's fence against Morocco to keep out refugees
26. Sri Lanka's fence against displaced Tamils
27. Turkey's wall against Syria to keep out ISIS terrorists
28. The Ukraine's fence against Russia to keep out Russian provocateurs
29. The United States' fence against Mexico to keep out migrants
30. Uzbekistan's fence against Afghanistan to keep out Taliban terrorists

More walls are going up all the time, due primarily to the threat of terrorists, or massive emigration, or economic migrants. The response to the *ICJ Wall Advisory Opinion* has been much muted, because there is no need for a strong response. Given the state of the world, it is extremely unlikely that any further lawfare challenge will be launched against Israel's security barrier in Judea and Samaria. If and when any such challenge arises, the Israel Law Center will be prepared to launch dozens of complaints at the ICC against states that have built berms/fences/walls to keep out provocateurs/terrorists/migrants, whether the barrier is built solely on the land of the builder or, in many cases, on land that is alleged to be "occupied." As a practical matter, the campaign to dismantle the Israeli security barrier has run its course, and has failed.

IV. A Summary of Chapter 3

Chapter 3 focuses on the struggle over the disputed land of Judea and Samaria / the West Bank. It starts by explaining that the Palestinians reject Jews in any part of what is often called the "Land of Israel" – that is, no State of Israel in any form, and ultimately no Jewish presence, would be acceptable anywhere between the Mediterranean Sea and the Jordan River. The core of the Israeli–Palestinian dispute is Palestinian rejectionism, and not any specific attitude or action of the Jews. The Palestinians express their rejectionism in explicit statements, in educating their children in the grossest forms of hatred against the Jews, and in the monstrosity, embodied in a Palestinian statute, of paying money to terrorists according to a sliding scale – the more Jews murdered and the more brutal the murders, the more money is paid to the terrorist.

Two cases are reviewed. The first, which is a charge of "population transfer" that the Palestinians will almost certainly make against Israel, is based on a section of the Rome Statute that was drafted and lobbied by the Arab states specifically in order to use in a lawfare attack against Israel. This statute is discriminatory on its face and may be categorized as a "bill of attainder," one of the hallmarks of a dictatorial perversion of law. To let the ICC, the UN, and all involved parties understand what is coming, the Israel Law Center filed a complaint against Turkey for its activities in northeastern Cyprus. Using the same section of the Rome Statute, and the same specific arguments that will be made against Israel, the Israel Law Center has shown that Turkey's activities are far worse than those of Israel. Ten additional instances are then listed of countries that might be called "occupiers" under this section of the Rome Statute; all of these countries may be charged if a complaint is brought against Israel and the ICC chooses to pursue an investigation.

The second case concerns Israel's security barrier, which has saved hundreds and possibly thousands of civilian lives since its construction began in 2002. A 2004 decision of the International Court of Justice found the barrier to be illegal, but this decision is an advisory opinion that binds no one, and the decision brushes aside Israel's right of self-defense in a cursory manner which, if applied consistently, will brush away rights of self-defense by states against armed rebellions and terrorist activities throughout Asia and Africa. Generally, both the State of Israel and the Israel Law Center have done very little in regard to this decision, and with good reason. There are at least sixty-five barriers in the world today, and more are going up as a result of global changes. All of the countries who have built, or who are building, or who intend to build such barriers may be charged as violators of international law under either the Geneva Conventions or the Rome Statute.

CHAPTER 4

The Sea: On Blockades and Flotillas

Introduction: The Nature of History

> [A]ll great events in world history occur ... twice ... the first
> time as tragedy, the second time as farce.
>
> – *Karl Marx*[138]

Subsequent to Egypt's homicidal threats against Israel and the massing of Egyptian troops on the Egypt–Israel border, the Six-Day War broke out, and Israel captured the Gaza Strip from Egypt. Israel controlled Gaza from 1967 until 2005. During August 2005, in an attempt to ease conditions for Palestinians and reduce tension, Israel withdrew completely from the Gaza Strip – every business, every soldier, every Israeli left. In January 2006, Hamas won the Palestinians elections, and formed a national unity government with Fatah, which later collapsed in civil war. In June 2007, Hamas seized control of the strip from Fatah, and has ruled continuously since that time.

---

[138] "Der achtzehnte Brumaire des Louis Bonaparte" ("The eighteenth Brumaire of Louis Bonaparte"), essay in the German language magazine Die Revolution, New York, 1852, http//www.mlwerke.de/me08/me08_115.htm. The quotation is from the first sentence of the first chapter, translated from the German by me.

In response to Hamas rocket firings on towns in southern Israel, and Hamas attacks on crossing points into Israel, Israel placed a blockade on Gaza, including a naval blockade that began on January 3, 2009. The blockade is not total, but applies only to items that are or may be used as offensive weapons, such as rockets and mortars. Since the implementation of the naval blockade, there have been eleven attempts to break the blockade. The attempts of relevance here are the attempt of May 2010, which will be called "Flotilla I"; the attempt of July 2011, which will be called "Flotilla II"; and the attempt of June 2015, which will be called "Flotilla III." Flotilla I resulted in armed conflict and several deaths. Flotilla II never sailed, in large part due to the active involvement of the Israel Law Center. Flotilla III occurred, but only as "the farce" in Marx's view of history. The subject of chapter 3 is lawfare in Flotillas I–III, and the likely results of future flotillas.

I. The Naval Blockade of Gaza and the Three Flotillas

This section describes the three significant attempts to break the naval blockade of Gaza and their relevance to lawfare. The discussion illustrates the powerful victories that can be achieved by operating through legal channels, particularly in combination with parallel political factors.

A. Flotilla I (2010)

Flotilla I initially included eight ships, with about seven hundred passengers, and with a stated intention to deliver "humanitarian goods" to Gaza. Prior to sailing, the Israeli government offered to allow the flotilla to dock at Ashdod harbor, where the Israelis, in coordination with the UN or another third party acceptable to both sides, would inspect the cargoes, select out military goods, and then send the humanitarian goods to Gaza. This offer was rejected by the organizers of Flotilla I. The chief organizer, IHH, was a Turkish organization with links to al-Qaeda.

Six of the ships sailed from Cyprus on May 30, 2011. (The seventh ship never arrived due to mechanical problems, and the eighth ship sailed later.) These six ships were boarded by Israeli naval forces on May 31, 2011. On five ships there was no opposition, but on the *Mavi Marmara* armed passengers attacked the Israeli forces, resulting in nine passengers dead and three soldiers wounded.

Many details of Flotilla 1, and of the confrontation on May 31, 2011, are not relevant here, since these details are not related to lawfare. In fact, there was no lawfare involved in Flotilla 1. The scope of Flotilla 1, the intention of the passengers to attack Israeli soldiers, and the presence of arms were not known or were not understood by the Israeli forces. However, Flotilla 1 is relevant here for four reasons.

First, the stated intention "to deliver humanitarian aid" was simply untrue. The real purpose of Flotilla 1 was to completely break the blockade, and to permit the importation of all goods without review (including, inevitably, mortars, rockets, rifles, ammunition, and other weapons intended to kill Israelis). Greta Berlin, one of the organizers of Flotilla 1, stated explicitly, "This mission is not about delivering humanitarian supplies, it's about breaking Israel's siege...." This intention was echoed by several other participants in Flotilla 1.[139]

Second, the UN published a report about Flotilla 1 and the incident of the *Mavi Marmara*. The UN report stated that the Israeli naval blockade of Gaza is legal.[140]

---

[139] "Tensions Rise over Gaza Aid Fleet: Israeli Army Intends to Halt Humanitarian Aid Mission Head for Palestinian Territory," *Al Jazeera Network*, May 28, 2010, available at http://www.aljazeera.com/news/middleeast/2010/05/2010528431964325.html. The article includes the quote attributed to Greta Berlin, a comment by an Irish activist that the activists "were determined to break Israel's blockade," and other hostile comments by organizers and by Hamas.

[140] United Nations, "Report of the [UN] Secretary-General's Panel of Inquiry on the 31 May 2010 Flotilla Incident," September, 2011, commonly known as "The Palmer Report," available at http://www.un.org/News/dh/infocus/middle_east/Gaza_Flotilla_Panel _Report.pdf, 38–45. The panel of inquiry found "that Israel's naval blockade was legal," p. 44, para. 81. The reason for this conclusion is that "Israel faces a threat to its security from militant groups in Gaza. The naval blockade was imposed as a legitimate security measure in order to prevent weapons from entering Gaza by sea and its implementation complied with the requirements of international law," p. 45, para. 82. The panel also found that there were serious questions about the nature and objectives of IHH (p. 4,

Third, a complaint was filed with the ICC, alleging that the actions of the Israel Defense Forces constituted a "war crime." The chief prosecutor of the ICC, Fatou Bensouda, ruled that even if there were a war crime, it was not of sufficient "gravity" to be pursued by the ICC. A panel of ICC judges has asked Chief Prosecutor Bensouda to reconsider this decision, but no further action has been taken.[141]

Fourth, and perhaps most important for the purposes of this book, Flotilla I set the stage for the further attempts, and for the entry of lawfare in Flotillas II and III.

B. Flotilla II (2011) and the Actions of the Israel Law Center

Flotilla II intended to sail to Gaza on July 5, 2010, slightly more than one year after Flotilla I. As with Flotilla I, although the stated intent was to bring humanitarian aid to Gaza, the actual intent was to break the Israeli naval blockade, and thereby enable the importation, without inspection, of all kinds of goods to Gaza.[142] The purpose of breaking the blockade is

---

para. 4), but that Israel's military action was premature and therefore excessive in the circumstances (p. 4, para. 6).

[141] Barak Ravid, "ICC Panel Orders Prosecutor to Reconsider Probe of Israel Over Gaza Flotilla Raid," *Haaretz*, July 16, 2015, available at http://www.haaretz.com/israel-news/.premium-1.666477. This is surely another example of severe bias against Israel, here in the form of a "double standard." The Rome Statute is intended to punish and deter atrocious crimes such as genocide, ethnic cleansing, and mass murder. In this case, there was a confrontation on a ship, in which a handful of people were wounded or killed due to the armed preparations of the ship's passengers and the ignorance of the other side. Could this incident honestly be called "genocide," "mass murder," "a war of aggression," or the like? Again, the overplaying of legal action shows that the intention is political, not legal, that the goal is to harm Israel, not to achieve "justice," and that in the end, the continuing abuse of the ICC is likely to weaken that court and severely damage its ability to achieve the objectives stated in the Rome Statute.

[142] For example, Paul Murphy, member of the European Parliament and activist who participated in Flotilla II, stated, "The aim of the Flotilla is to break that siege by delivering vital medical supplies and construction material and to highlight the ongoing blockade and impact on the population." "Paul Murphy Socialist Party MEP joins 'Freedom Flotilla II,'" Socialistworld.net, June 24, 2011, available at http://www.socialistworld.net/doc

clear and obvious – to allow the importation of weapons into Gaza. As the *National Post* writes:

> The real intention of the flotilla [Flotilla II] is to break the blockade and end Hamas' political isolation. There can be only one reason why anyone would consider such an outcome desirable: The absence of a blockade would allow the free passage of arms to the terror-embracing Hamas government, which has frequently demonstrated its goal of ending Israel's existence as a nation.
>
> Israel's blockade of Gaza is a direct consequence of attacks launched from within the territory. If flotilla participants really want to ease Gazans' isolation, they should encourage Hamas to acknowledge Israel's right to exist and to forswear terrorism.[143]

However, apart from sharing the basic motivation, these flotillas differ in two critical respects. First, Flotilla II was substantially larger and stronger than Flotilla I. Second, despite its relatively greater strength, Flotilla II was defeated by a combination of law and politics, because this time, with Flotilla II, the defenders of Israel were aware of what was to happen, and were prepared to act. The rest of the discussion about Flotilla II will focus on these two differences.

/5155. Israel does not prevent medicine or construction material from entering Gaza, even though much of the construction material is diverted from rehabilitation of civilian structures to building attack tunnels from Gaza into Israel. As Murphy stated, the true intent is to break the blockade. See also comments by Adam Shapiro, a founding member of the "Free Gaza Movement" – one of the sponsors of Flotilla II – and a participant on one of the ships of Flotilla II. In a speech to raise money for Flotilla II that he delivered at Rutgers University in November 2010, Shapiro stated, at time period 1:07–1:31, that "Free Gaza is one tactic of a larger strategy, to transform this conflict from one between Israel and the Palestinians, or Israel and the Arab world ... to one between the rest of the world and Israel," available at https://www.youtube.com/watch?v=okx5NwxAXVI. All three of the flotillas had no interest in delivering humanitarian aid or easing the plight of the Palestinians, but were intended rather to break the naval blockade as one step in a program to destroy Israel completely.

[143] "On Israel, Greece Gets It Right," Full Comment editorial, *National Post*, July 4, 2011, available at http://news.nationalpost.com/full-comment/national-post-editorial-board-on-israel-greece-gets-it-right.

1. THE STRENGTH OF FLOTILLA II

Flotilla II, intended to sail in July 2011, was stronger than the flotilla from 2010, in at least three respects. First, Flotilla II was substantially larger than Flotilla I. Flotilla II had ten ships, versus only eight in the earlier flotilla. The more ships, the greater the chance that one or more would succeed in breaching the naval blockade. Also, Flotilla II had more than one thousand activists, in comparison to less than seven hundred who participated in the earlier flotilla.

Second, Flotilla II had much greater international support than Flotilla I. Flotilla I was sponsored by four NGOs, but in reality, there were only two main sponsors – Free Gaza Movement (United States), which sponsored three ships; and IHH (Turkey), which also sponsored three ships, including the *Mavi Marmara*, by far the largest ship in Flotilla I, containing almost 90 percent of all the activists. The remaining two ships in Flotilla I were sponsored by Greek Ship to Gaza (Greece) and the European Campaign to End the Siege of Gaza, also known as "ECESG" (UK).[144] In contrast, Flotilla II was organized by twenty-two NGOs, but of these there were ten main sponsors, including the same four who had organized Flotilla I. Also, whereas Flotilla I had ships from four countries (Greece, Turkey, the UK, and the United States), the ships of Flotilla II originated in ten countries (Canada, France, Greece, Ireland, Italy, Norway, Spain, Sweden, Turkey, and the United States). In all comparable respects, Flotilla II had the greater international participation.

And third, there was strong political interest in Flotilla II. International interest in Flotilla II, and corresponding international press coverage, was massive from the very beginning. Flotilla I was also of interest, certainly,

---

[144] The European Campaign to End the Siege of Gaza, or ECESG, is headquartered in Belgium but is active mainly in Great Britain, with links to about thirty organizations that are overwhelmingly pro-Hamas, pro-Muslim Brotherhood, or pro-Palestinian generally, and of course virulently anti-Israel. See, for example, "The European Campaign to End the Siege on Gaza (ECESG) Is an Anti-Israel, Pro-Hamas Umbrella Organization which Participated in the *Mavi Marmara* Flotilla," Meir Amit Intelligence and Terrorism Information Center, October 5, 2010, available at http://www.terrorism-info.org.il/en /article/18014.

but to some degree it caught the world by surprise, whereas Flotilla II was expected to be a media event. To the extent that the organizers of Flotilla II wanted publicity, they got what they wanted.

Despite the much greater strength of Flotilla II in comparison to the earlier flotilla, Flotilla II failed utterly. Of the ten ships in Flotilla II, nine did not sail at all. The tenth ship, *Dignité Al Karama* from France, did sail, with a total of ten activists[145] in comparison to the more than one thousand who had originally planned to sail. The French ship was intercepted by the Israeli navy with no casualties, and it never reached Gaza. What accounts for this failure? There were political factors, and there were legal factors that were created and driven by the Israel Law Center.

2. POLITICAL FACTORS INSTRUMENTAL IN FLOTILLA II'S FAILURE

There were several political factors that made Flotilla II very different from the flotilla of the prior year. First, the stated purpose of Flotilla II – to provide humanitarian aid – was politically preempted, in two ways. Prior to the organization of the flotilla, both Egypt and Israel had eased restrictions, allowing more goods to be imported by land, so that at the time of Flotilla II there was no serious shortage of goods in Gaza.[146] Indeed, Turkey, which had supported Flotilla I, was opposed to Flotilla II, partly due to the fact that in response to civilian need, Egypt had opened the Rafah crossing into Gaza.[147] In addition, during final preparations for sailing, all of the countries directly involved in the sailing made offers to allow humanitarian goods to be delivered to Gaza – Greece offered to allow the goods to sail in Greek ships and under UN supervision; Egypt offered to receive the ships at El Arish port, and transship the goods to Gaza; Israel offered to receive the

---

[145] Sixteen people sailed on the ship, of whom three were crew members, at least three were journalists, and approximately ten were activists.

[146] Ethan Bronner, "Israel Warns of Using Force If New Flotilla Heads to Gaza," *New York Times*, June 16, 2011, available at http://www.nytimes.com/2011/06/17/world/middleast/17flotilla.html?_R=0.

[147] Hanan Greenberg, "Navy Gears for Turkish Flotilla," *Ynet News*, June 15, 2011, available at http://www.ynetnews.com/articles/0,7340,L-4082355,00.html.

ships at Ashdod port, and transship the goods directly to Gaza. All of these offers were rejected, because, after all, providing humanitarian aid was never the true purpose of the flotilla.

A second political factor distinguishing Flotilla II was Israel's policy in reaction to news of the flotilla. This factor must not be underestimated as one cause of Flotilla II's failure. Israel's policy was twofold: to ease restrictions of the blockade in order to preempt the need for humanitarian aid, but also to state strongly and repeatedly that any attempt to force the blockade would be met and rebuffed with force. For example, rumors were circulating that activists intended to attack Israeli soldiers, as they had done in Flotilla I. In response, Israel made clear that its soldiers would intercept the ships, defend themselves if attacked,[148] and arrest the activists. In the end, the only ship that sailed, the French *Dignité Al Karama*, was indeed intercepted by the Israeli Navy, and its passengers arrested. The firmness and constancy of Israel's opposition was almost certainly critical in enlisting the support of countries and also in demoralizing the activists. As one activist said, "Only a fool thought that we'd get to Gaza given what happened last year [to Flotilla I]. We knew we'd be stopped...."[149]

A third political factor, and perhaps in part a result of the first two factors, is that many governments expressed objection to Flotilla II in various ways, such as forbidding their citizens to take part, urging alternative action, or warning against possible harm. For example, negative comments were made about Flotilla II by the governments of Canada, Egypt, France,[150] Greece,

---

[148] Scott Sayare, "Israeli Advocacy Group Helps Delay Departure of Gaza-Bound Flotilla," *New York Times*, June 28, 2011, available at http://www.nytimes.com/2011/06/29/world /middleeast/29flotilla.html.

[149] Stated by Henry Norr, an activist present on the American ship *Audacity of Hope*, which managed to sail only ten minutes from Perama port before it was intercepted by the Greek Coast Guard. Kristin J. Bender, "Activist Talks about Failed Mission to Reach the Gaza Strip," *San Jose Mercury News*, July 8, 2011, http://www.mercurynews .com/breaking-news/ci_18442144.

[150] France, for example, called the flotilla a "bad idea...expected only to increase tension." "Another Ship Headed to Gaza Damaged," UPI, June 30, 2011, available at http://www.upi .com/Top_News/World-News/2011/06/30/Another-ship-headed-to-Gaza-damaged /UPI-55371309435411/. In addition, although Flotilla II was originally intended to include

the Netherlands, the United Kingdom, the United States, and of course Israel. Even Turkey, which had supplied the *Mavi Marmara* in Flotilla I, and which had subsequently broken diplomatic relations with Israel, urged the organizers to reconsider their intention to sail.[151] Of course Hamas supported the sailing, but its political influence is far inferior to that of the countries that openly expressed opposition.

Greece's role, in particular, was critically important. Several of the ships docked in Piraeus, or near Athens, and the Greek government would not permit them to sail for reasons of safety.[152] Indeed, ships of the Greek Coast Guard seized the US ship *Audacity of Hope* as it tried to sale from Perama, Greece, and later seized the Canadian ship *Tahrir* as it sailed from Crete.

3. LEGAL FACTORS INSTRUMENTAL IN FLOTILLA II'S FAILURE

The political factors, discussed above, set the stage for what happened. However, it is the legal factors, generated and managed by the Israel Law Center, which precipitated the ultimate failure of Flotilla II.

From the very beginning, the Israel Law Center's intention was to defeat this flotilla. As stated by its founder and director, "[T]he war on the flotilla should not be left for the [Israeli] Special Forces to fight alone. There are various ways to prevent, postpone, limit and avert the danger – and [physical] force isn't always the best way."[153] This comment correctly

---

fifteen ships, only ten ships arrived at the staging area. One of the five dropouts was stuck at the port of Marseille, having been seriously delayed as a result of a letter and lobbying campaign by French Jews. Ronen Medzini, "French Flotilla Ship Won't Sail," *Ynet News*, June 15, 2011, available at http://www.ynetnews.com/articles/0,7340,L-4082772,00.html.

[151] The Turkish foreign minister Ahmet Davutoglu urged the flotilla organizers to reconsider whether the flotilla was needed. Hanan Greenberg, "Navy Gears for Turkish Flotilla."

[152] The Greeks judged the mission to be "too dangerous." See Phil Black, "Greeks Arrest Captain of U.S. Ship Aiming to Protest Gaza Blockade," *CNN World*, July 2, 2011, available at http://edition.cnn.com/2011/WORLD/meast/07/02/israel.gaza.flotilla/index.html?hpt=hp_t2.

[153] Stated by Nitsana Darshan-Leitner, director of the Israel Law Center, in Ron Friedman, "Lawyers, not IDF, at Forefront of Battle against Flotilla," *Jerusalem Post*, June 6, 2011, available at http://www.jpost.com/Diplomacy-and-Politics/Lawyers-not-IDF-at-forefront-of-battle-against-flotilla.

reflects the attitude at the time – combative, because this was a war against Hamas and Hamas sympathizers, but also cooperative with the Israeli army. In this spirit, the Israel Law Center took four actions which, together with the intervention of the Israeli navy at the end, defeated Flotilla II.

First, the attorneys at the Israel Law Center considered what a ship must have in order to sail. Although none of these attorneys are specialists in maritime law, they understood that every ship must have commercial insurance before sailing. They therefore decided to attack this vital requirement. As nonspecialists, they did not know which companies provided such insurance, but that was a matter of basic research. They were able to identify fourteen ships that intended to sail as part of Flotilla II, but they did not know which specific companies insured which of the ships. In an act that I can only call "crowd investigating," or perhaps "crowd research," they placed on their website this announcement:

> Please help identify the insurance companies used by the following Gaza Flotilla boats. When you click on a boat on the list below, you will be taken to a web page where you can enter your comments.

Having identified all of the companies specializing in maritime insurance, and at least some of the companies insuring specific ships in the flotilla, the Israel Law Center then sent letters to each such insurance company, stating, in brief, that the company is (or may be) insuring a ship intended to aid the terrorist organization Hamas, and that the company would be liable for damage resulting from terrorist actions of the ship in breaching the blockade and delivering contraband goods, including deaths and injuries from contraband rockets fired at civilians.

Lloyd's of London, the world's largest maritime insurer, was one of the companies to receive such a letter. It responded:

> The Lloyd's Market has robust systems in place to ensure international sanctions are followed and therefore any underwriter identifying an insured or prospective insured acting on behalf of, or for the benefit of Hamas, would not insure such a risk.[154]

---

[154] Gil Ronen, "Maritime Lawfare Victory: Lloyd's Won't Insure Gaza Flotilla," *Arutz*

In other words, not only would Lloyd's itself not insure the ships, but in addition, none of the underwriters working with Lloyd's would insure the ships. This was a major blow to Flotilla II, particularly in view of Greece's refusal to allow the sailings for the reason that the ships were "not safe." The largest ship in the intended flotilla was again the *Mavi Marmara*, which had been the source of the deadly incident in Flotilla I – but this time it did not sail, due to its inability to obtain insurance.[155]

The Israel Law Center's second action to defeat Flotilla II occurred shortly after and as a result of the battle over insurance. Israel's Office of the Prime Minister contacted the Israel Law Center and offered assistance. The Israel Law Center responded, in essence, "Please tell us: What else do ships need, in addition to maritime insurance, in order to sail?" The prime minister's office responded that satellite communication was essential – to plot GPS coordinates (which is critical for sailing and also for safety), to contact port authorities (also critical for safety), and in this case, to contact international media in order to create political pressure on Israel.[156] Upon additional research, the attorneys of the Israel Law Center learned that the only company providing satellite communication services to ships in the eastern Mediterranean Sea was Inmarsat.[157]

Sheva (*Israel National News*), May 23, 2011, available at http://www.israelnationalnews.com/News/News.aspx/144423#.VrdDVBh97RY.

[155] Bronner, "Israel Warns of Using Force If New Flotilla Heads to Gaza." Further, it should be recalled that one of the fifteen ships intending to sail never left the port of Marseille. This was due in part to actions of French Jews lobbying insurance companies to deny insurance to the ship. In addition, at least one French insurance company denied maritime insurance to the same French ship, due to a letter from the Israel Law Center. "Shurat HaDin's Victories in the Struggle to Block the Anti-Israel Flotilla," Israel Law Center, June 19, 2011, available at http://israellawcenter.org/pr/shurat-hadins-victories-in-the-struggle-to-block-the-anti-israel-flotilla/. In the instance of insurance for the French ship, the Jewish community of France worked in parallel with the Israel Law Center – not in coordination but nevertheless toward the same goal, which was achieved. Here, again, is an example of the multiplicative power of political pressure combined with legal action.

[156] The interaction between the Israel Law Center and the office of the Israeli prime minister is detailed in Alana Goodman, "Meet the Legal Wonks who Brought Down the Flotilla," *Commentary Magazine*, August 22, 2011, available at https://www.commentarymagazine.com/culture-civilization/shurat-hadin-flotilla.

[157] The story of the Israel Law Center and Inmarsat is well explained in Kittrie, *Lawfare*,

Inmarsat is headquartered in London, with offices in Washington, D.C.;
Miami, Florida; and various countries around the world. On Sunday, June 5,
2011, the Israel Law Center sent faxes to nine senior executives of Inmarsat
in both the London and Washington, D.C., offices, stating the facts of the
flotilla planning to sail within the month, presenting evidence that Inmarsat
was providing satellite communication services to the ships in the flotilla,
and explaining that if Inmarsat continued to do so, the company would
be providing "material support and resources" to a terrorist organization,
which could result in any or all of the following:

1. Criminal liability for the senior executives of Inmarsat;
2. Civil liability of Inmarsat for all physical harm to American and Israeli
   citizens. In particular, if weapons or ammunition were smuggled into
   Gaza, the company would be liable for the damage caused in all attacks
   by Hamas.
3. The civil liability of the company would be shared by the senior executives of Inmarsat.[158]

The company answered very quickly. In a fax dated June 8, 2011, the company acknowledged receipt of the letter on June 6 and stated the company's
position:

> In this instance, it is our understanding that the vessel in question
> [the *Mavi Marmara*] is not registered, owned, controlled or operated
> by Hamas or any other designated terrorist organisation and, as a
> result, neither Inmarsat nor third parties in the distribution chain
> supplying airtime or terminals are in breach of any such restrictions
> [under international or other applicable sanctions legislation].

315–17. See also the relevant material in the Israel Law Center website, "Sinking the Gaza
Flotilla", at http://israellawcenter.org/war-zones/fighting-bds/the-flotilla.

[158] Corporate executives are typically immune from liability for damage related to acts
or omissions of the corporation, but that is not true for intentional torts or for crimes.
Further, the executives might be covered under Directors and Officers Liability Insurance
("D&O insurance"), but D&O insurance might or might not cover personal injury due
to a tort, and would almost certainly not cover damages caused by a criminal act. These
issues were not raised in the letter to Inmarsat, but it is a fair inference that the senior
executives were fully aware of the risks and liabilities.

In this answer, Inmarsat gave short shrift to the Israel Law Center's warnings. The center then responded on June 27, 2011, by filing a lawsuit in a state court of Florida against Inmarsat. The center requested a permanent injunction against the provision of satellite communication services to ships in the flotilla, and a declaration that the provision of such services would constitute a crime under United States federal law.[159] The case was ultimately not successful, and the requested relief was not granted. Nevertheless, Inmarsat understood the situation, and wisely chose to discontinue its service to ships in the flotilla.[160] If we can say that the lack of maritime insurance is a safety issue, even more so the absence of satellite communication service – without such service, a ship navigates with relatively primitive tools and is restricted in its ability to call for assistance.[161]

The Israel Law Center's third action, on June 17, 2011, was to file a request in a federal court in Manhattan to seize the ships in the flotilla. The center claimed that the ships had been outfitted with funds raised in the United States, and that such an act – the raising of funds for Flotilla 11 – was a violation of a federal statute that prohibits actions that fit or arm a ship intended to harm a nation that is at peace with the United States. Ultimately, this lawsuit was rejected, not because of its content, but because the statute allegedly violated allows only the United States government to sue and does not explicitly authorize a private party to sue.[162] Although this lawsuit lost,

---

[159] The lawsuit was *Fendel v. Inmarsat Inc. et al.*, Case Number 11-19912CA 15, Circuit Court of the 11th Judicial District, Miami-Dade County, Florida, action filed June 27, 2011, complaint available at http://www.investigativeproject.org/documents/case_docs/1594.pdf.

[160] Kittrie, *Lawfare*, 317.

[161] The satellite communication company Inmarsat provides a device called the "Inmarsat C," which reports the position of a ship, as determined by satellite communication, in case of emergency. This is clearly a safety measure. The ability to provide such a distress signal is a maritime requirement for ships above three hundred tons. Ari Bussel, "Taking the Legal Route: Suing Satellite Communication Providers," *News Blaze*, June 7, 2011, available at http://newsblaze.com/story/20110607042530buss.nb/topstory.html. Some of the ships in Flotilla 11 were small, and might not have met the threshold of three hundred tons, but the main ship, the *Mavi Marmara*, was over four thousand tons, and was required to be able to transmit such a distress signal.

[162] The statute allegedly violated is 18 United States Code sec. 962, and the final decision of the appellate court is *Bauer v. Mavi Marmara* et al., 774 F.3d 1026, United States Court

the attempt was a very creative action of lawfare, and other creative means may be found in the future.

The Israel Law Center's fourth action, after sending its letters to the maritime insurers and to Inmarsat, was to notify the Greek Ministry of Civil Protection that ships in the flotilla lacked insurance, might also lack satellite communications, and were improperly registered with the Greek port authorities – in that they stated, falsely, that they intended to sail for Alexandria, Egypt, when in fact they intended to run the Gaza blockade. The Israel Law Center demanded that the Greek Coast Guard check the ships. The ships were checked, and were prevented from sailing by Greek authorities because they lacked insurance, or dishonestly stated an incorrect destination, or were not seaworthy.[163] In the end, fifteen ships intended to sail, ten of these arrived in Greece or Corfu, but nine of these ten were blocked from sailing.

The only one of the fifteen ships that sailed for Gaza was the French ship *Dignité Al Karama*. This ship first sailed on July 5 from Athens and evaded the Greek Coast Guard, but turned back, apparently from a desire not to be the only ship to sail. The ship then tried to sail again, but was seized by the Greek Coast Guard. Finally, the ship stated dishonestly that its destination was Alexandria, left the Greek island of Kastellorizo on July 16, and sailed toward Gaza with sixteen people aboard. On July 19, 2011, the *Dignité Al Karama* was stopped by the Israeli navy, and then towed to Ashdod harbor. The passengers were released after being interviewed, and this was the end of Flotilla II.

What may be said about Flotilla II?

First, there is no doubt but that the legal actions of the Israel Law Center played a major role in the defeat of the flotilla. This was the opinion of a

---

of Appeals for the District of Columbia Circuit, decided December 19, 2014, judicial decision available at https://www.cadc.uscourts.gov/internet/opinions.nsf/E3AF1833 D3CD749085257DB30054B6BF/$file/13-7081-1528227.pdf.

[163] Jack Shenker and Conal Urquhart, "Activists' Plan to Break Gaza Blockade with Aid Flotilla Is Sunk," *Guardian*, July 5, 2011, available at http://www.theguardian.com /world/2011/jul/05/activists-gaza-blockade-aid-flotilla.

reporter for the *New York Times*, of the *Guardian* newspaper, and even of some of the flotilla activists.[164]

Second, legal action was not the only instrument used to defeat of the flotilla. In fact, Flotilla II was defeated by an extremely effective combination of politics and diplomacy on the one hand, and legal actions on the other. This is true not only in the details, such as the grounding of the French ship in Marseille for lack of insurance, but also in the broader strokes: the almost unanimous opposition of world governments (with the exception of Hamas), the preemptive actions of Israel and Egypt in lightening the land blockade, and the repeated offers to deliver the humanitarian goods after inspection all played a major part.

Third, the Israel Law Center was very effective in its management of the process. Its research was excellent, particularly the acquisition and use of intelligence from the Israeli government.

Fourth, creative thinking was required, and that was provided by the Israel Law Center. The use of crowd research is relatively new, perhaps completely new. The legitimate use of United States statutes and courts to protect American citizens, and to defeat the flotilla, was also innovative.

C. Flotilla III (2015) and the Actions of the Israel Law Center

The stated purpose of Flotilla III – to provide humanitarian aid to the people of Gaza – was the same as the stated purpose of Flotillas I and II. And like the earlier flotillas, the actual purpose of Flotilla III was completely differ-

---

[164] Many articles support this view. See, for example, Sayare, "Israeli Advocacy Group Helps Delay Departure of Gaza-Bound Flotilla"; Shenker and Urquhart, "Activists' Plan to Break Gaza Blockade with Aid Flotilla Is Sunk"; George Jonas, "Using Lawfare to Anchor the Gaza Flotilla," *National Post*, July 6, 2011, available at http://news.nationalpost.com /full-comment/george-jonas-using-lawfare-to-anchor-the-gaza-flotilla; Michael Jansen, "Greece Prohibits Gaza Boats from Leaving Its Ports," *Irish Times*, July 4, 2011, available at http://www.irishtimes.com/news/greece-prohibits-gaza-flotilla-boats-from-leaving -its-ports-1.591002; and Catrina Stewart, "Israeli Campaign Stops Gaza Flotilla Leaving Port," *Independent*, June 28, 2011, available at http://www.independent.co.uk/news/world /middle-east/israeli-campaign-stops-gaza-flotilla-leaving-port-2303675.html.

ent – that is, to break the naval blockade in order to allow the importation of unexamined goods (including offensive weapons) into Gaza. Apart from sharing these purposes, however, Flotilla III was different in its preparation, in its sailing, and in its consequences.

I. PREPARATIONS FOR FLOTILLA III

Flotilla III was organized by eleven NGOs, including ECESG, which had helped organize the second flotilla, and IHH. With close ties to al-Qaeda and Hamas, IHH was involved in all three flotillas and was the provider of the *Mavi Marmara*. This time there were only four ships involved. The lead ship, a Swedish fishing trawler named the *Marianne of Gothenburg*, contained approximately eighteen people. Most of these were activists, but several crew members and at least two journalists were also aboard during the final sail.[165] The flotilla included three smaller Greek ships as well.

Israel was also active prior to Flotilla III. As in earlier periods, Israel's policy was to provide humanitarian aid to Gaza but to strictly enforce the blockade against offensive weapons. Between the time of the Third Gaza War and the sailing of Flotilla III – that is, in the ten-month period of September 2014–June 2015 – Israel allowed the importation into Gaza, by land, of 1.6 million tons of building materials, humanitarian aid, and other supplies, equivalent to about 1 ton for each resident of Gaza.[166] Further, Israel offered then and continues to offer an option to ship humanitarian goods to Gaza through Ashdod port (*after* inspection for weapons).

At the same time, Israel remained adamantly opposed to a breaking of the blockade. In the days just before the sailing of Flotilla III, Israel's ambassador to the UN, Ron Prosor, emphasized to UN secretary-general Ban Ki-moon that the "maritime blockade has been proven necessary

---

[165] The exact number of people on the *Marianne* is not clear, and possibly varied over the course of its journeys. Various accounts number thirteen, fourteen, or eighteen people, the majority of whom were activist passengers, with about five crew members and apparently two journalists.

[166] Tamar Pileggi, "Israeli Navy Intercepts Gaza-Bound Ship, No Injuries Reported," *Times of Israel*, June 29, 2015, available at http://www.timesofisrael.com/israeli-navy-boards-ship-headed-for-gaza-no-injuries-reported/.

multiple times…[to prevent] smuggling arms and…terrorist attacks on Israeli citizens." Ambassador Prosor noted recent cases where gunrunning ships had been stopped by the blockade – including

- in 2009, the SS *Francop*, with five hundred tons of munitions;
- in 2011, the SS *Victoria*, with sixty tons of munitions; and
- in 2014, the *KLOS C*, with forty surface-to-surface missiles, one-hundred and eighty-one mortar shells, and four hundred thousand rounds of ammunition for assault rifles.[167]

2. THE SAILING OF FLOTILLA III AND ITS INTERCEPTION

The *Marianne* sailed from Sweden on May 10, 2015, heading for Greece. On June 25, the *Marianne*, accompanied by the three Greek ships, set out from Athens toward Gaza. At some point during the period June 26–June 28, the three Greek ships dropped out of the flotilla and turned back toward Greece. The Greek ships apparently did not hold any humanitarian aid, nor did they transfer such aid to the *Marianne*. On June 29, 2015, the *Marianne* was intercepted by the Israeli navy, its passengers were detained, and the ship taken to Ashdod port. During the period June 30–July 6, all of the passengers on the *Marianne* were interviewed and released. They all left Israel, with the exception of Basel Ghattas, a member of the Israeli Knesset (Joint Arab List), and Israeli journalist Ohad Chamo, who of course stayed in Israel.

The interception of the *Marianne* is of particular interest. It is described in the *Times of Israel* article entitled "Footage Shows Israeli Soldiers Debating Activists before Boarding Gaza-Bound Boat," which also includes a twelve-minute video of preparations on the ship, the humanitarian aid, and

---

[167] Both the quote by Ambassador Prosor and the list of terrorist ships appear in Stuart Winer, "Israeli Envoy Calls on UN Chief to Condemn Gaza-Bound Flotilla," *Times of Israel*, June 23, 2015, available at http://www.timesofisrael.com/israeli-envoy-asks-un-chief-to-condemn-gaza-bound-flotilla/. Many additional articles are available on the Internet about the terrorist ships *Francop*, *Victoria*, and *KLOS C* and their murderous cargoes. As to *KLOS C* in particular, see "Missile Shipments from Iran to Gaza Intercepted," Israel Ministry of Foreign Affairs, March 5, 2014, available at http://mfa.gov.il/MFA/PressRoom/2014/Pages/Missile-shipment-from-Iran-to-Gaza-intercepted-5-Mar-2014.aspx.

the interception of the ship.[168] As the Israeli navy approaches, a naval officer wishes the *Marianne* passengers good morning. Member of Knesset Ghattas answers, and the naval officer responds, "You are not a lawyer, and you do not know international law. Your intention to sail to Gaza is illegal. There is a naval blockade on Gaza, and it will continue." MK Ghattas says that the Israeli soldiers will be subject to trial at an international criminal court, and the naval officer responds, "As is well known to you, there is no shortage of anything in Gaza, except tools used for terror." Israeli naval commandos board the ship, and begin detaining the passengers. There is no resistance except for one activist, who refuses to be taken off the ship. In the video, this activist becomes erratic, perhaps a bit wild. The soldiers ask him several times to stop, they show him a Taser and state several times that they do not wish to use it, but when the activist continues, the soldiers taser him and take him into custody.[169]

3. THE DISPUTE REGARDING HUMANITARIAN AID

There was a serious dispute regarding the humanitarian aid on the *Marianne* – both whether it existed and, if so, the quantity and nature of the aid. In the video mentioned above, the camera panned to three plastic containers, each large enough to hold a pair of shoes. The containers were marked "Drugs," but their contents were not shown. Also in the video, an anti-Israel activist by the name of Dror Feiler was seen talking with the Israeli reporter and rummaging in a large bag. Feiler pulled out what he said was a solar energy panel (although the item is not visually identifiable in the video), and further said that there were two such panels which the activists intended to donate to Al-Shifa Hospital in order to enable the hospital to produce solar energy. Finally, Feiler said that the boat itself, which after all was a fishing trawler,

---

[168] Daniel Bernstein, *Times of Israel*, July 1, 2015. The article, with the embedded video, may be found at http://www.timesofisrael.com/footage-shows-voyage-interception -of-gaza-bound-ship/. Different conversations included in the video were conducted in English, Hebrew, and Arabic, and there are subtitles in Hebrew. Nevertheless, despite the absence of English subtitles, the video is sufficiently detailed so that a non-Hebrew speaker can obtain the essence of the story.

[169] The activists on the ship later alleged that Tasers were used against four of the passengers. The twelve-minute video shows a Taser being used against only one person, but presumably the video is not all inclusive, so the truth of the allegation is not clear.

would be given to Gazan fisherman, and that the value of all the intended aid was 100,000 Euros.

However, after the *Marianne* was taken to Ashdod, the contents were examined and Israeli defense minister Moshe Ya'alon stated, "There was no [humanitarian] aid on board." As a reporter for the *Washington Post* wrote, in direct response to the comment by Moshe Ya'alon:

> Not necessarily so – but pretty close. We checked. You decide [for yourselves whether or not there was humanitarian aid on the *Marianne*].[170]

The article by the *Washington Post* reporter did not confirm, and in fact contradicted at least in part, both the story of the activist Feiler and the comment by Ya'alon. One of the eleven NGOs that organized Flotilla III is the Freedom Flotilla Coalition (FFC). When requested to provide evidence of the humanitarian aid on the *Marianne*, Ann Ighe, a member of the FFC, sent a photograph of two brown shipping boxes, one box relatively large and the other box very small.[171] According to Ms. Ighe, the larger box contained one solar panel (presumably one of the panels mentioned by activist Feiler), while the smaller box contained one nebulizer – an inhaler of medicine to alleviate asthma attacks. The nebulizer was neither shown in the video noted above, nor mentioned by activist Feiler. Finally, Ighe confirmed Feiler's comment when she said that "the boat [*Marianne*] is cargo in itself, bound to be donated to a fishermen's organization in Gaza."[172]

---

[170] William Booth, "The 'Humanitarian Aid' Aboard a Recent Flotilla to Gaza Fit in Two Cardboard Boxes," *Washington Post*, July 1, 2015, available at https://www.washingtonpost.com/news/worldviews/wp/2015/07/01/did-the-flotilla-to-gaza-have-humanitarian-aid-aboard-or-not/.

[171] The photograph appears in the article by William Both, ibid. See also Stuart Winer, "Humanitarian Aid on Gaza Flotilla Fit in Two Boxes," *Times of Israel*, July 2, 2015, available at http://www.timesofisrael.com/humanitarian-aid-on-gaza-flotilla-fit-in-2-boxes/. It appears that the picture was originally received by *Washington Post* reporter William Booth from Ann Ighe of the Freedom Flotilla Coalition, and then copied in the *Times of Israel* article; neither the *Washington Post* nor the *Times of Israel* identifies a photographer or provides any other attribution.

[172] Booth, "'Humanitarian Aid.'"

This, however, does not end the story of the humanitarian aid. A few days before the *Marianne* was set to sail from Athens, on June 21, 2015, the Israel Law Center sent a letter to the CEO of Skandinaviska Enskilda Banken (SEB), which is the second largest bank in Sweden, and also the twenty-fourth largest Swedish corporation.[173] The letter contained the following points:

1. On August 27, 2013, SEB bank provided the funds by which activist Charles Bertel Andreasson purchased the *Marianne*. SEB granted a mortgage to Andreasson equal to about $36,000, and now holds a maritime lien on the *Marianne*.

2. Andreasson intends to use the ship, in the very immediate future, to run a lawful naval blockade. By international law, such a ship may lawfully be attacked or seized, which will likely result in the damage, destruction, or seizure of the ship, and hence the loss of SEB's lien property.

3. The use of the ship against an ally of the United States may be a violation of US criminal law.

4. Any aid provided to the terrorist organization Hamas, either by the ship itself or by any of its cargo, may be a violation of US law, subjecting the bank to civil liability.

5. Under Swedish criminal law, Swedish citizens may not undertake hostile acts for one foreign power against another foreign power. Since Sweden has recognized a "State of Palestine" as a "foreign power," the action of the *Marianne*, and SEB bank's assistance to the activist Andreasson, may violate Swedish criminal law.[174]

6. Therefore, the Israel Law Center demands that SEB take immediate action to seize the ship in order to prevent its sailing. The Israel Law Center also recommends that SEB cease all business with Andreasson

---

[173] The letter from the Israel Law Center to the CEO of SEB is available at http://israellawcenter.org/wp-content/uploads/2015/06/Marianne-Merged-Document.pdf. Appended to the letter is the *Marianne*'s ship registration as of April 27, 2015, in the original Swedish.

[174] The Israel Law Center's use of Swedish law against the Swedish bank SEB was a creative act, comparable to the use of Spanish law against Javier Solana, as discussed in chapter 1.

or his co-conspirators in the violation of international, American, and Swedish law.

Although no response was received from SEB bank, this was an admirable effort by the Israel Law Center, and may cause the bank to think twice before it further finances any flotilla against the naval blockade of Gaza.[175]

The story of the humanitarian aid aboard Flotilla III is complicated, but perhaps we can clarify it in a table.

Table 4.1: Humanitarian Aid for Gaza on Flotilla III

Type of Aid	Questions
Solar panel(s)	1. Were there any panels at all? 2. If so, one panel or two?
Nebulizer against asthma	1. Was there a nebulizer or not?
Medical drugs in three plastic containers, each one the size of a shoe box	1. Were drugs in the containers? 2. If so, what kind, and how many?
SS *Marianne of Gothenburg*	1. What is the value of a small and very old fishing trawler?[176] 2. Since the *Marianne* was the subject of a maritime lien, could the boat really be considered "aid"?

---

[175] The SEB bank, the financier of the *Marianne* ship against Israel, is controlled and partially owned by the Wallenberg family. Raoul Wallenberg, a member of the Wallenberg family, saved perhaps as many as one hundred thousand Hungarian Jews during World War II, and died apparently as a result of his efforts. The chairman of SEB bank is Marcus Wallenberg, a cousin of Raoul. Raoul saved Jews, while his family members are engaged in a bank that financed purchase of a ship to break a blockade against weapons that would be used to kill Jews. Perhaps the Wallenbergs did not personally know that SEB bank financed a ship against the blockade. There is no evidence that the Wallenberg family intended to break the blockade, let alone that they harbor animosity toward the Jews, but the situation is nevertheless more than a bit ironic.

[176] According to the ship registration appended to the Israel Law Center's letter to SEB, the *Marianne* is 20.43 meters in length and 5.31 meters in width, dimensions which are not large for a commercial fishing vessel. Also, the *Marianne* was built in Denmark in 1977, and was therefore thirty-eight years old when it led Flotilla III. Perhaps the ship's diminutive size and advanced age account for the sum of the mortgage – $36,000 is almost a trifling amount for a commercial fishing vessel. All of this information appears in the ship's registration, and has been translated from the original Swedish into English.

4. COMMENTS ABOUT FLOTILLA III

Three main comments may be made about Flotilla III.

First, Basel Ghattas, the Arab member of Israel's Knesset who participated in Flotilla III, stated that Israel and its commandos would be subjected to trial at an international criminal court. The only such court operating today is the ICC; since the Palestinian Authority became a member of the ICC a few months before Flotilla III, presumably that was the court intended. The UN has already decided that the naval blockade is legal. Therefore, actions in support of the blockade such as intercepting the *Marianne* and detaining its passengers are also legal. Perhaps the "international war crime" was the tasering of one wild and uncooperative activist on the ship, although it is not clear whether that crime would rise to the level of "ethnic cleansing," "genocide," and the other atrocities pursued by the ICC.

Second, the "humanitarian aid" of Flotilla III is simply not clear. If there was indeed any such aid, then the quantity is neither clear nor particularly impressive. Compare the actions of Israel to the alleged aid of Flotilla III. During preparations for Flotilla III, and during its sailing, more than five hundred trucks, loaded with building materials and humanitarian aid, crossed from Israel into Gaza *every day*.[177] The particular aid of Flotilla III would not seem to occupy even a small fraction of one truck. We could perhaps say that every little bit helps. On the other hand, given that the ship itself was in hock to the bank, and considering how many people were inconvenienced by Flotilla III, the organizers might have done better to send their humanitarian aid to Gaza via UPS.

Third, Flotilla III illustrates Marx's maxim that history repeats itself, "first as tragedy and then as farce." This flotilla illustrates that there was not at any time any interest in the welfare of the Gazans, or any intention to bring them aid. Flotilla III was a farce.

---

[177] In comparison to the tons of material permitted by Israel into Gaza every day, the so-called "humanitarian aid" of Flotilla III – possibly a solar panel or two, possibly a nebulizer, possibly a minor quantity of medical drugs, and a small fishing trawler that appeared, at the time, to be owned by the bank – may be considered pathetic. But then again, providing significant humanitarian aid to Gaza was never the point of Flotilla III.

II. Possible Scenarios for the Future of Flotillas to Gaza

Will there be additional flotillas to Gaza in the future? If so, with what effect?

There were no flotillas, and no blockade, prior to the Hamas seizure of Gaza in June 2007. With that seizure, and especially following the attacks made by Hamas against Israel, the naval blockade was initiated in January 2009. The earliest attempts to run the blockade were minor and insignificant. That changed in 2010, with what has been called here Flotilla I. That action produced deadly results because it was bigger, more organized, and much more hostile than prior flotillas, and more importantly, no one understood what was coming.

After Flotilla I, Israel and the world were prepared. Flotilla II, in 2011, was a smashing failure, due to the legal actions of the Israel Law Center combined with significant political opposition from many countries. On the political side, Israel's combination of its softness (allowing more goods into Gaza, and offering to transship humanitarian aid into Gaza) with its toughness (no compromise on refusal to allow uninspected ships to enter into Gaza) was understood and respected by the world.

Flotilla III was not a serious effort, and that almost surely reflects the understanding that Israel will not be moved on its military goal, and that the world supports Israel in its effort to prevent the importation of rockets and mortars into Gaza.

Is any of this going to change? Almost certainly not. Israel will continue to distinguish between killing weapons and civilian goods – the former will be identified and excluded; the latter will be allowed into Gaza. Similarly, the world will not change its opinion about weapons versus civilian goods, and serious international support will not be obtained for the importation of killing weapons into Gaza. Therefore, by logic, future flotillas would seem to be fated for failure, and activists would be presumed to stop these useless efforts. But that is not what has happened.

It has been noted that the Freedom Flotilla Coalition (FFC) was one of the organizers of Flotilla III. On its Facebook page, listed on November 1,

2015 – that is, *after* the failure of Flotilla III – FFC published what it has called its "strategy plan":

> The following strategic plan was adopted:
> 2016: Women's Boat to Gaza will sail to challenge the blockade.
> 2017: Focus will be on solidarity with the fishermen of Gaza.
> 2018: a large vessel carrying hundreds of supporters from around the world will sail to challenge the blockade.[178]

These have not been idle words. On September 14, 2016, two small vessels, the *Amal* and the *Zaytouna*, set sail from Barcelona toward Gaza, each with eleven female activists. This sailing was called by its organizers the "Women's Boat to Gaza." Almost immediately the *Amal* dropped out due to mechanical problems and returned to Barcelona.[179] The *Zaytouna* approached Gaza carrying thirteen women – eleven activists and two journalists from *Al Jazeera*. On October 5, 2016, the Israeli navy, spearheaded by women combat soldiers, intercepted the *Zaytouna* and brought it to Ashdod harbor. There was no violence, and there were no casualties.[180] The journalists were released immediately, and all of the activists were released within four days after the interception. Thus ended the latest effort to break the blockade against aggressive weapons to Gaza.

---

[178] See https://www.facebook.com/FreedomFlotillaCoalition/, entry for November 1, 2015. The strategic plan may also be found, with additional background information, at Freedom Flotilla Coalition, "New Strategic Plan Adopted by Freedom Flotilla Coalition," November 1, 2015, available at https://freedomflotilla.org/coalition-statements/30-new -strategic-plan-adopted-by-freedom-flotilla-coalition.

[179] There was no allegation of "Israeli sabotage" to the *Amal* on the website of the Women's Boat to Gaza, and, to the best of my knowledge, no such allegation was made. The truth seems to be that the *Amal* was simply not seaworthy for a trip from Barcelona to Gaza. A replacement vessel, which was named by the activists the *Amal II*, was acquired and sent from Barcelona to Palermo, Sicily, but could not continue because the original crew was no longer available for the delayed sailing. Syed C, "Women's Boat to Gaza: Hope is Lost," *Middle East Monitor*, October 4, 2016, available at https:// www.middleeastmonitor.com/20161004-womens-boat-to-gaza-hope-is-lost/. One must presume that the activists tried to find another crew, but were unsuccessful, for reasons unstated.

[180] "No Violence as Israel Intercepts Women's Boat to Gaza," *Times of Israel*, October 5, 2016, available at http://www.timesofisrael.com/israeli-navy-intercepts-gaza-bound -womens-boat/.

Some activists called this sailing a "fourth flotilla," or perhaps "Flotilla IV," but that is a rather grandiose name for a small boat with a handful of activists that failed without producing any real impact.[181]

What might have caused the organizers to think that this small sailing would succeed, in contrast to the failures of Flotillas I, II, and III? Neither Israel nor the world is likely to change its attitudes or actions about the importation of rockets, mortars, and ammunition into Gaza, so the blockade is likely to continue. For a flotilla, or even a small sailing, to succeed, there must be some kind of innovation that catches the world by surprise. What was new about the sailing of the *Amal and Zaytouna*?

First, all of the activists were women. That is an innovation, and it is indeed interesting, but its relevance to the goal of the sailing is not clear. Should future sailings be "all Italians," or "all left-handed people," or "all vegetarians"? There is no obvious connection between this innovation and the breaking of the blockade.

Second, the organizers of this sailing were very honest and very open. Each of Flotillas I–III masqueraded as a "humanitarian mission," allegedly launched to bring food and medicine to the ailing people of Gaza. This, of course, is a fraud – there is no shortage of these items in Gaza, multiple offers by multiple countries to transship all aid to Gaza were rejected by flotilla activists, and in any case there was very little in the way of "humanitarian aid" on Flotillas II and III. In contrast, the organizers of the *Amal* and *Zaytouna* sailing stated very clearly,

> The Women's Boat to Gaza is a solidarity, not an aid mission. . . . As such, the boats will only be transporting the women along with the hopes of an ever-growing international community to end the blockade.[182]

---

[181] The *Zaytouna* was described by one activist as "a 15-meter sailboat." "Seven Days on the Women's Flotilla to Gaza," *Israel Social TV*, September 22, 2016, available at 972mag.com/seven-days-on-the-womens-flotilla-to-gaza/122112 (presenting an edited version of a diary by Yudit Ilany). The *Zaytouna* was the equivalent of a private yacht, substantially smaller than even the fishing trawler *Marianne* in Flotilla III, and of course vastly smaller than some of the ships in Flotilla I. To say that this was a small boat that carried a handful of activists and that had no impact would be entirely accurate.

[182] Website of "Women's Boat to Gaza," answer to frequently asked question, "Will you be bringing aid to Gaza?" available at https://wbg.freedomflotilla.org/faq. See also the

Although this honesty is refreshing, one must wonder how it could contribute to the stated purpose. The Israelis have said repeatedly, and the world has understood, that the goal of the flotillas is not to bring aid, but to end the prohibition on the importation of weapons. The honesty of the current sailing simply strengthens that understanding.

The honesty does more still. The ultimate goal of all the flotillas and all the sailings is not merely to break the blockade and allow Hamas to receive weapons that will be used to kill Jews, but indeed to achieve one step in the destruction of Israel. This ultimate goal was never stated or even implied by the organizers of Flotillas I, II, and III, but the organizers of the *Amal* and *Zaytouna* sailing stated clearly on their website,

> We intend to raise awareness about the ongoing struggle that women in Gaza, in the West Bank, inside the Green Line and in the diaspora, have waged and continue to wage against the Occupation.[183]

If we take out superfluous words, the goal becomes, "to raise awareness about the ongoing struggle that women ... inside the Green Line ... continue to wage against the Occupation." By "inside the Green Line," the organizers presumably mean that the women of Tel Aviv, Haifa, west Jerusalem, Beersheba, and all other cities within pre-1967 Israel "struggle ... against the Occupation."[184] Again, this is completely new and unexpected honesty by

---

activist comment, "We are not here to bring 'aid' to the people of Gaza, but to contribute to an international effort to break the siege," by Lisa Gay Hamilton, "Why I Am on the Women's Boat to Gaza," *Counterpunch*, September 21, 2016, available at http://www .counterpunch.org/2016/09/21/why-i-am-on-the-womens-boat-to-gaza/. In contrast, another activist said, "We are carrying food and medicine on the boat that will be distributed to Gazans upon arrival," by Zohar Chamberlain Regev, in "Gaza-Bound Flotilla Sails Off from Spain's Barcelona," *Al Jazeera*, September 15, 2016, available at http://www .aljazeera.com/news/2016/09/gaza-bound-flotilla-set-sail-barcelona-160914144306403 .html. It is therefore not clear if there is any aid at all, but if there is, it is relatively minor, and the stated purpose of this sailing is not to bring aid, but rather to help break the blockade against killing weapons.

[183] Website of "Women's Boat to Gaza," answer to frequently asked question, "Why will there only be women participating on the boats?" available at https://wbg.freedomflotilla .org/faq.

[184] If this point needs reinforcement, in their website, the organizers refer repeatedly

the organizers of the *Amal and Zaytouna* sailing. The goal is not merely to allow weapons to enter Gaza, but rather to destroy the apparent "occupation" of Tel, Aviv, Haifa, etc., and hence to destroy Israel. The problem with this honesty, however, is that it extremely unlikely to convince Israel to terminate the blockade, and if anything is more likely to have the opposite effect.

The 2016 sailing ended in failure, like Flotillas I, II, and III. Nevertheless, the Freedom Flotilla Coalition is now planning an additional sailing in 2018, which they say will be "a large vessel carrying hundreds of supporters." Again, the innovation here is not known. The *Mavi Marmara*, in Flotilla I, was a large vessel with about six hundred activists. What will be new in 2018 about a "large vessel" with "hundreds of supporters"? If there is no innovation, how could activists expect a new flotilla to succeed in 2018, given the experiences of 2010, 2011, 2015, and now in 2016.[185] The lack of innovation by flotilla activists, together with Israel's integrated policy of being soft with people (by providing aid to Gaza) and hard on weapons (through the blockade) will almost certainly defeat future sailings by anti-blockade activists.[186]

---

to the Israeli army as the "Israeli Occupation Force (IOF)." This is a clever play on the phrase "Israel Defense Forces (IDF)," and it indicates very clearly the organizers' attitude – in their opinion, the IDF is only an occupation army. This is a consistent and sensible match with their general view – if the organizers include "inside the Green Line" as being "occupied," then of course any army that defends Israeli cities must also be an "occupation force."

[185] The "strategic plan" of the Freedom Flotilla Coalition says, "2017: Focus will be on solidarity with the fishermen of Gaza." I am frankly uncertain whether this means an intention to launch another ship in 2017. If that is the intention, such a sailing will also fail, unless the FFC presents a new and surprising innovation.

[186] The integrated policy is critically important to Israel's continuing success. The blockade alone is obviously essential, but it is not enough. Israel has permitted, and should continue to permit, the entry of food, medicine, and certain building supplies to Gaza. At the time of Flotilla III, more than five hundred trucks with supplies were arriving in Gaza every day. By the time of the *Zaytouna* sailing, Israeli security sources noted that "there is no siege on Gaza. Israel sends [to Gaza] between 800 and 1000 trucks with goods every day. Anyone can send goods to the Gaza Strip on the condition that they pass a regulated check; therefore, claims of a siege are baseless from the beginning." Zalman Ahnsaf, "Navy Stops Vessel Bound for Gaza," *Hamodia*, October 5, 2016, available at hamodia.com/2016/10/05/navy-stops-vessel-bound-gaza.

III. A Summary of Chapter 4

Israel has applied a naval blockade against Gaza. The sole goal of this blockade is to prevent the importation of aggressive weapons, such as rockets or
mortars, which will inevitably be used against Israel and particularly against
Israeli civilians. Non-military goods are not forbidden to Gaza, but they
are routed first to Israeli ports to ensure an absence of military weapons,
after which the goods are allowed into Gaza. The blockade of Gaza has
been found by the United Nations to be legal. Nevertheless, in the period
2010–2016, three flotillas and one small sailing were organized to break this
blockade. In all of the flotillas, there was a stated intention merely to bring
"humanitarian aid" to poor people, but the actual intent in both those flotillas and in the small sailing (as stated honestly and openly on the website
of the sailing's organizers) was to force Israel to allow uninspected cargoes
of weapons to enter Gaza.

Chapter 4 presents a short history of these three flotillas and the small
sailing: the 2010 flotilla led by the *Mavi Marmara*, the second flotilla of 2011
which ultimately did not occur (except for one small ship), the third flotilla
of 2015 (in which only a single ship sailed toward Gaza, but that was the
main ship), and the sailing of the *Amal* and *Zaytouna* in 2016.

Flotilla I had tragic consequences, because the flotilla organizers were
prepared for confrontation, while their opponents were not. Both Israel
and the world community were surprised by what happened on the *Mavi
Marmara*.

The organizers could not achieve surprise for Flotilla II. The world in
general was opposed to violence, particularly since three countries – Egypt,
Greece, and Israel – had each offered to accept the humanitarian goods and
deliver them to Gaza. Israel was prepared both diplomatically and militarily,
and used its political influence to maximum effect. The legal efforts of the
Israel Law Center – attacks on the insurance and communication service
providers, and alerting the Greek authorities – played a decisive role. It was
the combination of politics and law that defeated Flotilla II.

Flotilla III was a parody of a flotilla. The absurdity of the "humanitarian
aid" proved that the organizers were not serious about the effort, had no

expectation of success, and most particularly intended solely to embarrass Israel, rather than to help the people of Gaza.

The sailing of the *Amal* and *Zaytouna*, two small ships with a handful of female activists, does not rise even to the level of a parody. The *Amal* returned to port almost immediately. The *Zaytouna*, with eleven activists and two journalists, was stopped by the Israeli navy. This sailing presented several innovations, but the innovations either had no impact whatever (for example, the gender-specific nature of the activists, which seems simply irrelevant) or their impact is almost certain to strengthen the blockade and its international support (for example, the implied goal to use importation of weapons to Gaza as one step in the destruction of Israel).

The world is on notice. Israel is on notice. Without some kind of specific innovation that is relevant and that catches the world by surprise, future flotillas or future sailings are unlikely to have any impact on Israel's blockade against the importation of killing weapons into Hamas-controlled Gaza.

CHAPTER 5

The Air: Automation and the Future of War

Introduction: The Ultimate Fusion of Human and Machine?

> There is no security...against the ultimate development of
> mechanical consciousness.... Reflect upon the extraordinary
> advance which the machines have made during the last few
> hundred years, and observe how slowly the animal and
> vegetable kingdoms are advancing in comparison.... Where
> does consciousness begin, and where end? Who can draw
> the line? ... Is not everything linked with everything? Is not
> machinery linked with animal life in an infinite variety of
> ways?
>
> *– Samuel Butler,* Erewhon[187]

The futuristic novel *Erewhon* includes a section entitled "The Book of the Machines." In this section, the nineteenth-century novelist Samuel Butler sets out his vision of the future, and it is not a happy one. By his reckoning,

---

[187] Samuel Butler, *Erewhon* (London: Trübner, 1872), 192. Butler is perhaps better known for his satirical novel *The Way of All Flesh*, which had a significant impact in early-twentieth-century Edwardian England. However, his major contribution to our present, the twenty-first century, is undoubtedly the futuristic *Erewhon*.

machines were advancing at such a rate, particularly in comparison to the static circumstance of human beings, that a fusion of machine and human was inevitable at some point in the future. Butler died in 1902, his vision unrealized. We can say also that his vision was not yet realized in the twentieth or early twenty-first centuries, but what of the future?

The future of war is, without question, automation – in unmanned aerial vehicles (UAVs), in robotics, and in cyberspace. The most recent wars in the Middle East, and the asymmetric wars yet to be fought in the twenty-first century, have featured and will feature a fusion of identity such that the line between human and machine is no longer clear. In the modern age of warfare, what will be the respective roles of humans and machines? As a result of changing warfare, what new legal arguments will be raised on the lawfare front? How has Israel reacted to these technological, military, and legal challenges? These are the questions addressed in chapter 5.[188]

I. A Personal Story: Nocturnal Wanderings in Khan Yunis

During the Gaza War of 2014,[189] various units of the Israel Defense Forces were aligned against different fronts. The Paratroopers Brigade was positioned opposite Khan Yunis, in the southern part of the Gaza Strip. My youngest son was a soldier in this brigade, and fought in the war. During his service, for a period of five weeks my family and I had no contact with him. We knew he was well, but beyond that we knew nothing.

---

[188] Butler's vision – the blurring of the line between machine and human – is relevant particularly for the next thirty years, which is the time frame of the current book. However, Butler's general observation – that machines are advancing rapidly while people are not – will, if unchecked, result not in a fusion of man and machine, but rather in a dominance of machines over people. The point of machine dominance, sometimes called "singularity," or "technological singularity," will not occur within the immediate future, and may never happen at all, although some people feel it is a realistic possibility by the middle of this century.

[189] Also known as the Third Gaza War between Israel and Hamas, and as "Operation Protective Edge." The earlier wars between the same parties were the Second Gaza War of 2011, also known as "Operation Pillar of Defense," and the First Gaza War of 2008–2009, also known as "Operation Cast Lead."

When my son returned from the war, I asked him:

1. Where were you stationed?
2. What did you do?
3. Did you shoot anyone?
4. What was your biggest problem during the war?

This is what he told me:

The entire brigade was stationed on the Khan Yunis front. I was a member of a platoon of about thirty soldiers. We were divided into squads of six to twelve soldiers. During the entire time we were in Gaza, each squad in the platoon was positioned in a house on the outskirts of the city. Houses were changed, squads were reorganized, but always in a house facing into the city.

Our job was to observe actions within our field of vision, particularly the movements of enemy forces, and to report them to brigade headquarters. When we fired at enemies, it was mostly to pin them down and keep them away from our positions.

I honestly do not know whether or not I shot any terrorist. I hope I did, but I don't know. It was not our main responsibility to shoot the enemy. If we spotted hostile forces, we would report back, and the locations would be destroyed by artillery or tanks.

While we were in Gaza we had enough ammunition and food, but our main problem, particularly at the beginning of the war, was a shortage of water. The supply of running water to the area had been disrupted by the war. It's very hot in July and August, and we did not have enough to drink. This was not a matter of clean or dirty water, because we had pills that would purify just about anything, but there was no water of any kind.

In the evenings, we would go outside, searching for water in containers, going into empty houses to see if any water had been left. One night, I was with three other soldiers in an abandoned house. Suddenly we heard a loud *"Whoooosh!"* We went outside and we saw, about two hundred meters down the road, a group of terrorists firing rockets from Gaza into Israel.

I then asked my son if he and his comrades had chased after the terrorists. He responded:

We didn't chase after them, because we were in the last house. There is an electronic map, continuously updated, that shows the current and changing positions of all of our forces, all of our soldiers. It shows also all of the reported positions of the enemy. We had the map, and the same map was available to all of the ground forces – to the infantry units, the tanks, and the artillery. It might have been available to the navy and air force, too, but I don't know about that. On the map, we were at the very end of territory held by us. If we had chased after the terrorists, we would have crossed a line, not in real life but on the electronic map, from our territory into enemy territory. We would then be considered hostile forces, and our own army would kill us. You can't go beyond "the last house."

Upon hearing this, I feared that the terrorists had fled, but my son explained:

No, the terrorists didn't get away. Their position was blown up within thirty seconds of the time they fired the rockets.[190]

This story is a good framework for the discussion that follows. The Israeli army, and all Western armies, stand right now on the cusp between traditional war and that which is to come. We could note these lessons from the story:

1. Much of what combat soldiers do today is not really combat, as much as observation and reporting. A modern army does not need hands firing rifles – it needs eyes and ears to report enemy locations. Nevertheless, the soldiers are still at risk, due to their presence, and due to the need to supply them with food, ammunition, water, medical supplies, etc.[191]

---

[190] I should add that the importance of water is clearly understood in the IDF. The story related here is true, but the problem of water supply in the Third Gaza War was acute only at the beginning of the war. After secure supply lines were established, the situation became much better.

[191] My son's experience in Khan Yunis is not unique. In the Afghan and Iraqi wars, US forces expended about 250,000 bullets for each terrorist killed. Andrew Buncome, "US Forced to Import Bullets from Israel As Troops Use 250,000 Bullets for Each Rebel Killed," *Independent*, September 25, 2005, available at http://www.independent.co.uk /news/world/americas/us-forced-to-import-bullets-from-israel-as-troops-use-250000 -for-every-rebel-killed-314944.html. At $0.33 per bullet, the total cost to kill one terrorist, in bullets alone, was $82,500. "The Political Economy of the Bullet in Afghanistan," *Zero Anthropology*, August 18, 2009, available at http://zeroanthropology.net/2009/08/16

2. Once a target has been marked and communicated, it can be destroyed almost immediately. The precision is beyond anything that was available in the twentieth century, and beyond even imagination in the nineteenth and earlier centuries.[192]

3. The key to all of this is updated intelligence, created by a constant stream of reports from soldiers and aircraft, all of it processed in real time into a digital map which is distributed to units.

This last point, about intelligence, is critically important for the future of law and of lawfare. In the twenty-first century, there are other examples in which electronic communication is used to destroy enemy units.[193] These other examples, however, do not clearly capture what happened in the Gaza War of 2014, which was the first "network-centric war," the first time an entire ground campaign was linked in this way, and the first step toward what has been described as a "giant military iPhone."[194] The system used by my son and his comrades, called the "Digital Ground Army Command and

---

/the-political-economy-of-the-bullet-in-afghanistan/. Infantry soldiers still fire weapons, but as a general rule, they are no longer expected to actually hit the enemy. There are exceptions, to be sure – snipers are expected to hit their targets, special operations forces operating behind enemy lines are expected to kill the enemy, and frontline troops on specific missions will become engaged in deadly firefights. Regarding frontline troops, see, for example, Junger's book *War*, describing the active and persistent combat between US and Taliban forces in the Korengal Valley of northeast Afghanistan. These exceptions, as important as they are, do not subvert the general rule: in modern warfare, and certainly in warfare of the twenty-first century, combat soldiers are expected to defeat the enemy, but not by actually shooting him.

[192] For an excellent example, see Michael V. Hayden (director of the CIA, 2006–2009), "To Keep America Safe, Embrace Drone Warfare," *New York Times*, February 19, 2016, available at http://www.nytimes.com/2016/02/21/opinion/sunday/drone-warfare -precise-effective-imperfect.html?_r=0.

[193] See, for example, Rukmini Callimachi, "Kurds Team with U.S. to Combat ISIS in Syria," *New York Times*, August 10, 2015, available on the Internet as "Inside Syria: Kurds Roll Back ISIS, but Alliances Are Strained," at http://www.nytimes.com/2015/08/10/world /middleeast/syria-turkey-islamic-state-kurdish-militia-ypg.html?_r=0\. This article relates a story in which Kurds identify an ISIS position, transmit the GPS coordinates to US military command hundreds of miles away, and in about half an hour warplanes bomb the position, killing all of the ISIS fighters.

[194] Yaakov Lapin, "Network IDF," *Jerusalem Post*, September 28, 2015, available at http:// www.jpost.com/Israel-News/Security-and-Defense-Network-IDF-416497. To be sure, Operation Desert Storm (1991) and other military actions, particularly in the Middle East,

Control System," was deployed in mid-June 2014, three weeks before the war started on July 8. In the near future, the IDF will add all visual intelligence generated by cameras located with the ground forces, on ships, and on planes. All information will be processed immediately, and the resulting intelligence will be available, real-time and simultaneously, to the army, the navy, and the air force.[195] That is the future of war.

II. The Future of War: A Revolution in Military Affairs

The way in which war is conducted is undergoing enormous change. In the future, warfare will increasingly involve robotics – both in the air, as unmanned aerial vehicles (UAVs), and on the ground. Cyber warfare, too, will be playing a highly significant role in the coming years. As discussed below, the single most problematic issue regarding the advance of robotic and cyber war involves the question of machine autonomy.

A. Trends

The phrase "Revolution in Military Affairs" (often abbreviated "RMA") was coined in the 1990s to capture, in a single concept, the massive changes that were expected in warfare in the twenty-first century. The revolution was based on vastly improved intelligence (in quality, in quantity, and in timeliness), on the distribution of such intelligence to people who needed

---

have used electronic communication extensively, but the Third Gaza War nevertheless appears to be unique in its scope.

[195] Ibid. The program to create this all-services communication network is called "the Network Centric IDF Program (NCIP)." Shoshanna Solomon, "IDF Looks to a 'One-Network' Army to Fight Future Wars," *Times of Israel*, July 31, 2016, available at http://www.timesofisrael.com/idf-looks-to-a-one-network-army-to-fight-future-wars/. The intention is to construct "a digital military combat network that will see the air force, ground forces, and navy integrate with one another and with military intelligence in ways not seen in any other fighting force in the world." Yaakov Lapin, "IDF Using Relative Calm to Prepare for Future Threats," *Jerusalem Post*, August 3, 2016, http://www.jpost.com/Arab-Israeli-Conflict/Analysis-IDF-using-relative-calm-to-prepare-for-future-threats-463085.

to use it, and on the enhanced precision in the guidance of weapons.[196] Each of the legs of this stool was created from electronic networking, which became realistic as a military tool in the late 1990s, and which is being fully developed today.

There are many manifestations of the Revolution in Military Affairs, and we will look at three of them below: unmanned aerial vehicles (UAVs), robotic soldiers, and cyber war.

1. UNMANNED AERIAL VEHICLES (UAVS)

Unmanned vehicles are exactly what their name implies – machines without people. Humans may monitor a machine, or may control it, but they are not located in or beside the machine. There exist today unmanned vehicles for flight, called unmanned aerial vehicles (UAVs), and informally known as "drones." There are unmanned vehicles for movement or battle on the ground, which are "robots." There are also completely automated ships – this effort is only at the beginning stage, although major advances must be expected in the future.[197]

Drones are particularly important for several reasons. First, their growth in recent years has been massive, but this is almost minor in comparison to

---

[196] There are many summaries of the RMA concept. Several excellent discussions appear in various volumes of the *Journal of Military and Strategic Affairs* (published by the Institute of National Security Studies), all of which may be found at http://www.inss .org.il/index.aspx?id=4460. These include, for example, Lior Tabansky, "Basic Concepts in Cyber Warfare," vol. 3, no. 1 (May 2011): 75–92; Isaac Ben-Israel and Lior Tabansky, "An Interdisciplinary Look at Security Challenges in the Information Age," vol. 3, no. 3 (December 2011): 21–37; and Gil Baram, "The Effects of Cyberwar Technologies in Force Buildup: The Israeli Case," vol. 5, no. 1 (May 2013): 23–43.

[197] A prime example of an unmanned surface vehicle (or "USV") is the "Protector," a fully automated surface patrol ship developed by the Israeli company Rafael, whose main mission is to foil terrorists and pirates. "Unmanned Naval Patrol Vehicle," Rafael Advanced Defense Systems, 2010, at http://www.rafael.co.il/Marketing/288-1037-en /Marketing.aspx. As for the future, DARPA has funded an automated submarine tracker that may have a major impact on naval warfare. This ship, called the "Anti-Submarine Warfare Continuous Trail Unmanned Vessel," was launched in April 2016 for a test voyage, and may be deployed as early as 2018. Michael Nunez, "DARPA's New Autonomous Submarine-Hunter Could Change Naval Combat Forever," *Gizmondo*, February 12, 2016, at http://gizmodo.com/darpa-s-new-autonomous-submarine-hunter-could-change -na-1758778455.

the tremendous momentum expected over the next twenty years. In 2001, during the US involvement in Afghanistan, the United States operated about sixty UAVs. By 2012, the United States had seven thousand UAVs, comprising more than 30 percent of all aerial vehicles in the US Air Force. This represents a growth of more than 10,000 percent in a bit over a decade.[198] The impact in the future will be greater still. The US armed forces expect to use UAVs for at least seven air-force functions, including surveillance, C3 (command, control, and communications, which is the building block and prerequisite for intelligence), armed reconnaissance, attack, sustainment/ cargo, utility (including, typically, transport of valuable cargo such as communications equipment, and creation of an airborne command post), and medevac (air transport of wounded soldiers). As of 2010, drones carried the main burden of the surveillance function, but it is expected that by 2035 the great majority of operations will be conducted by UAVs, with the notable exceptions of utility (high-value cargos and airborne command) and medevac (which simply must have human involvement to deal with casualties).[199] UAVs will never replace humans, but in the future they will have a vastly more important role in the air forces of the United States and of other Western countries.

A second reason for the increasing importance of drones is that the tactical use of drones is on the verge of a fundamental shift. Most people are familiar with military drones from the Middle Eastern wars of the late twentieth and now the twenty-first centuries. UAVs are used today for observation, for spotting attacks, and for conducting precision strikes – in essence, assassinations – of enemy leaders. In all cases, UAVs are monitored remotely, by people. In almost all cases, drones operate individually, possible in contact with human strike forces but not deeply coordinated with other drones. In most cases, the UAVs are actually controlled remotely, in

---

[198] All statistics from Liran Antebi, "Changing Trends in Unmanned Aerial Vehicles: New Challenges for States, Armies and Security Industries," *Journal of Military and Strategic Affairs* 6, no. 2 (August 2014).

[199] General Martin E. Dempsey, commanding general, U.S. Army Training and Doctrine Command, "U.S. Army Unmanned Aircraft Systems Roadmap 2010–2035," 2010, pp 33, 50, 60, available at http://fas.org/irp/program/collect/uas-army.pdf.

which case they are a particular kind of drone known as a Remotely Piloted Vehicle (RPV).

In the future, however, drones will not come alone, but will rather attack in "drone swarms" with tens, hundreds, or even thousands of individual drones. The various units of a drone swarm will be in constant real-time communication with one another, coordinating an attack according to some kind of predefined plan but with flexibility to adapt to changing conditions. This is the vision of the Chinese People's Liberation Army,[200] and also of the United States Navy.[201] Other tactics are also possible, such as the so-called "kamikaze" or "suicide drone," which flies to a spot only to crash itself on a target.[202] This last tactic seems to have been ineffective to date, but would it still be ineffective if the "suicide" were committed by a swarm of drones, each packed with high-density explosives?

Third, global factors in play right now almost guarantee that the shift to drones will continue and even intensify. Among these factors may be noted (1) the rapid and dramatic rate of change in information and communication technologies; (2) the reduction in costs; (3) globalization; (4) the widespread and cheap availability of technology through the Internet; (5) a current absence of legislation or regulation that might stop or at a minimum inhibit the growth of drones; and (6) in the past decade, the proliferation of both the usage and the manufacture of drones to more

---

[200] Jeremy Hsu, "China's Drone Swarms Rise to Challenge US Power," *TechNewsDaily*, March 13, 2013, available at http://news.yahoo.com/chinas-drone-swarms-rise-challenge -us-power-173949154.html. See also Liran Antebi, "The United States: Prepared and Fit for Military Intervention in Iraq?" INSS *Insight* 567, July 1, 2014, available at http://www .inss.org.il/index.aspx?id=4538&articleid=7159, which notes that "China...has already declared its intention to develop the largest fleet of drones in the world and overtake the United States."

[201] Kris Osborn, "Future Carriers Built to Carry Drone Fleets," *Defense Tech*, July 19, 2013, available at http://www.defensetech.org/2013/07/19/future-carriers-built-to -carry-drone-fleets/.

[202] Rowan Scarborough, "Iran Creating 'Suicide' Drones that Threaten Israel, U.S. Navy: Pentagon," *Washington Times*, April 8, 2015, available at http://www.washingtontimes .com/news/2015/apr/8/iran-creating-suicide-drones-us-army-report-warns/?page=all; and also "Iran Helping Hamas, Hezbollah Build Fleet of Suicide Drones," *Jerusalem Post*, April 4, 2015, available at http://www.jpost.com/Middle-East/Iran-helping-Hamas -Hezbollah-build-fleet-of-suicide-drones-396673.

than fifty countries, as well as the adoption of drones by Hezbollah and other non-state actors.[203]

2. ROBOTS

Robots are a form of automation very similar to drones in some respects, but by definition they are limited to action on the ground. In many cases, robots are mobile, although fixed-position robots also exist.[204] All robots have at least three key components: sensors, processors, and effectors.[205] Sensors are apparent in every electronic measure, such as, for example, an electrified security fence. Such a fence might also have processors to determine, for example, whether a certain phenomenon should be reported, but the fence cannot take any action because it lacks "effectors," and hence the fence is not a robot.

There are five major advantages to military robots. First, because they are located remote from personnel, they eliminate, or at least greatly reduce, the chances of military casualties in the army using the robots. This is a tremendous advantage, particularly in democracies in which there is a strong natural reluctance to absorb military casualties. Second, in many cases, robots are significantly more precise than weapons manned by humans. Therefore, they can concentrate specifically on enemy military objectives, and can reduce the civilian harm. This advantage has major impacts on all four of the main legal principles used in lawfare, as discussed below. Third,

---

[203] These factors are summarized from Antebi, "Changing Trends," 23–28.

[204] For example, the Republic of South Korea is very active in using robotic firing systems to protect the demilitarized zone between the north and the south. See, for example, Mark Prigg, "Who Goes There? Samsung Unveils Robot Sentry that Can Kill from Two Miles Away," *MailOnline*, September 15, 2014, available at http://www.dailymail.co.uk /sciencetech/article-2756847/Who-goes-Samsung-reveals-robot-sentry-set-eye-North -Korea.html. The Korean robot sentry uses heat and motion sensors to identify targets, but cannot fire until commanded to do so by a person.

[205] P.W. Singer, *Wired for War: The Robotics Revolution and Conflict in the 21st Century* (New York: Penguin, 2009), 67. See also Liran Antebi, "Controlling Robots: It's Not Science Fiction," available at http://www.inss.org.il/uploadImages/systemFiles/liran .pdf, in *Arms Control and National Security: New Horizons*, Memorandum no. 135, ed. Emily B. Landau and Anat Kurz (Tel Aviv: Institute for National Security Studies, 2014), available at http://www.inss.org.il/uploadImages/systemFiles/memo135_final.pdf. Ms. Antebi's chapter appears on pp. 65–80 of the book.

robots are small, which means they are highly portable and often conceal-able. Fourth, although technical development of robots is very expensive, production is cheap and is likely to become even cheaper as more expe-rience is gained in the design and manufacture of robots. Maintenance, too, is likely to be much less costly than the actions required for larger and more complex systems. Fifth, as a result of the prior advantages, robots can execute some tasks that cannot be executed by people (or that are very difficult for human execution). This would include missions entailing great human risk, such as the dismantling of a live bomb. It would also include actions in which the risk of civilian harm is high, thereby requiring the greatest possible accuracy.

There are technical issues related to the deployment of military robotics, but these are likely to be solved in time.[206] There are also many moral and legal issues related to the rise of military robotics, which are discussed later in this chapter.[207]

3. CYBER WARFARE

What is "cyber warfare"? A colloquial understanding might be "the use of computers or computer networks to execute an act of war against an enemy." This, however, is not a legal definition of "cyber warfare." The law does not focus on the word "warfare," but rather on the word "attack," and the legal question is, "What kind of action is an 'attack' that triggers a right to respond?" The most accepted legal definition of the word "attack" appears in Article 49(1) of Additional Protocol I of the Geneva Conventions, which provides, "'Attacks' means acts of violence against the adversary, whether in offence or in defence." So an "act of violence" is an "attack," and an "attack" is an "act of war" that justifies a response.

The problem, however, is that the meanings of these terms, particularly

---

[206] Within the five-year period 2011–2015, the US Armed Forces invested about $30 billion in technology for unmanned systems, equal to about 8.5 percent of all military R&D in that period. Liran Antebi, "Who Will Stop the Robots?" *Journal of Military and Strategic Affairs* 5, no. 2 (September 2013): 68.

[207] The main moral issue – the relative autonomy of robotic systems – is discussed below in "Levels of Machine Autonomy." The legal issues are discussed below in "Legal Issues Likely to Arise in Future Warfare."

"violence" and "attack," were set in the era of physical war, or what is called "kinetic war," not in the age of "cyber war." There is, as yet, no accepted legal definition of the term "cyber attack," and hence no universal understanding of the term "cyber war." There are two competing views.

According to one view:

> A cyber attack is a cyber operation, whether offensive or defensive, that is reasonably expected to cause injury or death to persons or damage or destruction to objects.[208]

By this view, cyber actions are clearly acts of violence, hence acts of war, if they are performed with the intent to cause damage in the real world, and if they indeed cause some damage. Further, if such actions intend to cause damage, and are "reasonably expected to do so," they are acts of war even if the operation is blocked or fails for some other reason. The mere attempt to cause such damage is an act of war, similar, perhaps to the way that attempted murder is a criminal act, even if the attempt is unsuccessful. Note that this view makes no distinction between "military damage" and "civilian damage," because no such distinction is required – if a cyber action will likely harm a person or physical assets, it is an "attack."

This is only one view of "cyber warfare," and it is considered the narrow view. It is narrow because various cyber actions, including cyber espionage, cyber theft data, even the temporary destruction or disablement of data which can be reconstructed (but not including destruction of hardware), would not be an "attack," because there is no death or abiding injury.

A second and competing view of "cyber warfare" is that *any kind* of cyber intrusion is an act of violence, hence a "cyber attack," and hence an act of "cyber warfare." This would be true whether or not there was

---

[208] Michael N. Schmitt, ed., Tallinn Manual on the International Law Applicable to Cyber Warfare (Cambridge: Cambridge University Press, 2013). The Tallinn Manual is a two-hundred-page manual of recommendations – mainly rules and commentary – derived from a group of about forty legal, technical, and military experts who met several times over a three-year period to discuss the laws of cyber warfare. The rules proposed are not currently binding on anyone, but they do express one view of how the law of cyber warfare may develop. See also an explanatory video, "CyCon 2012 – Michael Schmitt: Tallinn Manual Part II," published September 29, 2012, from a conference in early June 2012, available at https://www.youtube.com/watch?v=f_TC3y7g4aA.

an intent to cause injury or damage, whether or not the cyber action is reasonably expected to cause injury or damage, and whether or not actual injury or damage was caused. In other words, the second view includes everything in the first view, plus much more. Consider this a kind of "cyber trespassing" view, which says that no one may intrude deliberately on my space, and such an action is an attack which entitles me to respond. This is the view of some observers,[209] and it appears to be the view also of the US Department of Justice.[210]

---

[209] For example, this is the view of Dr. Knut Dörmann, chief legal officer and head of the Legal Division of the International Committee of the Red Cross, who believes that cyber action directed at a civilian target is an "attack," even in the absence of physical damage. See Yonah Jeremy Bob, "The State of Cyber Warfare Law," *Jerusalem Post*, January 31, 2013, available at http://www.jpost.com/Features/Front-Lines/The-state-of-cyber-warfare-law. However, this view does not seem to extend to "cyber espionage" or the like, where the intent is specifically not to cause any damage or leave any sign of entry. Rather, it applies to cases where an action is taken that might create some kind of effect, either permanent damage or temporary disruption. An example of temporary disruption would be the temporary shutting down of a country's electricity system without causing permanent harm. In the first view of "attack" (that is, Professor Schmitt's view), this action with temporary effect only might not qualify as an act of war, but in the broader view of Dr. Dörmann it probably would qualify as an act of war. Dr. Dörmann's view seems to be that any cyber intrusion onto a civilian objective, or a cyber operation that will clearly impact civilian facilities even if such facilities are not the prime target, should be considered a "cyber attack." See Knut Dörmann, "Applicability of the Additional Protocols to Computer Network Attacks," in *International Expert Conference on Computer Network Attacks and the Applicability of International Humanitarian Law: Proceeding of the Conference*, edited by Karin Byström. Stockholm: Swedish National Defence College, 2004, available at https://www.icrc.org/eng/assets/files/other/applicabilityofihltocna.pdf.

The two views of "cyber attack" are sometimes called, respectively, the "permissive approach" (Professor Schmitt's view, allowing more freedom of cyber activity) and the "restrictive approach" (Dr. Dörmann's view, allowing less freedom of cyber activity in order to protect civilians). See generally, Michael N. Schmitt, "Rewired Warfare: Rethinking the Law of Cyber Attack," International Review of the Red Cross: Scope of the Law in Armed Conflict 96, no. 893 (2014): 189–206, available at https://www.icrc.org/en/download/file/11958/irrc-893-schmitt.pdf.

[210] In 2013, an Iranian hacker gained access to the monitoring and control system of the Bowman Avenue dam in Rye Brook, New York. Danny Yadron, "Iranian Hackers Infiltrated Computers of Small Dam in NY," *Wall Street Journal*, December 20, 2015, available at http://www.wsj.com/articles/iranian-hackers-infiltrated-new-york-dam-in-2013-1450662559. The dam is located only a few meters from a large grocery store and a residential area. No physical damage was caused, however, and in fact physical

For now, we may say that some cyber actions are clearly "cyber attacks," hence "cyber warfare," while other cyber actions will be classified only as the law of cyber evolves.

Apart from the exact legal definition of "cyber attack," what are the particular characteristics of cyber war that attract aggressors? The nature of cyber must be borne in mind. While machine war is an extension of conventional war, cyber war is completely different; it represents an entirely new reality. Whereas machine war and conventional war occur in the physical world, cyber war occurs in the ethereal "cyber space," which has been defined by one commentator as a world with three layers – the physical layer (hardware); the logic layer (software); and the data layer (information).[211]

Three characteristics of this new reality are attractive to potential aggressors. In particular, the targets themselves are attractive, the identity of the attacker may be hidden, and effective response by a defender is difficult.

1. The targets are very attractive. This is true for several reasons.

First, targets are ubiquitous. An activity or institution is vulnerable only if its information is stored and transmitted in digital form, but that is not a real limitation nowadays. In 1986, only 0.6 percent of data around the world was in digital format, but this became 24 percent in 2000, 93

---

damage could not have been caused, because at the time of the intrusion, the dam's sluice gate had been disconnected for maintenance. Nevertheless, the US Department of Justice charged that "hackers associated with the Iranian government attacked U.S. systems," and on this basis the DOJ filed an indictment against Iranian hacker Hamid Firoozi. Mark Thompson, "Iranian Cyber Attack on New York Dam Shows Future of War," *TIME Magazine*, March 24, 2016, available at http://time.com/4270728/iran-cyber-attack-dam-fbi/. The Department of Justice apparently thinks that intrusion without physical damage is a "cyber attack," although even this is unclear, since the formal charge states that the hacker caused $30,000 of damage in "remediation costs" – which are at least financial costs, whether or not they are "effects in the real world." United States v. Ahmad Fathi et al., Sealed Indictment by the Grand Jury of the United States District Court, Southern District of New York, March 24, 2016, Count Three, "Unauthorized Access to a Protected Computer," 14–16, available at https://www.justice.gov/opa/file/834996/download.

[211] Tabansky, "Basic Concepts in Cyber Warfare." A "cyber attack" occurs at the data layer, where information may be stolen, corrupted, or destroyed. The hardware/physical layer and software/logic layer are used by an attacker to enable the cyber attack on the data layer.

percent in 2007, and is virtually 100 percent today.[212] Additionally, the size of the market is about to expand tremendously. In the rapidly approaching "Internet of Things," essentially all electrical or electromechanical devices, from consumer refrigerators to private automobiles, will be connected to the Internet, and will be vulnerable to cyber attack.[213]

A second reason why cyber targets are attractive is that cyber attacks can be launched against what has been called "critical infrastructure." This is a crucial point. "Critical infrastructure" refers, at a minimum, to sites, assets, and networks that are critical to a country's security, economic welfare, health, or safety. This includes communication systems, ports, power stations and power distribution networks, dams, water supply, gas supply, transportation systems, hospitals, and nuclear facilities. Some people also include locations of extreme symbolic importance, such as heritage sites, museums, national archives, and monuments. All of these sites are vulnerable to cyber attacks.[214] The hacking of the computers of the US Democratic

---

[212] Guy-Philippe Goldstein, "Cyber Weapons and International Stability," *Journal of Military and Strategic Affairs* 5, no. 2 (September 2013): 124.

[213] Automobile hackers, or blackmailers, can turn off a transmission while a car is on the highway, disable brakes, turn on or off windshield wipers or defoggers, or sabotage just about any other electrical or electromechanical system of an automobile that is connected to the Internet. Andy Greenberg, "Hackers Remotely Kill a Jeep on the Highway – With Me In It," *Wired*, December 21, 2015, available at http://www.wired.com/2015 /07/hackers-remotely-kill-jeep-highway/. As if that were not sufficiently frightening, consider that terrorists could remotely take over a plane and create another 9-11, this time without any attackers on the plane. Mitch Ginsburg, "The Double-Edged Sword of Cyber Warfare," *Times of Israel*, June 24, 2015, available at http://www.timesofisrael .com/the-double-edged-sword-of-cyber-warfare/. It is estimated that by the year 2020, approximately twenty to thirty billion devices will be connected to the Internet of Things, which is to say, about three devices for each man, woman, and child living at that time. Venus Tamturk, "Internet of Things Forecasts & Best Practices," *CMS Connected*, August 30, 2016, available at http://www.cms-connected.com/News-Articles/August -2016/Internet-of-Things-Forecasts-Best-Practices. Every single one of these devices will be subject to a threat of cyber hijacking and other forms of cyber intrusion.

[214] On the definition of the term, see Harel Menashri and Gil Baram, "Critical Infrastructures and Their Interdependence in a Cyber Attack – The Case of the U.S." *Journal of Military and Strategic Affairs* 7, no. 1 (March 2015); and Lior Tabansky, "Critical Infrastructure Protection against Cyber Threats," *Journal of Military and Strategic Affairs* 3, no. 2 (November 2011). On the vulnerability of sites, see David E. Sanger, "Nuclear Facilities

National Committee in July 2016 raises an entirely new question: Can an electoral system be part of a nation's "critical infrastructure," and if so, how may the nation respond to an attack on this system?[215] The vulnerability of critical infrastructure is a major concern with cyber war.[216]

Third, as a result of the ubiquity of targets, and the ability to attack critical infrastructure, the potential scope of damage is very wide, comparable much more to the damage that might be caused by atomic, biological, or chemical weapons than the relatively minor damage of rockets or bullets. Cyber attacks against "critical infrastructure" may threaten an entire society.

Fourth, despite the widespread potential damage to a society, cyber attacks are not aimed at human beings, and the *direct* effect on humans may be small or nonexistent. In many cases, people will not even be present at the initial point of impact. A carefully crafted cyber attack may harm a society without causing death or physical injury to people. This in itself is an advantage in the international public-relations battle, and in addition

---

in 20 Countries May Be Easy Targets for Cyberattacks," *New York Times*, January 14, 2016, http://www.nytimes.com/2016/01/15/world/nuclear-threat-initiative-cyberattack -study.html; and Runkle, "Cyber Gap," which lists a Syrian cyber attack against the US army's website, a Hezbollah spying attack against Israel, Wikileaks' publication of Saudi Foreign Ministry secrets allegedly stolen by Iran, and Iranian attacks against oil and gas companies in Saudi Arabia and Qatar and against major American banks (Bank of America, Citigroup, and JPMorgan Chase).

[215] David E. Sanger, "U.S. Wrestles With How to Fight Back Against Cyberattacks," *New York Times*, July 30, 2016, available at http://www.nytimes.com/2016/07/31/us/politics /us-wrestles-with-how-to-fight-back-against-cyberattacks.html?_r=0.

[216] Apparently the first cyber attack specifically intended to bring down an electricity system occurred on December 23, 2015. Someone, presumably Russians but that is not known for certain, brought down the power grid of the Ukraine. Although this attack was very successful, the Ukrainians were able to recover quickly because much of their network is antiquated – it was restored by flipping on circuit breakers. American and European systems are more sophisticated, but also much less likely to recover quickly from a similar type of attack. David E. Sanger, "Utilities Concerned about Potential for a Cyberattack after Ukraine's," *New York Times*, February 29, 2016, available at http:// www.nytimes.com/2016/03/01/us/politics/utilities-cautioned-about-potential-for -a-cyberattack-after-ukraines.html?_r=0.

it gives the cyber attacker a chance to devise excuses and explanations for action which, after all, did not really kill anyone.

2. The second characteristic of cyber warfare that appeals to potential aggressors is that the attacker may hide his identity. Formally, this is known as the "attribution problem," or informally, as "masking." Who actually attacked? The specific identity of the attacking persons is difficult to determine, and the exact nature of the attacker (i.e., individuals, a criminal organization, or a state) may be easily concealed. In some cases, even the geographic source of the attacker cannot be determined. For purposes of war and lawfare, the question of governmental sponsorship is critical, but government involvement may be concealed.

To further complicate the attribution problem, cyber attacks can be and often are outsourced. Cyber mercenaries, also known as cyber soldiers of fortune, will prepare and launch cyber attacks for money.[217] The prices are set according to what kind of attack is desired, for how long, against what defenses, against what target, etc. Typically an offer is made and accepted on an exclusive basis, but proposed attacks can also be put to bid. If a country, or a non-state actor, lacks the expertise to prepare and launch its own attack, but has some money (and not a lot of money is required), the attacker can find someone to do the work. These services are often hired on what is called the "dark net."[218]

3. The third characteristic of cyber warfare that appeals to potential

---

[217] Argentina, for example, has become a world leader as a cyber mercenary. It even holds annual "hacking conferences." Nicole Perlroth, "In a Global Market for Hacking Talent, Argentines Stand Out," *New York Times*, November 30, 2015, available at http://www .nytimes.com/2015/12/01/technology/in-a-global-market-for-hacking-talent-argentines -stand-out.html?_r=0.

[218] The "dark net" refers to websites with privately encrypted servers that cannot be monitored by government. It is said to offer many types of illegal services, including cyber attacks. For example, mercenary cyber attacks may be purchased by Hamas or the Islamic state for a few thousands to tens of thousands of dollars. Benjamin Runkle, "The Cyber Gap: The Internet Is the Middle East's Next Battleground, But Are We Prepared?" *Tablet Magazine*, August 13, 2015, available at http://www.tabletmag.com/jewish-news -and-politics/192360/cybergap-internet-middle-east. It is believed that ISIS uses the dark net to distribute attack plans for terrorists located outside territory controlled by ISIS. "IS Plans to Hit US Air Bases in Mideast, Warn Israelis who Hacked into IS Web

aggressors is that effective response by a defender is very difficult. This is true for at least two reasons.

First, all or almost all preparatory steps can be completed by an attacker without any tip-off to the intended target. Compare this to conventional warfare. When the Egyptian army massed on Israel's border in May 1967, everyone saw the Egyptians assembling. Israel and the world knew what was likely to follow. Not so with cyber. A cyber attacker can complete most preparations – including recruitment, training, financing, communicating, identification of targets, building weapons, and testing methods – with no notice to the intended target.[219] Sometimes the attacker's preparations can be tracked, but often not.

Since the attacker's preparations are usually hidden, a preemptive attack by the defender against a cyber threat is very difficult to justify. A preemptive attack, also called an "anticipatory attack," is one that is launched in the face of imminent harm, with the sole intention of preventing the harm. How can such a preemptive attack be made, when the target does not know who presents the threat or even whether or not a threat exists? Retaliation may be made, but only after the harm has occurred, and even retaliation depends on knowing who the attacker was.

Second, cyber favors the weak. It is a cliché that war favors the strong, and that may be accurate in regards to physical warfare, but it is not true with cyber. The cost of trying to defend computer systems and critical infrastructure may be massive, in comparison to relatively minor costs for mounting an attack.[220] For example, a "cyber rifle," comprised of an antenna, a radio, a very small minicomputer, and a metal frame, may be assembled

---

Group," *Times of Israel*, August 3, 2016, available at http://www.timesofisrael.com/israeli-company-claims-hack-on-is-chat-group-with-list-of-future-targets/.

[219] This list of preparatory steps for a cyber attack was adapted from a list in Yoram Schweitzer, Gabi Siboni, and Einav Yogev, "Cyberspace and Terrorist Organizations," *Journal of Military and Strategic Affairs* 3, no. 3 (December 2011), 42.

[220] As stated by one technical expert, "The nature of cyber…is [that] offense is *really* easy…and defense is *really* hard." Joshua Corman, Chief Technology Office for Sonatype, in the video "Zero Days – Security Leaks for Sale," published by VPRO Backlight on July 14, 2015, available at https://www.youtube.com/watch?v=4BTT iWkdT8Q, time duration thirteen seconds, at 16:30–16:43. This is not idle chatter – indeed, it reflects the fundamental asymmetry of cyber war.

for $150 in outlay and ten hours of work. Such a rifle may be used to turn off a drone's power, to open locked doors, or to connect secretly to wireless networks.[221] It is perhaps fitting that in an era of asymmetric war, cyber – the most modern arena of warfare – favors those who are prepared intellectually and not those with the most powerful armies.[222]

B. A Timeline of Modern Warfare, 1800–2050

The discussion in this chapter highlights that we are currently in the midst of a transition from one form of "modern warfare" to a completely new form. Let us illustrate this transition in table 5.1.

Table 5.1: A Timeline of Modern Warfare, 1800–2050

Type of War	1800–1950	1950–2015	2015–2035	Post 2035
Human/Kinetic	Yes	More Intensive	Declining	Specialized
Robotic/Cyber	No	Initial	Big Boost	Predominant

Some people believe that modern war began before 1800, but that particular question is irrelevant here. We can say that in the 150 years from 1800 to 1950, war was human and kinetic – in particular, human beings fought with weapons that fired metal projectiles. Such weapons were initially muskets, then rifles, machine guns, tanks, planes, etc., but in all cases people were involved and they fired metal projectiles. With the exception of science-fiction writers, no one thought about "robotics" or "cyber."

---

[221] Stacey Higgenbotham, "The Army Built a Wi-Fi 'Gun' that Shoots Drones from the Sky," *Fortune Magazine*, October 19, 2015, available at http://fortune.com/2015/10/19/army-wifi-gun/.

[222] I have listed here three primary advantages of cyber war – attractive targets, concealed identity of attackers, and difficulty of response by defenders. A slightly different view might be taken. For example, one group of commentators has listed five advantages, including (1) absence of human presence at the target; (2) potential for wide scope of damage; (3) concealed identity of the attacker; (4) cost-effective cyber attacks, and (5) harm to a society without death or physical injury to persons. Adapted from Schweitzer, Siboni, and Yogev, "Cyberspace and Terrorist Organizations," 40–41. Other lists may be cited, but the general characteristics of cyber war, and its advantages in some cases over physical war, are generally understood and agreed.

In the next stage, 1950–2015, human and kinetic war became much more intensive, with vastly improved firepower and accuracy. In most cases, it was the predominant form of warfare.[223] At the same time, both robotics and cyber began to enter the arena; their use then intensified, particularly in the years 2000–2015. Robotic soldiers and drones have become much more active on the battlefield, but they do not dominate, and robotic naval forces are in their infancy. Still, ordinary people understand what robotic warfare is, and that was not true even twenty years ago.

Similarly, although the first computers began in the late 1940s and early 1950s, the age of cyber war really began with the first serious networking – DARPA's Advanced Research Projects Agency Network (ARPANET). This led to the first commercial Internet service in the late 1980s, and then the tremendous explosion of networked data in the 1990s and 2000s. Cyber did not become a major form of warfare in the period 1950–2015, but the stage was set.

We are now in the transition period. Will it actually last twenty years? That seems to be the prediction. During this transition period, conventional warfare operations – manned aircraft, human soldiers, manned warships, etc. – will continue, but they will become progressively less prevalent and more specialized.[224]

At the end of the transition, in the post-2035 world, robotics and cyber

---

[223] The "ABCs" – atomic, biological, and chemical weapons – are not under discussion here.

[224] Dempsey, "U.S. Army Roadmap," suggests a massive reorientation of air assets from manned to unmanned by 2035. See also "Israelis Urged to Prepare for Battlefields Dominated by Robots," *Space Daily*, February 3, 2014, http://www.spacedaily.com/reports/Israelis_urged_to_prepare_for_battlefields_dominated_by_robots_999.html, in which Liran Antebi "estimated that within two decades [that is, by 2033] unmanned systems will be capable of performing 70–80 percent of 'classic military tasks [whereas] human fighters…will be trained to execute specific tasks that have been determined to be better for humans to execute, and this is because of morals and ethics.'" The 2033 time estimate tracks almost exactly with the estimate in the US army roadmap noted above. The article in *Space Daily* is based on an extensive research project conducted by the Institute for National Security Studies, entitled "The Use of Unmanned Military Vehicles in 2033: National Policy Recommendations Based on Technology Forecasting Expert Assessments," ed. Yoav Zacks and Liran Antebi, Memorandum no. 145 (Tel Aviv: INSS, 2014), available in Hebrew only at http://www.inss.org.il/uploadImages/systemFiles/memo145_7%20%20%D7%A1%D7%95%D7%A4%D7%99%20%D7%9C%D7%90%D7%AA%D7%A8%20.pdf.

will dominate, "eliminating the need for large armies with fighter jets, tanks, and warships."[225] There is no doubt that at the end of the transition period, conventional warfare will continue – for special tasks that only humans can execute and for tasks more suited to human execution due to ethical or legal issues.[226] Conventional warfare will not be dominant after the transition, however. War will be, for the most part, robotic and cyber. After the transition, the legal issues of warfare will increasingly involve robotic and cyber war.

C. Levels of Machine Autonomy

Probably the single major issue regarding the advance of robotic and cyber war, and really the only serious threat that may retard or stop their growth, involves the question of machine autonomy. "Machine autonomy" refers to the degree to which machines – here robots or cyber machines – can act independently of human beings. The levels of machine autonomy are summarized in table 5.2 below.

Table 5.2: Levels of Machine Autonomy[227]

Level	Summary	Degree of Autonomy for the Machine	Examples
I	Platform controlled by human	None	Automobiles; handguns
II	Platform authorized by human	Minimal	Self-moving vacuum cleaner
III	Platform supervised by human	Substantial	Remotely Piloted Vehicles
IV	Human sets targets; then machines operate independently	Maximal	Search and destroy robots

---

[225] Antebi, "Israelis Urged to Prepare for Battlefields Dominated by Robots."

[226] According to Liran Antebi, ibid., "We'll need human fighters in this era too [after the transition], but they'll serve within very specialized frameworks and will be trained to execute tasks that have been determined to be better for humans to execute, and this is because of morals and ethics."

[227] Information to create table 5.2 was derived primarily from Antebi, "Who Will Stop

At the lowest level of machine autonomy, level I, a human makes all the decisions, and the machine merely carries out the person's instructions. That is true, for example, of private cars, and also of handguns. The machine, be it a robot or a cyber machine, has no autonomy.[228]

At level II of machine autonomy, a machine has a programmed and fixed routine, and once a human authorizes the machine to act, the machine executes the routine with no further human involvement. "Authorization" may mean to simply power on the machine, as in the cases, for example, of a self-moving vacuum cleaner, or an automatic swimming-pool cleaner.

At level III of machine autonomy, a machine has multiple programmed routines, some of which may be relatively complex. Through its sensors, or possibly through other data input sources, the machine assesses a current situation and conveys that assessment to people. The human supervisor then selects and activates a particular routine to authorize a particular action, which may be surveillance, attack, or other. Once a routine has been selected, the machine carries it out without further human intervention, unless and until the human cancels the action. This is the way in which Remotely Piloted Vehicles operate today.

At the highest level of machine autonomy, level IV, a machine has full autonomy. A human operator sets targets, or defines other objectives, after which the machine acts completely independently by planning and then executing its tasks to achieve the objective. In some instances, the human role ends with setting the target or objective, and the machine does all the rest – this is full autonomy. This would be the case, for example, with search

---

the Robots," 64–65. There are alternative names for the levels appearing in table 5.2. Level II, which I have called "human authorized," has also been called "semi-autonomous operation" and "human *in* the loop"; Level III, which I have called "human supervised," has also been called "supervised autonomous operation" and "human *on* the loop"; Level IV, which I have called "independent machine operation," has also been called "fully autonomous operation" and "human *out of* the loop." Paul Scharre, "Autonomous Weapons and Operational Risk," *Center for a New American Security*, February, 2016: 9, available at https://s3.amazonaws.com/files.cnas.org/documents/CNAS_Autonomous -weapons-operational-risk.pdf

[228] Vehicles as they are currently operated, and as they have been operated for the past one hundred years, have no autonomy, and are at level I. Self-driving vehicles, which are predicted to arrive in the 2020s, will be at a higher level of autonomy, presumably level II or level III.

and destroy robots, which seek out a target, identify an image as a target, and then attack the identified target with no further communication to or from a human being.

There is a strong feeling among some proponents of international humanitarian law that level IV is not morally acceptable, and should not be permitted legally. This opposition focuses specifically on robotics, calling level IV machines "killer robots," but the argument could be made equally for cyber machines. The opponents of such "killer robots" state four arguments.[229]

First, a machine cannot make correct judgments in a human situation, and is therefore defective as the decider of life and death. For example, only a human can read faces and body language to understand whether a person is terrified, or about to attack.

Second, machines have no compassion, and will therefore kill without emotional restraint.

Third, specifically because machines will reduce military casualties, political leaders will not be required to face public backlash resulting from military casualties, and therefore such leaders will be more likely to go to war.

Fourth, if machines identify and attack targets, human accountability becomes unclear. To say "the robot is responsible" would be nonsense, but is the responsible party the manufacturer of the hardware, the software programmer, the military commander who chose the mission, or someone else?[230]

The question then, as stated by Liran Antebi, is "Who can stop the robots?" The answer is, in my opinion, "No one can stop the development

---

[229] These arguments are summarized from Bonnie Docherty, "Losing Humanity: The Case against Killer Robots," *Human Rights Watch* and *International Human Rights Clinic of the Harvard Law School*, November 4, 2012, available at https://www.hrw.org/sites/default/files/reports/arms1112ForUpload_0_0.pdf, particularly pages 3–4.

[230] The report "Losing Humanity: The Case Against Killer Robots" (ibid.) mentions also that "fully autonomous weapons [those of Level IV] would likely contravene the Martens Clause," which, as stated in chapter 1, forbids actions or weapons that run counter to "public conscience." It is not clear to me whether the writer considered this a separate argument, although in my mind it is rather a conclusion that is supported (or not supported) by the four arguments listed above.

of robots, or of cyber." The reason is that the increasing use of machines and the decreasing use of human soldiers in the field will reduce military casualties.

> [T]he ability to use force while minimizing the risk to soldiers is very useful for any Western democracy that is forced to defend itself against terrorist and guerilla organizations.... It lessens the impact of the Achilles' heel of democracies...: sensitivity to military casualties.[231]

I am the father of three frontline combat soldiers. I strongly encourage these children to accept the responsibility of military service, and they do accept it, together with the risks, because there is no alternative if we wish to continue as a society. But if the army needs only their eyes and ears, not their hands, and if in fact machine eyes and ears can do the job equally well or even better, then why should they put their lives in jeopardy? Machines will drastically reduce military casualties, and for that reason they cannot be stopped.[232] There are still technical obstacles,[233] but these will be over-

---

[231] Antebi, "The United States: Prepared and Fit for Military Intervention in Iraq?"

[232] There would be an argument against this, perhaps even a strong argument, if the widespread adoption of machine warriors would increase the level of civilian casualties. In that case, the P principle, proportionality, would require that a balance be made between the saving of military lives on one side, versus the loss of civilian lives on the other side. This, however, is a false choice, because it is a fact, almost universally recognized, that in most cases machines are *more precise* than humans, *more accurate* in their use of weapons, and hence *likely to reduce* civilian casualties of the attacked party at the same time that they reduce military casualties of the attacker. For example, "A.I.-based [Artificial Intelligence] weapons... offer the possibility of selectively sparing the lives of noncombatants." Jerry Kaplan, "Robot Weapons: What's the Harm?," *New York Times*, August 17, 2015, available at http://www.nytimes.com/2015/08/17/opinion/robot-weapons-whats-the-harm.html. Also, "[T]o compare different air operations in densely populated areas... shows that in operations in which extensive use is made of UAVs for intelligence gathering and/or attack, fewer civilians are hurt than in airborne operations in which attacks are conducted mainly by manned aircraft." Liran Antebi, "It's Not the Tool, It's the System: Use of UAVs by the United States," Institute for National Security Studies, INSS Insight no. 766, November 12, 2015, available at www.inss.org.il/index.aspx?id=4538&articleid=10932. However, the use of machines to reduce civilian casualties raises more questions, which are discussed in the section "Legal Issues Likely to Arise in Future Warfare," below.

[233] For example, robots have limitations of vision, and difficulties in movement on rough terrain or under the surface of water. Antebi, "Who Will Stop the Robots?" 69–70.

come, and the incentive to use robots and cyber will be overwhelming. Would it be possible, then, to stop only level IV – that is, to outlaw the use of fully autonomous robots or autonomous cyber machines? That issue is not yet resolved.

III. Legal Issues Likely to Arise in Future Warfare

The new legal issues derive specifically from the nature of the new forms of warfare. One new form of warfare, "machine war," encompasses both robotics and UAVs.[234] The other new form of warfare is cyber.

A. Machine War

Machine war is an extension of the old forms of war, rather than something completely new. Identifying and destroying the enemy on a field of battle is the main objective of machine war, as in conventional war. Machine war is different, however, because it greatly reduces or even removes the presence of human soldiers, thereby reducing the military casualties of the attacker. At the same time, machine war is also much more precise, because machine precision exceeds human precision. There are two implications of enhanced precision. First, in the age of machines, there is no doubt whatsoever: if the enemy can be identified and located, he can be neutralized or killed. Second, in many cases it may be possible to reduce, perhaps dramatically, the number of civilian casualties. It is these characteristics of machine war that drive the new legal issues.

I. MACHINE AUTONOMY

The transition to machine war is unavoidable, but the permissible level of machine autonomy has not been resolved. In particular, is level IV legally permissible, or does it constitute a "war crime," or does it constitute a war crime only in specific cases? Today, war robots and drones operate indi-

---

[234] UAVs, or drones, are in essence flying robots.

vidually. They can be programmed to be extremely inflexible, acting only according to clearly defined parameters. For example, the Iron Dome Air Defense System, employed very effectively in the Gaza War of 2014, identifies an incoming rocket, tracks it, estimates its point of impact, and destroys it with an interceptor missile but only if the rocket will hit a populated area. In the Gaza War of 2014, about four thousand six hundred rockets or mortars were fired at Israel from Gaza; about 18 percent were determined to be on a lethal trajectory, and of these, approximately 87 percent were destroyed by interceptor missiles. This system is entirely automated, that is, it is level IV, but there is no legal issue because the system is solely for defense.

Individual drones are in operation all over the Middle East. Sometimes their mission is solely surveillance. Other times they target enemy personnel in what some activists have called "assassinations" or "extrajudicial killings." These attacks are not, however, level IV operations, because humans either authorize the actual firing of the weapon (which would be level II), or supervise the machine activity and choose not to intervene (which would be level III).

What will happen, however, when modern armies realize the vision of drone swarms – when hundreds or thousands of machines execute a coordinated attack, communicating with each other in real time and changing tactics according to changes on the battlefield? As a practical matter, humans cannot match the speed of the machines, and therefore human involvement would simply slow down the attack.

Let us take another scenario, which is almost certain to happen by the middle of the twenty-first century. Two combatants, either the armies of two nations or a nation versus a non-state armed group, each have their own drone swarms, and launch them at each other. Active human involvement on one side would almost certainly degrade reaction time, possibly with deadly consequences for that side. In other words, the absence of level IV machine autonomy for the drone fleet of one side may cause that side to die. Is level IV autonomy still forbidden?

One might argue that this is not a real dilemma, that level IV is not a problem in this context, because a drone fleet against a drone fleet does not have direct human consequences, and hence there is no chance for a war crime. But let us change the facts slightly. What if one of the drone fleets is targeting a manned control center, or an aircraft carrier, or another objective with enemy soldiers and possibly also enemy civilians? Is it legally permitted for this drone swarm to attack? In formal terms, what type of drone attack is militarily necessary (the necessity principle), and what action is proportional (the proportionality principle)? These questions are not resolved.[235]

2. SHIELDING

In an age of machine war, the targeted combatant, particularly a combatant that is not a nation but rather an armed group, realistically has no physical defense against the attack of machines. This is exactly the situation likely to arise in asymmetric war, which is now, and will likely continue to be, the dominant form of warfare in the twenty-first century. The only real defense is to hide.

There are three ways to hide. First, the armed group can simply choose not to engage in armed action. That is effective in terms of avoiding machine retaliation, but not effective in advancing the group's goals. Second, the group can hide physically, waiting for its chance to act. This is what Hamas does in Gaza. Not only do they use attack tunnels to infiltrate into Israel, but they also hide from bombardment in intra-Gaza defense tunnels. Hiding is effective as long as the combatants cannot be physically located, but again, it is a purely defensive tactic, and cannot, by itself, advance the group's goals. Third, they can hide among civilians and civilian infrastructure, firing their rockets and mortars, hoping that the other side will choose not to fire. In other words, the armed group uses shielding (a violation of the

---

[235] In his opinion review for the *New York Times*, Michael V. Hayden, former head of the CIA, remarked about drone attacks on al-Qaeda, "[U]nmanned aerial vehicles carrying precision weapons and guided by powerful intelligence offer a proportional and discriminating response when response is necessary" ("To Keep America Safe, Embrace Drone Warfare"). It is proper, in fact legally required, that the proportionality and distinction principles be considered. Hayden's statement, however, is not a legal opinion, and even if it were, the facts could be changed slightly to cast doubt in a specific case. The reality is that legal issues of machine warfare have been introduced, but not resolved, and the issues will become more pressing in years to come.

shielding principle of law). Since there is no physical defense against an attack by robots, shielding is likely to become more and more prevalent in the asymmetric battles of the twenty-first century.

Shielding puts the opposing army in a dilemma: on the one hand, it must respond in order not to concede military advantage to the armed group; on the other hand, it must separate the civilian from the military (the distinction principle) or risk losing in the court of international public opinion and in lawfare counterattacks. The tension between the desire to respond and the need to exercise restraint has been apparent in the three Gaza wars, and will likely become much worse in future asymmetric conflicts.[236]

3. PRECISION TARGETING

Under the laws of war, an attacker must do everything reasonable to reduce civilian harm. This, indeed, is the "humanitarian" aspect of "international humanitarian law," an equivalent name for "laws of war." Machines are much more accurate. There are still issues of choice of armament, the decision to attack based on intelligence (which may be faulty), and the target's use of civilian shielding, all of which are not resolved by machines. However, once these issues are resolved by people, machines are much more likely to conduct an attack that successfully neutralizes the target but reduces civilian damage (subject to the type of armament used, correct identification of the target, and the degree of shielding). That being so, are Western armies *required* to use robots when conducting an attack against armed insurgents? Or stated in the alternative, if an army fails to use a robot, and civilians are

---

[236] A very different scenario may be inferred from a recent article by Arthur Herman, "The Pentagon's 'Smart Revolution,'" *Commentary Magazine*, June 16, 2016, available at https://www.commentarymagazine.com/articles/pentagons-smart-revolution/. Herman posits a world in which extremely miniaturized killer drones will use face-recognition intelligence to locate, identify, and kill specific targets, the last step achieved when the drone attaches itself to the target and then either blows up or injects a fatal toxin. This is not science fiction – it is being developed right now, and will be available soon. In such a world, predictions as to the continuation of "shielding" are almost impossible. If enemies can be visually identified at a very short range, and then eliminated with no damage to surrounding people or property, can "shielding" continue to be an effective strategy for terrorists and guerilla groups? Advancing technology will have a massive impact on war, on the interpretation and application of the laws of war, and on lawfare.

harmed, is the army guilty of a "war crime" for failing to minimize civilian damage? Three of the four fundamental principles of war might be invoked – failure to attack only necessary targets (the necessity principle), failure to distinguish a legitimate military target from non-combatant civilians (the distinction principle), and failure to act proportionally (the proportion- ality principle) by using a blunt weapon – that is, humans – when a more precise weapon, machines, would have reduced the harm. To the best of my knowledge, this claim has not yet been made, but it is likely to come up in the future.

B. Cyber War

Cyber war has at least three particular characteristics – attractive targets, concealable identity of attackers, and difficulty of response – that dis- tinguish it from physical war, and that attract possible aggressors. Given these unique characteristics of cyber, several unique and unresolved legal issues arise. Six such issues may be noted here. The first four are discussed in a seminal article appearing in the *Harvard International Law Journal* of December 2012.[237]

1. THE DEFINITION OF "ATTACK"

What is an "attack" by a cyber operation? The waging of offensive war is illegal, but a party always has a right of self-defense under Article 51 of the United Nations Charter. What, then, is a "cyber attack" that justifies a defen- sive response? As noted previously, there is no accepted legal definition of "cyber attack," with two competing views – the narrow view requiring actual or likely damage, and the broader view including any cyber intrusion.

Whichever of these views (or a third view) is accepted as the definition

---

[237] Harold Hongju Koh, "International Law in Cyberspace," *Harvard International Law Journal* 54 (December 2012): 1–12, available at www.harvardilj.org/2012/12/online_54 _koh/. Professor Koh was the legal advisor to the US Department of State at the time this article was published, and is currently professor of international law at Yale Law School. The specific part of the article of interest here is "II. International Law in Cyberspace: Challenges and Uncertainties," 7–9, which lists and discusses "unresolved questions."

of "cyber attack," can there be forms of "illegal force" that do not rise to the level of "attack"? The traditional US view does not recognize a distinction between "illegal force" and "attack," since all "illegal force" is an "attack." Other countries do recognize a distinction between the two terms, and specifically allow a response to an "attack" but not to an "illegal force" that does not achieve the level of attack. Let's illustrate this difference with a chart.

Chart 5.1: Illegal Force vs. Attack in Cyberspace

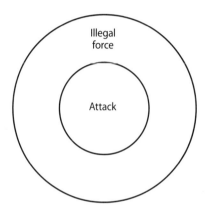

Whether there is a difference between "illegal force" and "attack" is another unresolved legal question.

2. PERMITTED RESPONSE

Assuming that there was some kind of "attack," how may the attacked party respond? Without doubt, any response by the attacked party must comply with the principles of international humanitarian law: necessity, distinction, and proportionality.[238] How would that work in specific cases of cyber attack? Even assuming an "attack" has occurred, must the response be limited by the nature and effect of the attack?

---

[238] In his article (ibid., 7–8), Professor Koh notes that the US view has been that "*any* illegal use of force" is an attack, triggering a right of self-defense. Under this view, there would not be concentric circles in chart 5.1, but rather only one circle, where "attack" and "illegal force" are equivalent. Nevertheless, under either view (i.e., that whether or not "illegal force" and "attack" are equivalent), the right of self-defense permits a forceful response, but in all case the response "must still be *necessary* and of course *proportional*." (Italics in the original.)

For example, assume that an attacker has intruded into a financial system and gained access to sensitive records, but did not erase the records or cause damage to the hardware. If this is an "attack" that permits a response, is the permissible response limited by the nature of the attack? That is, would the victim be permitted, legally, to do the same thing – to go into the aggressor's financial system and steal sensitive information? Would the victim be limited to this response, and legally barred from further action? And here is the most difficult question: The general rule of international humanitarian law is that an attacked party may act in self-defense, but may not act in retaliation. How exactly does that work in the context of a cyber attack? All of these questions remain unresolved.

3. DUAL-USE INFRASTRUCTURE

What can be done about what is called "dual-use infrastructure"? In conventional and machine war, an attack is against a military objective. In cyber war, an attack is against a network, which might be entirely military, but will likely have some kind of connection, and hence an impact, in the civilian realm. An attack against a military objective, such as a military communication system, would be permitted under the necessity principle (assuming the other laws of war are observed). Conversely, an attack against civilian "critical infrastructure" would clearly be forbidden. The problem of dual-use infrastructure arises when an attack is directed at the military objective, but also impacts civilian infrastructure. There are at least three questions:

First, critical infrastructure may not be attacked legally, but what exactly is "critical infrastructure"? The definition of this key term has not been clearly established in international law.

Second, if a particular system serves both military and civilian needs – that is, if a system is "dual use" – is it a legitimate military target or not? In other words, could an attacker target a military objective, knowing but ignoring the effects on civilian infrastructure? For example, could an attacker bring down a mobile communication system, knowing that the system is relied upon by both the military and civilian sectors but ignoring the harm to civilian communication? Or if the civilian harm is not ignored, how can an attacker weigh harm to the military objective against unintended harm to the civilian sector? What kind of attack would be proportional (P)?

Third, even if a particular infrastructure is not "critical," it may have connections to and effects on other infrastructure that is "critical." This is called "interdependence of infrastructure." For example, could a cyber attacker bring down the electricity at a military base, either knowing, or simply being indifferent to the possibility, that destroying electricity at one location will have a cascading effect through a city, a state, or an entire region? How can the attacker weigh the benefit of achieving a military objective against the possibility of a cascading effect in the civilian realm?

These questions are not resolved. Some commentators feel that the questions are not resolvable in a general way, but rather must be asked and answered in every specific case.[239]

4. ATTRIBUTION: WHO IS ATTACKING?

Who exactly is attacking? If the attack cannot be attributed to anyone in particular, what can the targeted party do? Is nothing at all permitted? May the targeted party launch its own cyber response to attempt to both identify, and then sabotage, the attacking party? Or perhaps this is not a legal issue at all, and must be left to the technical experts?[240]

5. PREEMPTION: ANTICIPATORY SELF-DEFENSE

Is military preemption permitted, and if so, when? In legal literature, this is sometimes called "anticipatory attack," and it is one of the extremely

---

[239] At p. 8 of his article, Professor Koh discusses the unresolved question of dual-use infrastructure, but from the opposite view. He states that "civilian infrastructure [must] not be used to seek to immunize military objectives from attack, including in the cyber realm." That is, he recognizes that some parties will attempt to use a form of shielding by deliberately tying their military systems to civilian systems, and then daring, so to speak, the other side to attack the military system and cause massive civilian harm. This is the same issue, but from the opposite viewpoint, and again, the issue is not resolved. Professor Koh recommends "a careful, fact-intensive legal analysis in each situation."

[240] Professor Koh (ibid.) suggests, "[C]hallenges... [such as] attribution... are as much questions of a technical and policy nature rather than exclusively or even predominantly questions of law.... [W]e cannot expect that all answers to the new and confounding questions [in cyberspace] will be *legal* ones." (Italics in the original.)

important unresolved issues in cyber war. The general rule, established in the *Caroline* case of 1837 (also known as the *Caroline* affair or the *Caroline* incident), is that an anticipatory attack is allowed only when a state has "a necessity of self-defence, instant, overwhelming, leaving no choice of means, no moment for deliberation."[241] Although it occurred almost two hundred years ago, nevertheless the *Caroline* case was applied at the Nuremberg Military Trials following World War II,[242] and the case is still valid law today. However, a doctrine that is very sensible for kinetic attacks may be less relevant for attacks in cyberspace.

There are two main problems with anticipatory attacks in cyber war. First, the effects of a cyber attack, particularly against critical infrastructure, are akin more to a nuclear, biological, or chemical attack than to a physical attack against a military target. Second, the time frame of a mass attack – cyber, nuclear, biological, chemical – is much more difficult to determine than the time frame of a conventional attack. The mass attack, when it happens, can be immediate and pervasive.[243] Analogies to conventional war are therefore simply misplaced. The doctrine of anticipatory self-defense in the context of cyber war is not yet defined.[244]

---

[241] Letter of July 27, 1841, by US secretary of state Daniel Webster to Lord Alexander Ashburton, including Enclosure 1 to Mr. Henry Fox, Her Britannic Majesty's Minister to the United States, regarding the seizure and destruction of the merchant vessel *Caroline* (destroyed by the British Navy on December 29, 1837), available at http://avalon.law .yale.edu/19th_century/br-1842d.asp. This case is discussed in Dinniss, *Cyber Warfare and the Laws of War*, 82–83, as part of an excellent discussion of anticipatory self-defense in the context of cyber warfare at 82–95.

[242] *Nazi Conspiracy and Aggression*, "International Military Tribunal at Nuremberg, Opinion and Judgment," Office of United States Chief of Counsel for Prosecution of Axis Criminality (United States Government Printing Office, Washington, D.C., 1947), at p. 36, quoting the *Caroline* case that "preventive action in foreign territory is justified only in case of 'instant and overwhelming necessity for self-defense, leaving no means and no moment of deliberation,'" https://www.loc.gov/rr/frd/Military_Law/pdf/NT _Nazi-opinion-judgment.pdf.

[243] These two differences between a conventional attack and a mass attack – that is, greatly enhanced gravity of damage and immediacy of impact – are discussed in Dinniss's book at pp. 87–88, relying in part on Christopher Greenwood, "International Law and the Pre-Emptive Use of Force: Afghanistan, Al-Qaida, and Iraq," *San Diego International Law Journal* 4 (2003): 7.

[244] However, Dinniss in *Cyber Warfare and the Laws of War*, analogizes anticipatory

6. NON–LETHAL FORCE

As with machine war, are there times when cyber war is not only permitted, but actually *required* instead of physical or "kinetic" war? This argument is more of a stretch than with machine war. It relates not to the precision of cyber (for indeed, cyber is less precise in separating civilian from military), but rather to the fact that cyber can be "non-lethal" whereas physical attacks are specifically intended to cause death or damage. In particular, if an initial action is an "attack" but does not cause physical damage (such as a cyber attack that does not kill or damage, or a physical attack that is intended to kill but fails in its purpose), should the response be limited to an action that by its nature will almost certainly be non-lethal? To the best of my knowledge, this claim has not yet been made, but it may be raised in the future.[245]

---

self-defense in the context of nuclear war to the use of the doctrine in cyber war. The International Court of Justice issued an advisory opinion entitled *Legality of the Threat or Use of Nuclear Weapons*, Advisory Opinion, I.C.J. Reports 1996, p. 226, International Court of Justice (ICJ), 8 July 1996, available at http://www.icj-cij.org/docket/index.php?p1=3&p2=4&case=131&p3=4, in which the ICJ split evenly – seven judges declaring that a state may *never* introduce nuclear weapons and seven judges saying a state may introduce nuclear weapons if the existence of the state is threatened. Dinniss states, at p. 86,

> This [recognition of anticipatory self-defense as a legitimate exercise of a state's right to ensure its survival] accords with the advisory opinion in the *Nuclear Weapons* case, [in] which . . . the majority of judges were unable to conclude that the first use of nuclear weapons would invariably be unlawful if the very existence of the state were threatened.

Hence, by analogy, if a state threatened with total destruction could use nuclear weapons, which is the implicit ruling in the ICJ advisory opinion (since such weapons were not forbidden), then a state could presumably use a cyber attack, even a massive cyber attack with large-scale damage, if that is the only reasonable way for the state to defend its existence. If this is true, then a state that is threatened with a massive cyber attack could preempt the attacker with its own cyber attack. None of these inferences, however, are firmly established in international law – cyber is simply too new, and too different from what has occurred before, for present conclusions. The law will be established only in the future.

[245] As noted above, in 2013, Iranian hackers took control of the Bowman Avenue dam in Rye, New York, which is located only a few meters from a large grocery store and a residential area. Yadron, "Iranian Hackers." Apparently no physical damage was caused, but this is still considered an "attack" under traditional US doctrine. The incident was likely a probe to learn the parameters of what can be done. May the United States respond

C. A Summary of Legal Issues in Machine and Cyber War

Let us summarize the legal issues of machine and cyber war in a table:

Table 5.3: Legal Issues of Machine and Cyber War

Issue	Machine War	Cyber War
1. What is an "attack" that would justify a response?	(Usually not an issue.)	Major issue: there is no clear and accepted definition of "cyber attack."
2. What is legally permitted?	Is level IV full machine autonomy permitted?	What response is permitted to a cyber attack?
3. Shielding	Major issue, and will likely become much worse.	Dual-use infrastructure may be a type of shielding.
4. Who is attacking (attribution)?	(Usually not an issue.)	Anonymity is a major issue.
5. Preemption	(Usually not an issue.)	One of the most pressing issues in cyber.
6. Is it ever required legally, rather than merely permitted?	It might be required, instead of a human response, to achieve precision targeting.	It might be required, instead of physical force, in response to "illegal force" that is not an "attack."

There are fewer general issues in machine war than in cyber war, at least partly because machine war is far closer to conventional war than cyber war, both in character and in effect. This does not mean, however, that legal questions will arise less often in machine war – the frequency and severity of legal issues will be fact specific, and are likely to be as pressing in machine war as in cyber war. Shielding will probably become a major problem in machine war, even more so than it is today, as all parties come to recognize that there is no military defense to machines, only a legal and public relations defense.[246] Shielding will also be an issue in cyber war, particularly

---

at all? If so, would the doctrine of proportionality require that the United States respond only by taking over control of an Iranian infrastructure? Could the United States cause damage to the attacking computer network?

[246] I do not hold cheaply the legal, political, and public-relations defense that armed insurgents and terrorists are likely to assert against Western armies. Israel, in particular,

in the form of critical infrastructure that is dual use and/or interdependent with other critical infrastructure. While that is a major problem, probably the most significant problem in the realm of cyber is likely to be preemption, which, as noted above, is both a legal and a technical issue.

IV. Future Arguments by Lawfare Activists against Western Armies

We may assume that, in the future, lawfare activists will use every argument they can to embarrass or inhibit Western armies, to hold them liable at the International Criminal Court, and to damage their international standing as part of a political attack. Given the legal issues expected in machine and cyber war, as discussed above, what might these arguments be? We can identify at least four arguments that are likely to become increasingly common over the next few years.

A. Too Much Machine Autonomy

The increasing use of machines in warfare is inevitable. By about 2035, robots and drones are likely to play the dominant role in physical/kinetic war. There are different levels of machine autonomy, in particular, level II – human authorizes specific action; level III – human supervises but only intervenes to prevent an action; and level IV – full machine autonomy, without human involvement (after the initial objectives have been defined).[247]

Whatever the level of human involvement in a robot or drone attack, we may expect lawfare activities to say, "Killer robots," "Machines out of control," "Extrajudicial assassination by heartless machines." These arguments are likely to be heard even if there are no civilian casualties, and even more so if there is damage to civilians or to civilian buildings.

---

will be subject to claims and charges at both the United Nations and the International Criminal Court.

[247] See "Levels of Machine Autonomy," earlier in this chapter.

B. Not Enough Machine Involvement

The argument that there was not enough machine involvement is approximately the opposite of the first argument, but will almost certainly be heard in specific cases. It is widely recognized that in most cases, machines are more precise and more accurate than persons. When humans are involved in an attack and civilians are unintentionally harmed, which will without doubt happen in some military actions, the argument will be, "If humans had been less involved in this case, there would have been no miss," hence the attacker has violated the rule of distinction (D) by causing needless civilian casualties. Or perhaps the argument will be, "If machine surveillance and attack had been used, only the exact amount of force required would have been used"; therefore, the human attackers used too much force and violated the rule of proportionality (P).

In cyber war, if an initial attack is a cyber attack, even one that causes serious damage to civilians and to what has been called "critical infrastructure," any military response in the physical world will be deemed "excessive" by lawfare activists. They will claim, "The response to a cyber attack may only be a cyber counterattack. Any physical/kinetic counterattack is disproportionate, and hence violates the rule of proportionality (P)."

C. Failure to Respect Civilians

In asymmetric war, the increasing use of shielding by terrorists or other non-state armed groups is inevitable. In very many cases, armies facing such groups will need to decide whether to attack (even though civilian damage is very likely) or to allow the terrorists to get away. In some cases, the armies will attack, and civilian damage will be caused. Lawfare activists might say, "There was no 'shielding' at all, and hence the attack was simply murder against civilians." Or they might say, "Shielding cannot be avoided in the circumstances of an overcrowded population/urban environment/ refugee settlement/etc., but this is the not the fault of non-state actors, and therefore there is no justification to attack when local civilians will be harmed." Or they might say, "Yes, in this case the armed group used illegal shielding, but that does not justify an illegal counterattack. The correct thing to have done would have been to file a legal charge against the shielding offenders, not to kill innocent civilians." Again, these arguments involve the principles of distinction (D) and proportionality (P).

In the cyber realm, the basic problem is again shielding. Western countries are likely to separate their own military and civilian cyber networks, or at least design their information systems such that civilian networks are insulated from an attack on the military network. In contrast, terrorists and non-state armed groups are likely to do nothing – that is, to leave in place one cyber structure servicing both military and civilian needs, so that an attack on the one will cause damage on the other. Sophisticated armed groups might go further – they might deliberately tie together the military and civilian networks, so that an attack on the military network will *necessarily* cause planned and serious civilian damage.[248] This is a form of "shielding" which to the best of my knowledge has not yet occurred, and is therefore completely new to the world, but it is likely to occur in the future. In either of these cases – where the two networks grow together and are not separated, or where the armed group deliberately shields its military network with a civilian network – any cyber response by a Western army will cause civilian damage. Lawfare activists will exclaim, "Failure to distinguish civilians (D)," or "Attack with disproportionate force (P)," or even, "There was no need for a cyber action, hence the army violated the principle of military necessity (N)."

D. There Was Never a Cyber Attack

It is still unclear, under the current state of the laws of war, what constitutes

---

[248] Even with the best of intentions, there is still the problem of a backbone network that services both military and civilian needs, and is therefore an example of dual-use infrastructure. If a backbone network is attacked, there may be a problem of "cascading failures" from "interdependent infrastructures" (different networks that are connected and work together). A party with bad intent, such as an armed group using cyber shielding, can design its information networks so that any attack on the military network will cause significant civilian damage.

a "cyber attack" or a "threat of cyber attack." Therefore, any response by an army will be denounced as "unjustified," "lacking military necessity (N)," and "aggressive war" under Article 2, paragraph 4 of the United Nations Charter. Several specific arguments are likely to be made.

First, whatever the cyber threat or cyber attack by the other side, no response is permitted unless the attacking party is clearly identified. (This is called "attribution.") It is almost certain that in many cases, lawfare activists will claim, "Guilt has not been proven," or "Even if a place of origin is identified, that does not mean the attacker was the nation-state, so no response is permitted against such a state."[249]

Second, cyber theft, cyber spying, cyber probing for system weaknesses, and even cyber seizure of physical assets (such as networks, or dams, or power plants) might not be considered "attacks" unless identifiable and serious damage occurred. Therefore, according to the activists, any cyber response to any of these actions would be disproportionate and unjustified.[250]

Third, the question of launching a cyber preemption (that is to say, an anticipatory attack in self-defense), is very complicated. The possible damage of a cyber attack is very severe, and there is very little or no advance

---

[249] For example, if a cyber attack is prepared by cyber mercenaries, the typical procedure is for the mercenaries to first identify a system vulnerability, then to "write the exploit" (meaning to write code to attack this vulnerability), then to transfer the "exploit" to the client in exchange for money. In a typical case, the client then "weaponizes the exploit" (meaning that he places the malicious code into the target system). In other cases, however, the exploit is weaponized by the mercenaries rather than by the client, in which case discovering the true source of the attack can be extremely difficult. The level of evidence required to attribute the attack to a specific party is not clear under the current state of the law. Lawfare activists will always say, "Not enough evidence," or "Not proven," or "Unclear."

[250] Dinniss uses the term "pinprick attacks" to refer to probes and to cyber entries without damage. She analogizes these cyber pinpricks to pinpricks in the physical world, and cites specific cases of countries in the past – the UK, the US, and Israel – that have tried to justify military responses to multiple small-scale physical attacks. In all the cases she cites, the argument to justify military response was rejected by the United Nations Security Council. Dinniss, *Cyber Warfare and the Laws of War*, 93–94. In the cyber realm, the law is not settled. Could a nation legally respond to "cyber pinpricks" by launching its own cyber counter-pinpricks? There is, as of yet, no clear answer to that question.

warning. Assuming that the threatening party could be identified, would a threatened target have the right to preempt the attack by launching its own cyber attack? Lawfare activists are certain to argue along these lines:

> The clear standard for a preemptive attack, which has been settled law for almost two hundred years under the *Caroline* case, is that the need for such an attack must be "instant, overwhelming, leaving no choice of means [and] no moment for deliberation."[251] That standard was not met here – the possible cyber threat was not "instant," the threatened damage was not "overwhelming," and there was certainly time for both "deliberation" and "non-aggressive means." Hence, the preemptive attack was not legally justified, and constituted a war crime.

Although there is much superficial appeal in this argument, it is not clear whether the *Caroline* case, which sets the legal standard for preemptive attack in the kinetic world, should apply also to the cyber world.

V. The Israeli Response

With the great changes in modern warfare, both those that have occurred in the past few years and those expected during the transition to robotics and cyber war, legal issues have become an increasingly important factor in warfare. How has Israel responded to these changes? There have been significant responses in the Israel Defense Forces, in the Israeli government, and in Israeli military research and development (R&D).

A. The Israel Defense Forces (IDF)

The Israel Defense Forces have responded to the changes in warfare by reorganizing the army to emphasize cyber capabilities and by appointing a new military advocate general specifically suited to meet the challenges ahead.

---

[251] This was the specific standard set forth in the *Caroline* case (1837), and it is still the law today for conventional threats, but the *Caroline* case occurred before anyone had heard of cyber, atomic, biological, or chemical attacks.

I. REORGANIZATION

In early 2015, Lieutenant-General Gadi Eizenkot was appointed the twenty-first chief of staff of the Israel Defense Forces. On August 13, 2015, in an unprecedented action, General Eizenkot published the army's strategic focus. The focus is explained in a thirty-three-page document entitled "The Strategy of the IDF."[252] One commentator has summarized the three imperatives listed in the document as "safeguarding Israel's international standing, response to terror groups, and fending off cyber attacks."[253] Each of these imperatives relates directly to the changing laws of war.

The "response to terror groups" relates to asymmetric war, which is the essence of the battle environment today. The document states that both "conventional and nonconventional threats" have declined in importance, but they have been replaced by "sub-conventional threats" such as terror and by "cyber threats."[254]

Both "international standing" and "regional standing" are discussed.

---

[252] The original of General Eizenkot's document, in Hebrew, is available at http://www .idf.il/SIP_STORAGE/FILES/9/16919.pdf. It would not be an exaggeration to say that this is an extraordinary military document, providing unprecedented insight into the strategic thinking of the Israel Defense Forces. All of the references herein are based upon my reading of the document in the original Hebrew. However, the document has recently been translated from Hebrew into English by the Belfer Center for Science and International Affairs, and is available at http://genius.it/belfercenter.org/IDF_Strategy .html?filter=annotator:BelferCenter, or in a pdf version at http://genius.it/belfercenter .org/files/IDFDoctrineTranslation.pdf. "Deterring Terror: How Israel Confronts the Next Generation of Threats, English Translation of the Official Strategy of the Israel Defense Forces," Belfer Center, August, 2016. The Belfer Center is the main source of research, teaching, and training in international security, diplomacy, environmental issues, and science and technology, of the John F. Kennedy School of Government at Harvard University. On the basis of this English translation, Graham T. Allison, Director of the Belfer Center and Professor of Government at Harvard, has written an outstanding article on Israel's thus far successful policy in deterring aggressive action by ISIS, Hamas, Hezbollah, al-Qaeda, Iran, and others. "Why ISIS Fears Israel," Graham Allison, *National Interest Magazine*, August 8, 2016, available at http://nationalinterest.org/feature/why -isis-fears-israel-17286. See also "C3R" and "Deterrence" in the Glossary.

[253] Judah Ari Gross, "In Rare Disclosure, IDF Sets Out Its Strategy, Admits Flawed Response to Hamas, Hezbollah," *Times of Israel*, August 13, 2015, available at http://www .timesofisrael.com/better-us-ties-tackling-terror-and-cyber-warfare-idf-reveals-strategy/.

[254] "The Strategy of the IDF," 3.

Law and the legal environment, including international law, are mentioned fifteen times. It is clear that the chief of staff wishes to preserve and even strengthen Israel's international legal standing.

Of the three imperatives noted here, cyber is by far the most prominent – "cyber threats" are mentioned eight times. General Eizenkot's response, stated in the document, is to raise cyber as a fourth branch of the military, equal in status to air, land, and sea, with the creation of a new "cyber corps" to defend the army and the country against cyber attacks. The new cyber corps was announced on June 15, 2015.[255] The intention, stated at the time, was to do two things: First, to unify cyber security, which has been divided between offensive operations in Military Intelligence and defensive operations in C4I;[256] and second, to significantly raise the importance of cyber operations in the army. Indeed, on December 1, 2015, General Eizenkot appointed the new head of the cyber corps, with the rank of brigadier general.[257]

The creation of the cyber corps is at the macro level of the IDF. At the micro level, the IDF has recently created a cyber-defense brigade, which it calls informally the "cyber-fire squadron." Composed of both conscripts and reservists, the brigade is intended to protect both the army and the state. The brigade currently has one "cyber intervention team," and the intention is to create additional teams both to respond to large cyber attacks and to proactively thwart cyber threats.[258] Exactly how this will play out is not yet known, but the very creation of such a brigade underscores the seriousness with which the IDF considers the cyber threat.[259]

---

[255] Mitch Ginsburg, "Army to Establish Unified Cyber Corps," *Times of Israel*, June 16, 2015, available at http://www.timesofisrael.com/army-to-establish-unified-cyber-corps/.

[256] "C4I," an acronym for "Command, Control, Communications, Computers, and Intelligence," or *cheil hatikshuv* in Hebrew, is the corps responsible for all communications within the army.

[257] "IDF Appoints First Head for Unified Cyber Warfare Corps," *Times of Israel*, December 1, 2015, available at http://www.timesofisrael.com/idf-appoints-first-head-for-unified-cyber-warfare-corps/. The officer's identity is classified for reasons of security.

[258] The concept of the IDF cyber-defense brigade is explained in Gili Cohen, "Cyberattacks Waned Amid Iran Nuclear Talks, Israeli Officer Says," *Haaretz*, February 16, 2016, available at http://www.haaretz.com/israel-news/.premium-1.703816.

[259] The general goal is to create "a single unified cyber authority" within the IDF. This is

2. THE APPOINTMENT OF A NEW MILITARY ADVOCATE GENERAL (MAG)

On October 22, 2015, a new chief of the IDF Military Advocate General (MAG) Corps was appointed. Brigadier-General Sharon Afek was selected by Defense Minister Moshe Ya'alon specifically to enhance Israel's ability to defend itself in international legal forums such as the International Criminal Court.[260] General Afek has been a military lawyer for twenty-five years, in the international law department of the MAG (rising to deputy head of the department), as chief legal counsel to the Israel Air Force, and as chief legal counsel to forces in Judea and Samaria / the West Bank. He is also the sole author of a 144-page study of cyber law, entitled "The Cyber Attack – Legal Guidelines: Applying Principles of International Law to Warfare in Cyberspace."[261]

General Afek's specific work background would seem to be ideally suited to lead the battle at the ICC and in international forums, and to defend Israel's actions both in asymmetric war and in the cyber battle. This is the task for which he was chosen, and his background highlights the areas that Israel believes will be the legal battlegrounds going forward.

---

intended to be achieved by the end of 2016, but as of the current writing, "there were still open questions about where it [the unified cyber authority] would be located [within the IDF] and how best to combine cyber and intelligence capabilities." Yonah Jeremy Bob, "Former Shin Bet Head 'Bursts Myth' on Cyber Hackers Who Attack Israel," *Jerusalem Post*, June 21, 2016, http://www.jpost.com/Israel-News/Former-Shin-Bet-head-bursts -myth-on-cyber-hackers-who-attack-Israel-457355.

[260] See Yonah Jeremy Bob, "Facing ICC, Ya'alon Appoints Veteran Sharon Afek as New IDF Head Lawyer," *Jerusalem Post*, August 17, 2015, available at http://www.jpost.com /Arab-Israeli-Conflict/Facing-ICC-Yaalon-appoints-veteran-Sharon-Afek-as-new-IDF -head-lawyer-412347; and also Judah Ari Gross, "New Military Advocate General Prepared for ICC fight," *Times of Israel*, August 18, 2015, available at http://www.timesofisrael.com /new-military-advocate-general-prepared-for-icc-fight/.

[261] Eshtonot 5 (October 2013). To the best of my knowledge, this study appears only in Hebrew. The title was translated by me. The study is available at http://maarachot.idf .il/PDF/FILES/4/113504.pdf.

B. Actions by the Government of Israel

The government of Israel, like the IDF, has demonstrated its readiness to meet the new challenges of robotic and cyber warfare – through the appointment of key legal and intelligence officials with cyber experience, through investment in programs geared to cyber technology and robotics in the business sector, and through the development of new weapons.

I. KEY APPOINTMENTS

Surprisingly, or perhaps not so surprisingly given the tenor of what is happening in warfare, many of the recent appointments to major legal positions in the Israeli government have gone to people with experience in the laws of war or in cyber war. The appointment of General Sharon Afek as the new MAG is noted above.

On January 3, 2016, Avichai Mandelblit was appointed as the fourteenth attorney general of the State of Israel. This is the highest legal position in the country. Prior to this appointment, Attorney General Mandelblit was the military advocate general in the period 2004–2011, and thereafter legal advisor to Prime Minister Netanyahu. He is a military attorney through and through, the longest serving MAG in forty years, and only the second chief military attorney to become the attorney general.[262] He is one of the most powerful, and arguably the single most powerful MAG in the history of Israel.[263] Further, and this is the most interesting point for present purposes, his specific area of expertise is international law,[264] which is the law of the ICC and the law misused by lawfare activists.

---

[262] Apart from Avichai Mandelblit, Meir Shamgar was the only MAG to become the attorney general. Also, Meir Shamgar, like Avichai Mandelblit, served seven years as the MAG, although the average tenure is less than five years, and only one person served as the MAG longer than Mandelblit and Shamgar. Meir Shamgar ended his term as MAG in 1975, and since that time, in the past forty years, no MAG has served as long as Avichai Mandelblit.

[263] Yonah Jeremy Bob, "Rule of Law: Attorney-General on Deck," *Jerusalem Post*, January 11, 2016, available at http://www.jpost.com/Israel-News/Politics-And-Diplomacy/Rule-of-law-Attorney-general-on-deck-440813.

[264] Yonah Jeremy Bob and Lahav Harkov, "Avichai Mandelblit Nominated as Next Attor-

In Israel, the chief intelligence agencies, apart from Military Intelligence, are the Mossad (roughly equivalent to the CIA or MI6) and the Shin Bet (roughly equivalent to the FBI or MI5). On December 7, 2015, Yossi Cohen was appointed as the new head of the Mossad. At the time of his appointment, Prime Minister Netanyahu stated that the Mossad had three tasks: operations that will foil threats to state security, contacts with countries that do not currently have formal relations with Israel, and "on the intelligence side, the Mossad must adopt itself to the cyber and advanced-technology era."[265] For many years, Cohen was the head of the Mossad division that recruited and ran human agents. Although the recruitment of agents will continue, Cohen understands that the focus of war has shifted. Shortly after his appointment, he said,

> What is a conventional war? Tank versus tank battles aren't expected to occur in the next five years. There's not even someone to have one with.... Instead, Israel is destined to fight asymmetric wars, of formal armies against non-state, terror organizations.[266]

The problem in this century is not conventional war, but rather the new war of robotics, cyber, and lawfare. Agents will still be vitally important in the Mossad, but without doubt there will be a rise in the relative importance of electronic intelligence and cyber skills.

On February 11, 2016, two months after Cohen was appointed head of the Mossad, Nadav Argaman was appointed as the new head of the Shin Bet. His background is unique. Although he has significant experience running agents, his main experience is in the operations department, which is trending more toward signals intelligence (SIGINT) – that is to

---

ney-General," *Jerusalem Post*, December 20, 2015, http://www.jpost.com/Israel-News /Politics-And-Diplomacy/Avichai-Mandelblit-chosen-as-next-Attorney-General-437855.

[265] Barak Ravid, "Netanyahu Names National Security Council Advisor Yossi Cohen as Next Mossad Chief," *Haaretz*, December 7, 2015, available at http://www.haaretz.com /israel-news/premium-1.690575.

[266] Judah Ari Gross, "Yossi Cohen Has Had Iran in His Sights for Over a Year," *Times of Israel*, December 8, 2015, available at http://www.timesofisrael.com/yossi-cohen-has -had-iran-in-his-sights-for-over-a-year/.

say, communications intercepted by computers or radio installations. This appointment represents a major reorientation of focus. As journalist Yossi Melman noted:

> His appointment indicates the sea change the agency has been undergoing in the recent years. Since the 1967 Six-Day War, the Shin Bet has occupied itself primarily with the struggle against Palestinian terrorism. Accordingly, the three chiefs over the past 16 years have emerged from that field.[267]

Argaman, however, does not fit the standard mold for head of the Shin Bet. Although he has worked against Palestinian terrorists, that is not Argaman's primary area. His chief specialty, signals intelligence, is particularly well suited to fight against cyber terrorism. Also in this regard, the Shin Bet has created a unit devoted to providing cyber security to the main utilities in Israel – the national water company, the national electric company, and the major suppliers of natural gas.[268]

Finally, as a result of the incident of the *Mavi Marmara* (part of Flotilla I described in the previous chapter), an Israeli investigative body called the Turkel Commission recommended that a new unit be set up at the Department of Justice, whose sole task would be to overview the Shin Bet and ensure that its practices were in accordance with international law. The intention, of course, is to ensure that Israeli investigations are honest and real, so that there will be no need to involve the International Criminal Court. The head of that unit in the Department of Justice is Colonel (res.) Jana Modgavrishvili, who was formerly the chief prosecutor at the MAG under Avichai Mandelblit.[269] Here, too, the intention is to strengthen Israel's ability to defeat charges under international law.

---

[267] Yossi Melman, "Netanyahu Names Nadav Argaman as the New Head of the Shin Bet," February 12, *Jerusalem Post*, 2016, available at http://www.jpost.com/Breaking-News/Netanyahu-names-Nadav-Argaman-as-the-new-head-of-the-Shin-Bet-444617.

[268] Amitai Ziv, "Israeli Startups Arm World for the Online Wars to Come," *Haaretz*, January 14, 2016, available at http://www.haaretz.com/israel-news/business/premium-1.697575.

[269] Yonah Jeremy Bob, "Rule of Law: Transforming the Shin Bet," *Jerusalem Post*,

In all of the above cases, the intention is to strengthen Israel's ability to fight the next war – the war of robotics, cyber, international lawfare activists, and the ICC. I have no evidence or reason to believe that these actions were coordinated, and I doubt that they were. Rather, the senior people in government understand, I believe correctly, that the old paradigms of symmetric war and standard rules of engagement are no longer sufficient for what is come. For that reason, they are changing focus and staffing up, to deal with the challenges of the future.

2. INVESTMENT

The Office of the Chief Scientist of Israel ("OCS") helps develop technology by advice, contacts, and financial support, in order to foster economic growth and encourage innovation and entrepreneurship.[270] The National Cyber Bureau, created in 2012, is part of the Prime Minister's Office. It is specifically charged with advancing defense and building national strength in the cyber field, building up Israel's lead in the cyber field, and advancing processes that support the first two tasks.[271]

In a marriage of technology, entrepreneurship, and defense, the OCS and the National Cyber Bureau jointly created a program called "Kidma." Over a 2.5-year period to the end of 2015, Kidma invested about $34 million (that is, about $13 million/year) in companies developing cyber-security technology "deemed to be groundbreaking or disruptive."[272] The initial program was very successful, and Kidma's annual budget was approximately doubled to $25 million/year.

The Kidma program demonstrates that the government is not just

---

June 13, 2013, available at http://www.jpost.com/Features/Front-Lines/Rule-of-Law -Transforming-the-Shin-Bet-316488.

[270] The OCS achieves these goals through its executive agency, "MATIMOP – Israeli Industry Center for R&D," http://www.matimop.org.il/ocs.html.

[271] Prime Minister's Office: The National Cyber Bureau – Mission of the Bureau. http:// www.pmo.gov.il/English/PrimeMinistersOffice/DivisionsAndAuthorities/cyber/Pages /default.aspx.

[272] Niv Elis, "Israel to Invest NIS 100m in Cyber-Security Fund Kidma," *Jerusalem Post*, December 21, 2015, available at http://www.jpost.com/Business-and-Innovation/Israel -to-invest-NIS-100m-in-cyber-security-fund-Kidma-437981.

speaking about cyber, nor is it content solely to appoint legal officers with international law and cyber law experience. The government is also investing money and providing direct assistance to boost Israel's cyber capability and, in the words of the National Cyber Bureau mission, "to build Israel's lead in the cyber field." The significance is that not only is the government changing its own focus, as discussed above, but in addition it is working with private industry to change the orientation of the society outside of the government.[273]

3. R&D: THE DEVELOPMENT OF NEW WEAPONS

The reality is that the old army – of tanks, planes, and ships – is gradually being obsolesced by robotics and cyber. Israel has reacted in two ways. First, resources cannot be made available unless the old is sloughed off. Therefore, since 1985, Israel has reduced its total number of tanks by 75 percent, and its manned planes by 50 percent.[274]

Second, war of the future will be conducted by swarms of unmanned devices. As Israeli defense analyst Yuval Azulai states, "Hundreds of devices,

---

[273] The various government bodies responsible for cyber security in Israel should not be confused. Overall responsibility lies with a "National Cyber Directorate" (NCD), which is part of the Prime Minister's Office, and which includes exactly two divisions. One division, the National Cyber Bureau (NCB) sets overall cyber policy and increases cyber capabilities in Israel. The second division, the National Cyber Authority (NCA, alternatively called the "National Cyber Security Authority"), is responsible for protection of critical infrastructure and for national cyber defense. The NCA was created in February 2015, and as of this writing is still evolving in its responsibilities and its relationships to other bodies within the government. See "Cabinet Approves Establishment of National Cyber Authority," Israel Ministry of Foreign Affairs, February 15, 2015, available at http://mfa.gov.il/MFA/PressRoom/2015/Pages/Cabinet-approves -establishment-of-National-Cyber-Authority-15-Feb-2015.aspx; Barbara Opall-Rome, "Interview: Eviatar Matania, Head of Israel's National Cyber Directorate," *Defense News*, July 11, 2016, available at http://www.defensenews.com/story/defense/policy-budget /leaders/interviews/2016/07/11/israel-cybersecurity-directorate-matania/86445128/; and Judah Ari Gross, "Israel lawmakers advance bill to streamline cybersecurity," *Times of Israel*, August 1, 2016, available at http://www.timesofisrael.com/israeli-lawmakers -advance-bill-to-streamline-cybersecurity/.

[274] Yossi Melman, "The Gideon Doctrine: The Changing Middle East and IDF Strategy," *Jerusalem Post*, September 13, 2015, available at http://www.jpost.com/Jerusalem-Report /The-Gideon-Doctrine-412594.

of different kinds, will communicate with one another in real time, will react to the changing reality, and will attain the desired outcome on the battlefield, with no human presence on the scene."[275] Swarms of UAVs, hundreds or thousands of drones coordinating with each other in real time, has not yet been achieved, but as noted, that is the vision of the Chinese People's Liberation Army and of the US Navy. It will be achieved.[276]

Israel is already one of the leading countries worldwide in the design and production of drones, which are unmanned vehicles specifically for air combat, and it has increased its own fleet of drones by 400 percent over the past twenty years.[277] The country is now actively integrating robots into the ground forces, currently in the form of "advanced guards" to open attack corridors through areas infested with booby traps and snipers. In the future, "robot battalions" will be deployed.[278]

Many Israeli robotic programs could be noted, but I will mention two here. The first is a program called, colloquially, "She sees, she shoots." Robotic sentries are positioned on the border with Gaza, with visual communication to an operations room in Israel staffed with women soldiers. If a target is identified, the responsible soldier, acting in accordance with predefined rules of engagement, presses a button, and the robotic sentry fires a heavy machine gun with extreme accuracy.[279] The second program is

---

[275] *Space Daily*, "Israelis urged to prepare for battlefields dominated by robots."

[276] There are technical obstacles to the achievement of this vision. Perhaps the greatest obstacle is the need to increase significantly what is called "energy density," which is roughly the amount of energy available per volume. Drones today are relatively large, which is due in part to the constraint of low energy density. To create swarms of small drones will require that energy density be increased – this is a major technical challenge, but eventually the challenge will be met.

[277] Melman, "Gideon Doctrine."

[278] On the army's current and future use of robots, see, for example, "IDF Begins Integrating Robots into Ground Forces," *Israel Today*, May 7, 2015, available at http://www .israeltoday.co.il/NewsItem/tabid/178/nid/26564/Default.aspx.

[279] The formal name of this program is the "Spot and Strike System," but it is staffed solely by women soldiers, and in Israel it is known colloquially as "*Ro'ah, yorah*," literally "She sees, she shoots." See Anshel Pfeffer, "Lethal Joysticks," *Haaretz*, July 2, 2010, available at http://www.haaretz.com/israel-news/lethal-joysticks-1.299650. Although I have not seen statistics, the program is said to be extremely effective.

what I would call a "snake robot" – a six-foot-long robot, covered in military camouflage, that moves along the ground taking video pictures which it conveys in real time to a command position.[280]

There is no doubt, given its investment in unmanned military systems and cyber war, that Israel will be one of the leading countries in military technology of the future.

C. The Secret of Israeli Creativity: A Father's Story

When my children were small, I used to go to school performances in the Israeli elementary school system. The first time I attended a performance, I was appalled. The "play" seemed to be chaotic – no plan, no order, people coming on and off stage, basically incomprehensible. Had this same performance been mounted at an American school, the parents would have been outraged – they would have demanded, and received, the teacher's resignation, and probably the principal's, too. Afterwards, I talked to my children, and asked what they thought of the performance. "It was great! Just right!" I thought about this for a moment, and realized that my kids were right, and I was wrong. I had seen the performance through American eyes, and heard it through Western ears.

People talk frequently about the source of Israeli creativity, the "start-up nation," etc.[281] I am not a psychologist, but I am a father and a person who deals with innovation in my profession. It seems to me that the source of Israeli creativity is here, in the "balanced chaos" of Israeli childhood. Children from the earliest age are taught to be self-confident and assertive, to fight for their ideas. Systems here, such as the school system, sometimes appear chaotic, but the chaos has a certain order. Spontaneity is encouraged; uniqueness in thought and behavior is tolerated in Israel to a degree far

---

[280] A video of the snake robot, entitled "Israel: Military Robot Snake," may be viewed at https://www.youtube.com/watch?v=8t2nFHjtIJQ.

[281] Dan Senor and Saul Singer, *Start-Up Nation: The Story of Israel's Economic Miracle* (New York: Hachette Book Group, 2009).

beyond what is typical in the United States; failure is accepted; and second or third efforts are not just permitted, they are expected.

The battles of the future will be based far more on creativity and innovation than upon massed numbers of soldiers or tanks. A small number of people, with good ideas and adequate funding, will triumph over nations much larger in population. For that reason, Israel will survive the upcoming wars, which will be wars primarily of automation and cyber. For the same reason, Israel will fight and triumph in the lawfare conflict of the twenty-first century.

VI. A Summary of Chapter 5

Warfare has changed over the past few years, and is currently in the midst of an upheaval that will essentially revolutionize war over the next twenty years. Human soldiers will continue to be essential, but only in specialized roles. The main burden of war will be carried by machines.

Chapter 5 begins with a story of soldiers at war on the outskirts of Khan Yunis, in Gaza. Their mission, their actions, and their limitations highlight the role of soldiers today, and the need for a new paradigm. The second section of chapter 5 explains the main trends in warfare, which are unmanned aerial vehicles, robots, and cyber war. The section ends with a discussion of the various levels of machine autonomy, and a timeline of modern warfare covering 1800 to 2050.

The third section discusses the legal issues of modern warfare, for which there are as yet no clear answers. Issues discussed include the level of machine autonomy, shielding as a main weapon of war, definition of "cyber attack," attacks on dual-use military-civilian infrastructure, the uncertainty as to who is attacking, anticipatory self-defense against cyber threats, and the possibility that future law will permit machine or cyber response but forbid human response.

Not all of these issues will be taken up by lawfare activists, but almost certainly some of them will. Lawfare activists will likely claim that "no attack was made" so no response is allowed, that "the attacker cannot be identified" so any response is a war crime, that anticipatory self-defense against cyber threats is illegal, that Western armies that ignore shielding commit war crimes, and that dual-use infrastructure may never be attacked. The question of different legal consequences for choosing human response or machine/cyber response is particularly difficult – it is likely that whatever choice is made, activists will allege that the choice taken was a "war crime."

Chapter 5 continues with a discussion of actions taken by Israel with regard to future warfare. By its key appointments in law and intelligence in both the army and the government, and by its investments and its R&D, Israel has indicated very clearly that it understands the trends of warfare and is taking action now to meet the new challenges. Ultimately, the ability of Israel to survive depends on the people rather than the army or the government. In the new age of modern warfare, creative thinking and innovation will be critical to the success of a society.

Chapter 5 ends with a father's story intended to illustrate what I consider to be the key to what has been called the "start-up nation."

Summary of Key Points

I. The Revolution in Modern Warfare

Three trends have created a revolution in modern warfare. These are first, the shift in emphasis from symmetric to asymmetric warfare; second, the digitization and globalization of information; and third, the automation of war.

Asymmetric war – a war between a state and a non-state armed group – has existed alongside symmetric war – a war between two states – for centuries. However, in modern times, and certainly in the nineteenth and twentieth centuries, symmetric war has been dominant. That is no longer true. Asymmetric war is dominant now, and is fated to be the main form of warfare in the future. The breakup of failed states, multiple armed groups in conflict, and shifting alliances will not be exceptions, but rather the norm in the asymmetric wars of the twenty-first century.

The rise of the Internet and the globalization of information are obvious to everyone. The result of this trend is that modern war is fought not only on the battlefield, but also in the media, at the UN, and in international courts such as the International Criminal Court (to hear charges of war crimes) and the International Court of Justice (which deals with civil claims and advisory opinions).[282] The rise of the ICC in particular is likely to be a major factor in the conduct of war.[283]

---

[282] In the first years of this century, 2000–2015, we have seen also numerous cases of what is called "universal jurisdiction," which is the exercise of jurisdiction by the courts of a nation over defendants who are not necessarily connected with that nation, but who are charged with war crimes. However, in light of the defeat of universal jurisdiction – in Belgium, in Spain, and in the UK, as discussed in chapters 1 and 2 – it is not clear how serious a factor universal jurisdiction will be going forward.

[283] However, the ICC has not yet realized its potential in terms of number of cases

The automation of war is manifested in the increasing use of robots – both ground robots, and flying robots known as unmanned aerial vehicles ("UAVs," also known as "drones"). The rise of cyber war, which has only just started, is another manifestation of automated war. Over the next twenty years, robotics and cyber will become increasingly important aspects of war, not as a complete substitute to human soldiers, but certainly in a predominant position over the increasingly specialized human involvement.

It is the confluence of these three trends – asymmetric war, the globalization of information, and the automation of war – that has created the modern battlefield. Similarly, it is the combination of these three trends that has created "lawfare," which is, in essence, the use of law as a weapon of war. In an asymmetric war, the terrorists or non-state armed group cannot win a physical contest against a modern army. Further, as a result of the tremendous changes in military technology, and the changes expected over the next twenty years, the combatants of a non-state armed group cannot hope to hide from the machine technology of the opposing army. If a combatant can be identified and located, he can be killed, and eventually, if he reveals himself by attacking, *he will indeed* be identified, located, and killed. This reality is widely understood. The result is that the non-state armed groups have come to rely increasingly on non-physical means of war, including shielding behind civilians (a clear example of a war crime, but widespread nevertheless), management of foreign journalists and news sources, political attacks at the UN and other international bodies, and increasingly, resort to the International Criminal Court.

This is the reality not only for the non-state armed groups, but also for the Western armies opposing such groups, including the armies of Israel, the United Kingdom, the United States, and other states fighting in the

---

brought or convictions. Further, as discussed in chapter 2, the eventual success or failure of the ICC will likely depend, to a large degree, on the way it handles the Israeli-Palestinian dispute. If the ICC is found to apply one standard to the world and a totally different, more rigorous standard *against* Israel, then the ICC will likely be seen as a sham, just another anti-Israel mouthpiece. The responsibility on ICC chief prosecutor Bensouda weighs very heavily at the moment – her performance now may determine the ultimate acceptance or rejection of the ICC by the international community.

Middle East, in Africa, in Asia, and elsewhere. Each country must decide, in these circumstances, what it will do. Israel's response has been a reorganization of the Israel Defense Forces to emphasize cyber capabilities; the appointment of key legal officials (the attorney general and the IDF military advocate general) and key intelligence officials (the Mossad and Shin Bet) with cyber and computer experience; major investments in cyber technology and robotics; and the encouragement of the business sector to pursue these same areas.

II. The Approach of the Israel Law Center

The three trends of modern warfare create reality also for organizations fighting on the lawfare front. In Israel, the chief such organization is Shurat HaDin – Israel Law Center. Various cases initiated and prosecuted by the Israel Law Center are discussed in this book. These cases reveal the Israel Law Center's basic approach, and the keys to its great success. We can identify four aspects of this approach: creative thinking, intensive research, the interweaving of law and politics, and the understanding that success is best measured in broad terms.

A. Creative Thinking

In area after area, in case after case, the Israel Law Center has demonstrated creative thinking and an innovative spirit typical of "the start-up nation."

Chapter 2 discusses the Spanish complaint against Israeli government and military officials, in which the Israel Law Center responded not by defending the Israeli officials but rather by using the same Spanish law against Javier Solana, one of the most well-known and beloved Spanish politicians.

Chapter 3 discusses the complaint filed at the ICC against Turkey for its occupation of northeast Cyprus. This was only the opening salvo, but it made clear to the ICC and other involved parties that the ICC would either apply the same standards to Israel as to the rest of the world, or the ICC would be revealed as a hypocritical sham.

Chapter 4 discusses the Israel Law Center's involvement in flotillas, particularly its use of maritime and insurance law to attack the organizations that enabled Flotilla II in 2011. The use of "crowd research" to identify the insurers of the flotilla ships was extremely innovative, and may be unprecedented.

In July 2016, the Israel Law Center sued Facebook for allowing hate speech on its pages, and thereby enabling terrorist attacks against Israelis. Damages are sought in the amount of $1 billion.[284] This case may be won or lost, but the fact that it was launched testifies to the creative thinking of the Israel Law Center. Similarly, in early March 2016, the Israel Law Center announced that it was preparing a lawsuit against the heads of Palestinian Television, for their persistent screening of vicious threats to murder Jews. This lawsuit will be filed in the International Criminal Court, one of the key battlegrounds in the lawfare conflict.[285]

B. Intensive Research

Even the greatest and most creative idea amounts to little without amassing the information needed to implement it. The Israel Law Center has demonstrated high ability to find and use relevant research. The degree to which

---

[284] Reuters, "$1 Billion Lawsuit Accuses Facebook of Enabling Palestinian Attacks," July 11, 2016, available at http://fortune.com/2016/07/11/facebook-lawsuit-hamas-attacks/.

[285] Specifically, names are being gathered to join an intended class action lawsuit against Riyad Al-Hassan and Ahmed Assaf, heads of Palestinian Broadcasting Corporation. The argument will be that incitement on television has encouraged Palestinians to murder Jews, in the same way that the heads of Rwandan television were tried by a specially created international court, and sentenced to thirty years' imprisonment, for their role in the 1994 genocide against the Tutsi population of Rwanda. Ruthie Blum, "Lawfare Group Pursuing Class-Action 'War Crimes' Suit at International Criminal Court Against Palestinian Broadcasting Chiefs (VIDEO)," *Algemeiner*, March 2, 2016, available at http:// www.algemeiner.com/2016/03/02/lawfare-group-pursuing-class-action-war-crimes -suit-at-international-criminal-court-against-palestinian-broadcasting-chiefs-video/. See also the website of the Israel Law Center, "A Worldwide Campaign to Prosecute the Heads of Palestinian Television in the Hague," Israel Law Center, available at http:// israellawcenter.org/legal_action/a-worldwide-campaign-to-prosecute-the-heads-of -palestinian-television-in-the-hague/. The current intention is to file a complaint with the ICC in late 2016 or early 2017.

the Israel Law Center generates its own research depends on the degree to which it is an expert in the subject. For example, the ICC complaints filed against Turkey, Khaled Mashal, and Mahmoud Abbas all demonstrate deep research executed and integrated by the Israel Law Center. Conversely, the attorneys of the ICC are not experts in maritime law, but they generated an initial idea to attack the insurance coverage of the ships, and then worked with Israeli military intelligence in attacking the ships' telecommunication links and the false sailing manifests that the ships filed with local port authorities – it was a combination of efforts and expertise by the Israel Law Center and by outside parties that created the necessary information.

Finally, in some cases, the Israel Law Center must rely extensively on outside parties. For example, it was possible to identify Javier Solana as a possible "war criminal" under Spain's impossibly broad law of universal jurisdiction,[286] but beyond that, the Israel Law Center understood it would need to rely on Spanish attorneys to prepare, file, and prosecute a specific complaint.[287]

C. The Interweaving of Law and Politics

Lawfare does not operate in a political vacuum. In fact, the opposite is the case. It is most successful when it is tied, as intimately as possible, to parallel efforts in the political realm. One example is the victory in the Javier Solana case, which occurred even before the filing of the complaint. The legal pressure brought by the Israel Law Center complemented the very severe political pressure exerted by the United States and China against universal jurisdiction in Spain.

Another case, possibly the chief example presented in this book of the combination of law and politics, is the saga of Flotilla II. The political environment

---

[286] The Spanish law permitting the exercise of universal jurisdiction by Spanish courts was later amended, two times, with a severe narrowing of the scope of the statute.

[287] Although the Israel Law Center was not sufficiently expert to prepare and file a Spanish-language complaint in the Spanish courts, it was able to perform the research necessary to locate, hire, and work with local Spanish counsel. Similarly, in Flotilla III, the Israel Law Center noted possible legal consequences to SEB Bank *under Swedish law*, which demonstrates again the organization's expertise in finding and using information.

was created by the Israeli government, particularly in its wise policies of limiting the blockade only to offensive weapons, offering repeatedly to transship to Gaza all humanitarian aid on the ships, allowing the entry into Gaza of five hundred fully loaded trucks per day during the time of Flotilla II, and most importantly, repeatedly insisting that it would not under any circumstances lift the blockade against offensive weapons. This was a political story that had great appeal internationally, as reflected in the strong political support for Israel's positions by various nations during both Flotilla II and Flotilla III.

The Israel Law Center capitalized on this environment by threatening the supporting companies (the insurers and Inmarsat) with potential financial liability for supporting Hamas – an armed group that was and still is widely recognized as a terrorist organization. In this political environment, the Israel Law Center's attacks upon the ships' insurance, telecommunications, and deceptive filings with port authorities found a ready audience.

The Israel Law Center has never claimed that its victories are independent of the political environment, and indeed, it recognizes that the combination of law and politics creates the most potent form of lawfare.[288]

D. The Definition of Success

What is the meaning of "success" with regard to lawfare waged by an organization such as the Israel Law Center? Certainly the winning of lawsuits

---

[288] Conversely, when the Israel Law Center is not aligned with the political environment, the results may not be as successful. In 2009, the Israel Law Center, working with American attorneys, sued the Bank of China for providing monies that ultimately funded terrorist actions in Israel that killed American citizens. The Israeli government promised support, and initially did provide intelligence, but ultimately chose not to allow its officials to testify, presumably because of severe political pressure from China. "[T]the plaintiffs dropped the case because no one from the Israeli, US or Chinese governments would testify." Yonah Jeremy Bob, "Exclusive: Historic Case against Bank of China for Millions in Terror Financing Dismissed," *Jerusalem Post*, November 8, 2015, available at http://www.jpost.com/Israel-News/Politics-And-Diplomacy/Exclusive-Historic-case-against-Bank-of-China-for-millions-in-terror-financing-dismissed-432381. The political and legal interests were initially aligned, but the case was lost when the political environment changed. I do not consider this a defeat for the Israel Law Center – the legal case was lost, but there were, in my opinion, serious political gains, as discussed in the next footnote.

is one measure of success, but that cannot be the only measure in an area characterized by the interweaving of law and politics. The result in Flotilla II was a smashing success in both the legal and political realms. What about the ICC filings in 2014 against Turkey and against the leaders of Hamas (Khaled Mashal) and the Palestinian Authority (Mahmoud Abbas)? If the definition of success is solely "to stop the Palestinian Authority from joining the ICC," the filings were a failure – the PA joined the ICC in early 2015.

However, a broader definition of "success" would judge these filings much more positively. The ICC has been put on notice, and everyone is now aware that Palestinian filings at the ICC will generate multiple counter-filings. If the ICC intends to be accepted in the international community, it would do well to treat Israel's counterarguments and counter-filings fairly. The Rome Statute has not been adopted by several major countries that together represent the majority of the world's population. Demonstrated bias by the ICC would do nothing to expand its membership or influence.

Similarly, a lawsuit against the heads of PA television for anti-Semitic and anti-Israel incitement cannot realistically hope to stop such incitement. The lawsuit can, however, make very clear to wide segments of the international legal and political community the true nature and severity of the hatred generated by the Palestinian Authority. A "legal victory" from this suit is very difficult to imagine, but a political victory is certainly achievable, and could have major political and public-relation benefits for Israel. Such a political victory will require the support of the Israeli government, and that is very likely to come – Israel has much to gain from such a lawsuit, and there is no countervailing political pressure.[289]

---

[289] As noted above, there was countervailing political pressure from China in the Bank of China case, which ultimately caused the Israeli government to withdraw its political support, and the lawsuit was consequently dismissed. Legally, this was a defeat. Politically, however, the Bank of China is on notice that it will be monitored and, if it continues to support terrorism, it will be sued again. I doubt that the Bank of China will be supporting terrorism in the near future. Indeed, after this lawsuit was launched, the financial accounts that supported terrorism against Israel were terminated by the Bank of China. Many other international banks are also on notice that if they support terror, they may be sued for hundreds of millions of dollars. Further, by terminating its support of the lawsuit, Israel performed a political favor for China – in reaction to China's political

III. The Laws of War and NGOs

The traditional principles of the laws of war – necessity (N), distinction (D), proportionality (P), and shielding (S) – will continue to apply in one form or another both now and through the future forms of warfare. The function of pro-Israel and pro-Western non-governmental organizations (NGOs), such as the Israel Law Center, is to use these principles to protect Western armies and states. These NGOs will fight discriminatory laws (especially "bills of attainder" targeting Israel), double standards in the enforcement of law, and *ex post facto* applications of law. Organizations such as the Israel Law Center will fight on the lawfare front with creative ideas, in-depth research, and coordination with political authorities to produce both legal and political success.

---

pressure to be sure, but nevertheless a favor, and that fact may help Israel in the future. It would have been better for the Israel Law Center had the Bank of China case gone to trial, and the ultimate result cannot be called a "legal victory," but nevertheless, serious political benefits were derived. This case was not a complete success, but neither was it a complete failure, if "success" is defined, properly in my opinion, to include both legal and political impacts.

Afterword

In a speech delivered on May 21, 2015, Colonel Richard Kemp (ret.), CBE, formerly commander of British Forces in Afghanistan, spoke about the change in Western values over the past thirty years. The speech, a bit more than a half hour in length, is entitled "The Amoral Revolution in Western Values, and Its Impact on Israel."[290]

Colonel Kemp discusses the decline in Western values such as democracy, freedom of speech, family values, respect for the state, loyalty, and "traditional Judeo-Christian values" generally. In parallel, there has been a rise in political correctness and moral relativity. Although one might think that "moral relativity" implies equal judgment of all, that is surely not the case for Israel, which is viewed as a "Western colonial outpost" and as a "true evil to be attacked at every opportunity." The assault is not aimed primarily against Israel, nor even against Western countries. Rather, as Colonel Kemp says, "The target is Western values themselves." Perhaps most pernicious of all, the assault is being led not by fringe elements, but rather by the Western media, "especially broadcast media, especially television," which, ironically, seeks to destroy the very values that have made the West great and that have enabled the Western media to exist.

---

[290] Colonel Kemp's talk is available at https://www.youtube.com/watch?v=IsJDbnZjQik. A transcript of the talk is available at http://besacenter.org/perspectives-papers/col-richard-kemp-the-amoral-revolution-in-western-values-and-its-impact-on-israel/. There are a few minor discrepancies between the talk on YouTube and the transcript, but these have no effect on the overall message.

Colonel Kemp states very clearly, and correctly in my opinion, that "history has proven time and again Arab nations cannot defeat Israel on the field of battle, and this will always be the case." For that reason, the Palestinians resort to "terrorist methods…missiles…and attack tunnels." Also for that reason, the Palestinians resort to using human shields "in the hope that Israel will attack and kill their [civilian] people," thereby achieving global condemnation of Israel, and exploiting anti-Israel pressure at the UN, the International Criminal Court, the European Union, the universities, businesses, [and] trade organizations.…" This is the Palestinian approach to the outside world. Internally, the Palestinian authority "[incentivizes] terror by paying terrorists and the families of terrorists killed or imprisoned for attacking Israelis," and "[incites] anti-Israel hatred through speeches, newspapers, broadcast media, school textbooks, and school teachers."

This is the entire problem. The problem is most explicitly not "occupation" by the Jews of any person or any land. It is rather the "rejectionism" by the Palestinians of any Jewish presence in any part of Israel. And more, it is the rejection by the Palestinians of the West, of Western values, of democracy, of free speech, of non-corrupt government, of every value that makes the West what it has been and what it is now. Among these values we must include the laws of war, which are called also, for good reason, international *humanitarian* law, for these are the human values that are denied in the cynical use of lawfare by non-state terrorist groups against Western armies.

Through force of historical circumstances, Israel is at the forefront of this battle, but it is not Israel's fight alone. It is the fight also of every country in Europe, the Americas, Asia, and Australia, that lives by and supports these same Western values. In the end, the countries of the West will live or die together. As Colonel Kemp concludes his speech,

> Israel's fight is the Western world's fight. Upon Israel's survival depends the survival of Western civilization.[291]

---

[291] The same point was made by the great American longshoreman-philosopher Eric Hoffer. Speaking about the Six-Day War, he said, "I have a premonition that will not leave me; as it goes with Israel, so will it go with all of us. Should Israel perish, the holocaust will be upon us." Eric Hoffer, "Israel's Peculiar Position," *Los Angeles Times*, May 26, 1968,

Survival requires a willingness to defend oneself. This is true for Israel, but ultimately it is true for every country and every civilization. Willingness of self-defense means willingness to fight. The modern age – characterized by asymmetric war, globalization of information, and the revolution in military affairs created by robots and cyber – requires that new tools be used. The use of law, and lawfare, is one tool of self-defense. Lawfare will certainly be used *against* the West, and therefore it must also be used *by* the West in order to ensure the survival of our civilization and of the great moral values bequeathed by that civilization to the world.

---

reprinted in the *Wall Street Journal* on July 30, 2014, and available at http://www.wsj .com/articles/notable-quotable-eric-hoffer-on-israel-1968-1406761244.

The Debate about the Relevance of Internal Reality to the Laws of War

---

The legal scholars Michael N. Schmitt and John J. Merriam[292] have recently published three essays concerning Israeli targeting in the Third Gaza War of 2014 ("Operation Protective Edge"). All three essays arrive at the same conclusions, but they are directed at different audiences. The publications are as follows:

1. "A Legal and Operational Assessment of Israel's Targeting Practices"[293] – a short essay of about four pages, which is essentially a summary of the authors' approach;

2. "Israeli Targeting: A Legal Appraisal"[294] – a twenty-page essay directed at a "military-policy audience"; and

---

[292] Michael Schmitt is a professor of international law at the US Naval War College, a professor of public international law at the University of Exeter, UK, and one of today's leading scholars on the laws of war. John Merriam is a US army judge advocate, who is currently serving as a military professor and the associate director of the Stockton Center at the US Naval War College.

[293] *Just Security* (online publication), April 24, 2015, available at https://www.justsecurity.org/22392/legal-operational-assessment-israels-targeting-practices/.

[294] *Naval War College Review* 68, no. 4 (Autumn 2015): 15–33, available online in pdf format at http://papers.ssrn.com/sol3/papers.cfm?abstract_id=2596836.

3. "The Tyranny of Context: Israeli Targeting Practices in Legal Perspective"[295] – an eighty-eight-page essay published in an academic law journal, and hence intended for an academic and legal audience.

For present purposes the short essay is sufficient, so I will use that here, but I note that parallel citations may be found in any of the three writings.

Professors Schmitt and Merriam perform a detailed review of Israeli targeting practices, and conclude that Israeli targeting in the Third Gaza War accords with the laws of war. They mention specific factors that, in their opinion, seem to be unique to Israel. Here is their language, quoted at length:

> Several key factors inform IDF decision-making in this regard. The first is the extraordinary degree to which the Israeli population views itself as "under siege" — Israel is surrounded by foes, and both of its chief antagonists (Hamas in Gaza and Hezbollah in Lebanon) possess vast quantities of cheap, widely available, and highly inaccurate rockets that they regularly launch at Israeli population centers.... [T]he destruction of rockets and rocket-launching infrastructure (often in the form of civilian houses converted to military use in order to deter Israeli attack) has a high degree of "anticipated military advantage," such that it may justify (from the IDF's standpoint) levels of collateral damage that may strike outside observers as potentially excessive.
>
> The second factor that figures prominently in the IDF approach to targeting is the acute casualty aversion in Israeli society writ large, coupled with a pervasive fear of IDF soldiers being taken prisoner and used to exert strategic leverage over Israel.... The difference in perspective [between the view of the IDF and that of the US Armed Forces] can be explained in part by the fact that, unlike the all-volunteer professional military the United States fields, the IDF is a conscript force; nearly every Israeli family has loved ones who

---

[295] *University of Pennsylvania Journal of Law* 37, no. 1 (2015): 53–139, available online in pdf format at http://papers.ssrn.com/sol3/papers.cfm?abstract_id=2593629.

have confronted, are confronting, or will confront the risk of capture or death in combat.

Because Hamas well understands this particular characteristic of its Israeli foe, it employs an extensive network of infiltration tunnels and masks its fighters among the civilian population close to Israeli communities in an effort to surprise and overwhelm isolated IDF positions. Therefore the IDF places a high priority on the destruction of tunnels and the infrastructure that supports them, and is willing to operate aggressively both by ground and by air to root out Hamas fighters from the civilian population among which they hide. Strikes on tunnel entrances, on cement plants that Israel claims are used to construct the tunnels, and on Hamas concentrations in civilian settings sometimes lead outside observers to question the degree to which Israel honors the principle of distinction, the rule of proportionality, and the requirement to take precautions in attack.

Professors Schmitt and Merriam hereby identify three factors that are unique to Israel and that impact the internal environment of Israeli mentality, and *that therefore create a standard in the application of the laws of war for Israel that could be different if the same laws were applied to another party.* Here are the three factors, according to the professors:

1. The *"Israeli population views itself under siege"*: This is not just an external view, but rather is the internal environment – the way the Israelis view their world. According to Professors Schmitt and Merriam, this internal understanding will justify attacks by Israel against rockets and rocketry infrastructure that might entail civilian casualties "that may strike outside observers as potentially excessive" if the same attacks had been made by parties who do not view themselves as under siege.

2. *Israel's "acute aversion" to casualties*: Israel has a very high aversion to casualties, which is derived, according to the professors, from the nearly universal conscription of the IDF. Hamas understands this unusually high aversion of the Israelis, and exploits it by acting, through tunnels, to target and overwhelm small army units. The implication from the professors, not stated but clearly implied, is that attacks against small IDF units, even if

successful, can have no impact on the result of the war, but such attacks are planned and executed by Hamas for psychological, not military, reasons. The Israelis, understanding this, target the tunnels in ways that make sense for the Israelis but which others might question under the laws of war. Since the professors justify Israeli targeting practices in the Third Gaza War, it may be understood that they support the Israeli view – that is, the internal reality, i.e., high aversion to casualties, can justify actions that might not be justified for other parties in other contexts.

3. *Israel's "pervasive fear" of losing soldiers to captivity*: Israel also has a "pervasive fear" of soldiers being taken captive, and this, according to the professors, for two reasons – first, the captives may be used as "strategic leverage" against Israel, and second, again the conscript army. In this context, an interesting question is the legality of the IDF's "Hannibal Directive," which allows intense bombardment of an area to prevent the capture of a soldier (or to enable the return of a seized soldier). This question is not discussed at all in the short summary, and is mentioned only in passing in the twenty-page article, but is discussed in depth in the eighty-eight-page article. The Hannibal Directive was allegedly invoked by Colonel Ofer Winter during the Third Gaza War, in an attempt to return the seized soldier Lieutenant Hadar Goldin. The professors do not render a final decision on the Hannibal Directive in the case of Lieutenant Goldin, but they state that while the Hannibal Directive does not (indeed it cannot) "dispense with the rule of proportionality or any other...[legal] norm [of war],"[296] the directive "relaxes the rules of engagement in these cases [and thereby] demonstrates the military advantage the IDF attributes to keeping its soldiers out of enemy hands."[297]

Although, as noted, the professors do not express an opinion about the

---

[296] Schmitt and Merriam, "Tyranny of Context," 129.

[297] Ibid. It should be noted that upon recommendation of the Israel State Comptroller, IDF chief of staff Eizenkot revoked the Hannibal Directive in June 2016. The army is currently considering possible revisions, and is expected to issue a new anti-kidnapping directive that will be clearer in its formulation and that will specifically integrate the principles of international law. See Amos Harel, "Israel's Military Chief Orders to Revoke Controversial 'Hannibal' Directive," *Haaretz*, June 28, 2016, available at http://www.haaretz.com/israel-news/.premium-1.727479.

Hannibal Directive, they do reference the "relative values placed by each adversary on particular points of political and military objectives," which lead to "the manner in which combat operations are conducted to achieve them [the objectives of each adversary]."[298] All of this simply illustrates the principle, stated by von Clausewitz, that war is an interaction, "always the collision of two living forces."[299]

I am in general agreement with the professors that the Israelis feel "under siege," and that they are highly averse to both casualties and captives. I agree also that the aversion to casualties stems, in part, from the conscripted nature of the army, but I think far more important, not mentioned by the professors, are the ever-present thoughts of religion (particularly the great value placed on human life by the Jewish religion) and of the Holocaust memory. Similarly, the pervasive fear that soldiers may be seized stems in part from the conscript army and the desire not to relinquish strategic leverage, as the professors noted, but even more so, in my opinion, from the near-mystical belief in the obligation not to lose a comrade. In my opinion, this belief derives primarily from the memory of the Holocaust and the feeling that, ultimately, the Jews can rely only on themselves.[300]

The general theme presented by Professors Schmitt and Merriam was challenged by two Israeli academics: Amichai Cohen, dean of the Law Faculty at the Ono Academic College, Israel, and Yuval Shany, dean of the Law Faculty at the Hebrew University in Jerusalem.[301] Professors Cohen and Shany challenge the theme in two ways:

One idea in the Schmitt-Merriam publications, according to Professors Cohen and Shany, is that the factors used in proportionality (P) are

---

[298] Ibid., 58.

[299] Ibid.

[300] The obligation of loyalty to one's comrades inheres in all armies, but even more so in the IDF, as implied (although not stated explicitly) by Professors Schmitt and Merriam. It is my firm opinion, although of course others may disagree, that it is the memory of the Holocaust that causes this extreme loyalty in the IDF and throughout Israeli society.

[301] Cohen and Shany's challenge to the Schmitt-Merriam model appears in "Contextuality Proportionality Analysis? A Response to Schmitt and Merriam on Israel's Targeting Practices," *Just Security* (online publication), May 7, 2015, available at https://www.justsecurity.org/22786/contextualizing-proportionality-analysis-response-schmitt-merriam/.

broad strategic considerations, such as the effect on Israel's siege mentality. There are four problems with this idea, according to Professors Cohen and Shany:

1. Proportionality analysis is already difficult. The factors proposed here are abstract, indirect, and non-military. The addition of factors such as the "Israeli siege mentality" would make a proportionality analysis "hopelessly ambiguous."

2. This idea confuses "*jus ad bellum*" and "*jus in bello*." The psychological threat posed by a rocket infrastructure may be a reason for going to war ("*jus ad bellum*"), but it is an inappropriate consideration in the conduct of war ("*jus in bello*").

3. The introduction of broad strategic considerations necessarily hampers soldiers in their planning of operations, particularly in the application of the proportionality principle to decide whether the operation may proceed, and if so, how. The use of such broad strategic considerations would unduly burden the planning of operations.

4. There is no evidence that the strategic threat of Hamas rockets caused any change in the proportionality analysis of the IDF. In fact, the highly effective defensive weapon, the Iron Dome anti-rocket system, suggests that if there is any change in Israel's proportionality analysis to attack the Hamas rocket system, the change would seem to suggest a lower need of attack rather than a heightened need as implied by Schmitt-Merriam.

A second idea in the Schmitt-Merriam publications, according to Professors Cohen and Shany, is that culture-specific factors – in this case Israeli aversion to casualties and to captives – may impact the proportionality analysis. To add such factors would, according to Professors Cohen and Shany, open the door to cultural relativism. This would cause proportionality analysis to be much more subjective, less predictable, more complicated, and possibly unequal (in that different parties, using different culture-specific factors, would arrive at different conclusions). Professors Cohen and Shany question why a civilian population should bear the burden of a more complicated proportionality analysis being conducted by an opposing army.

Professors Cohen and Shany then summarize as follows:

In short, we believe that a contextualized proportionally analysis framework, which incorporates broad strategic and cultural sensitivities, risks obfuscating and skewing IHL [international humanitarian law] proportionality analysis.

Four days after publication of the Cohen-Shany response, Professor Schmitt published a counterresponse.[302] In this counterresponse, Professor Schmitt maintained the following:

1. Israel's enemies, Hamas and Hezbollah, can strike Israel's population centers with rockets. Hamas exploits this ability by rocketing Israeli civilians, in order to offset Hamas's own conventional weakness and to exploit what Hamas perceives as an Israeli weakness. By this action, Hamas raises the military advantage for Israel of attacking Hamas rocket infrastructure, because stopping attacks on civilians is a legitimate military objective. Further, these attacks by Hamas are intended to spread terror among Israeli civilians, and stopping terror is also a legitimate military objective.

2. Israel has a strong aversion to both casualties and captives, derived in part from the frequency of combat in which Israel is engaged, the large-scale conscription of the population into the IDF, and Israel's inability to sustain heavy casualties due to the small size of its population.[303] Hamas, which in a conventional battle would lose catastrophically, tries to exploit the Israeli aversion, both by attacking isolated IDF outposts and by trying to snatch

---

[302] Michael Schmitt, "*The Relationship Between Context and Proportionality: A Reply to Cohen and Shany*," May 11, 2015, *Just Security* (online publication), available at https://www.justsecurity.org/22948/response-cohen-shany/.

[303] In fact, "frequency of combat" was not discussed in the prior Schmitt-Merriam publications, although it seems to make sense in this context. Conscription is very widespread, but it is not "universal" nor even "near-universal." The current conscription rate in Israel is running at 50 percent of eligible men and women in the 2015–2016 cohorts, and this is expected to fall to about 40 percent in the cohorts in the decade of the 2020s. Nevertheless, I think the more general point that Professors Schmitt and Merriam have made is correct, namely, that almost every Jewish family in Israel has a blood relation who is in, or who has been in, or who will be in military service. However, I also believe, contrary to the opinion expressed by Professors Schmitt and Merriam, that the main sources of aversion to casualties and captives are primarily found not in the army, but rather in the memory of the Holocaust and in Judaism's core values (in particular, the value of life, and the great need for freedom). That is my opinion, as I discussed in section III of chapter 1.

IDF soldiers. In an asymmetric battle such as the one waged between Hamas and Israel, the seizure of enemy soldiers yields a great military advantage.[304] Since the seizure of Israeli soldiers is clearly a military advantage for Hamas, therefore the opposite – that is, foiling seizure attempts – must constitute a great military advantage for Israel. According to Professor Schmitt,

> [I]t is not the Israeli population's perception of the operation that affects military advantage, but rather that of Hamas or Hezbollah.... I struggle to see how denying the enemy [that is, Hamas or Hezbollah] an avowed military aim achieved by military means cannot constitute military advantage [to the Israelis].

In general, Professor Schmitt's main thesis in his counterresponse parallels the same argument made in the twenty-page article "Israeli Targeting: A Legal Appraisal"[305] and in the eighty-eight-page article, "The Tyranny of Context: Israeli Targeting Practices in Legal Perspective"[306] To the best of

---

[304] The reference to "asymmetric battle" is Professor Schmitt's language, not mine, but I agree with him, and I repeat that these asymmetric conflicts will be the dominant form of war for all Western societies throughout the twenty-first century.

[305] War is "the interaction between adversaries" (Schmitt and Merriam, "Israeli Targeting: A Legal Appraisal," 18, second full paragraph).

[306] Professors Schmitt and Merriam ("Tyranny of Context," 58) quote the great military theorist von Clausewitz as stating that war "is always the collision of two living forces" (Carl von Clausewitz, On War, translated from the German and edited by Michael Howard and Peter Parent [Princeton: Princeton University Press, 1976]). From this statement, the professors conclude that war is an

> interaction between adversaries ... [that] impacts the relative values placed by each adversary on particular political and military objectives and, accordingly, the manner in which combat operations are conducted to achieve them.... [Further, this principle applies also to] both Israel and its adversaries. ("Tyranny of Context," 58, first and second paragraphs)

In short, since war involves "living forces" and their "interaction," objectives and methods of war will change depending on the nature of the parties fighting. By implication, the legal results should also be influenced by these party-specific considerations.

This argument – that war involves a duality of "living forces" whose interaction will affect both the context of the war and its legal consequences – does not appear clearly in the brief summary "A Legal and Operational Assessment of Israel's Targeting Practices." Its absence from the summary may be part of the reason for the dispute between Schmitt-Merriam and Cohen-Shany.

my understanding, this is the Schmitt-Merriam basic argument: Although the principles of waging war – necessity, distinction, proportionality, shielding, and others – are fixed, their application in specific wars and in specific situations in specific wars will be affected by the context of the war, and particularly by the parties, by the parties' relative positions, and by their relative goals. I am in substantial agreement with what I perceive to be the Schmitt-Merriam basic argument. For that reason, I believe that the internal environment of combatants is relevant, and I have therefore discussed, in chapter 1, Israel's internal environment.

As with many legal issues, however, the "right" and the "wrong" are not always clear. Professors Cohen and Shany fear, rightly, that introducing into the calculations of a party at war factors such as "broad strategic sensitivities" and "cultural sensitivities" (what I have called the "internal environment") can easily degenerate into a cultural relativism that would sweep away all of the principles of war. While this fear is legitimate and well founded, nevertheless in my opinion one cannot arrive at a conclusion that the parties' backgrounds and experience are irrelevant. War is not between machines, it is between peoples, and human factors will always play a part. In the end, there must be a balance between the application of the universal principles of war (such as necessity, distinction, proportionality, and shielding) on the one hand, and subjective human intention on the other hand.

Perhaps the solution to this problem lies in the application of the oldest principles of criminal law – *actus reus* (literally, "guilty act," meaning there is no crime without an action that is objectively judged to be "criminal") and *mens rea* (literally "guilty mind," meaning that there is no crime unless there is also a criminal intent, although the intent of the party may be inferred from the circumstances). Whether actions are "criminal" or not will be determined on a case-by-case basis, decided possibly by a judicial authority such as the International Criminal Court, but here, too, the intent (or "*mens*") of the charged party will bear on that party's guilt or innocence, as in all criminal cases. For that reason also, Israel's internal environment is relevant to the application of the laws of war.

Glossary

(Including Abbreviations and Acronyms)

ACCOUNTABILITY: If a semi-autonomous (levels II or III) or fully autonomous (level IV) machine executes an action – which could be anything
from spying or theft of information to killing an enemy combatant –
who is responsible for that action? Is it the designer of the machine? The
manufacturer? The direct operator? The person who gave the command
to launch the machine? Questions of human accountability for machine
action are not entirely resolved in the laws of war. See "Machine Autonomy." Compare "Attribution Problem."

ACTUS REUS: Latin for "guilty act," *actus reus* is a concept in criminal law
according to which there cannot be a crime without an action that is
objectively judged to be "criminal." However, a "crime" requires both a
guilty act (*actus reus*) and a guilty intent (*mens rea*) – if either is missing,
there is no crime. A guilty act, but without criminal intent, may be a
mistake or negligence, but it is not criminal. Conversely, a guilty intent
without a guilty act cannot be a crime, since people are not punished
for intents not acted upon.

A major question in the laws of war is whether the exact same laws
must be applied in exactly the same way for all parties, or whether there
may be a difference based upon the internal environment of the alleged
war criminal. As to the *actus reus*, guilty act, there is no difference – all
parties are judged according to the same standard, and in the same way.
As to *mens rea*, guilty mind (that is, criminal intent), the conclusion is

much less clear. On the one hand, the laws of war must be applied in an equivalent manner. Otherwise, there is a risk that cultural relativism will render the laws of war meaningless (since each party will claim that different laws apply to that party). On the other hand, parties to a conflict are human, and they will have different perceptions based on who they are and their history. These human differences should be considered in some way when judging a party's possible guilt for war crimes. This book includes, in section III of chapter 1, a discussion of the "internal environment of Israeli Jews," on the assumption that different peoples may be viewed differently under the laws of war. However, this assumption is disputed between Professors Schmitt and Merriam on the one hand (who appear to support the assumption), and Professors Cohen and Shany on the other hand (who appear to reject the assumption), as discussed in the appendix. See "Cultural Relativism," "Internal Environment of Israeli Jews," and *"Mens Rea."*

ANTICIPATORY SELF-DEFENSE: This term, which is also called "anticipatory attack," or "preemption," has at least two meanings. First, it may be the action by a state that, in the face of a clear and immediate military threat, acts first and with the intention of thwarting that threat. Although not explicitly included in "the inherent right of self-defence" recognized by Article 51 of the UN Charter, commentators have suggested that Article 51 must include a right of anticipatory self-defense in the face of an overwhelming, possibly even an existential, threat.[307] However, is there a right of anticipatory self-defense when the attack is not kinetic (that is, not physical destruction) but rather cyber? That is a complicated legal question for which there are as yet no clear legal answers. See "Cyber Attack."

The second meaning of "anticipatory self-defense" relates to lawfare; it is a strategy used by organizations such as the Israel Law Center to anticipate where anti-Israel lawfare activists will attack, and to thwart

---

[307] See, for example, Leo Van den hole, "Anticipatory Self-Defence Under International Law," *American University International Law Review* 19, no. 1, art. 4 (2003): 69–106, particularly the conclusion at pp. 105–6, http://digitalcommons.wcl.american.edu/cgi/viewcontent.cgi?article=1160&context=auilr.

or blunt the attack by launching a similar attack first. For example, in anticipation that activists may attack Israel under Article 8, section 2(b)(viii) of the Rome Statute regarding direct "or indirect" transfer of population into a territory, the Israel Law Center has filed a complaint with the ICC against Turkey's occupation of northeast Cyprus, and may file multiple complaints against alleged occupiers in Asia, Europe, the Middle East, North Africa, South America, and Antarctica. If the ICC chooses to deal with a complaint against Israel, the ICC will know, for a certainty, that every action or decision it takes will be echoed back in complaints against multiple parties from around the world. This strategy is not intended to stop the ICC from investigating Israeli activity, which cannot be done; rather, it sends a clear message to the ICC: "If you, the ICC, choose to act in an unfair and discriminatory manner, your actions will be published widely and they will bring disrepute on a court that has still not gained full international acceptance." See "Israel Law Center."

ARPANET: An abbreviation of "Advanced Research Projects Agency Network," this was a multi-computer network characterized by data packet switching (not circuit switching) and the TCP/IP computer protocol. The network was established in 1969, and developed, eventually, into the Internet. It may therefore be said that ARPANET was the precursor to the entire cyber world – cyber attacks, cyber mercenaries, cyber operations, cyber shielding, cyber tools, etc. ARPANET was funded by DARPA. See "Cyber Attack," "Cyber Mercenaries," "Cyber Operation," "Cyber Space," "Cyber Shielding," "Cyber Warfare," and "DARPA."

ASYMMETRIC WARFARE: See "Symmetric versus Asymmetric Warfare."

ATTRIBUTION PROBLEM: One of the advantages of a cyber attack is that the victim often cannot know who exactly launched the attack, and hence is unable to respond effectively. Even if an attack may be identified by source location, the victim cannot always know if the attacker was a private party, a non-state armed group, or the government of a state. This lack of knowledge, which is called the "attribution problem," may be exacerbated if the attacker employs cyber mercenaries to create the attack. If an attacker makes specific efforts to obscure its identity, this is often known as "masking." See "Cyber Attack" and "Cyber Mercenary." See also "Back-hack" and "Hack-back." Compare "Accountability."

BACKBONE NETWORK: A general network that provides a communicative link to various sub-networks. If the backbone links both military sub-networks and civilian sub-networks, it becomes an example of "dual-use infrastructure." If the backbone network is attacked in order to harm the military sub-network, there may be collateral damage to the civilian sub-network. Even if the attack is launched solely at the military sub-network, the civilian sub-network may also suffer, because of the linkage of the two sub-networks. See "Cascading Effects/Cascading Failure," "Collateral Damage," "Critical Infrastructure," "Cyber Shielding," and "Dual-Use Infrastructure."

BACK-HACK: The process of determining that a cyber attack has been made, and then using bits of digital information left by the attacker to identify the source of the attack. Back-hack helps resolve the attribution problem by identifying the source of the attack, but it does *not* include retaliation by the victim of the attack. See "Attribution Problem." Compare "Hack-back."

BDS: See "Boycott, Divestment, and Sanctions."

BILL OF ATTAINDER: A statute or other legal command that is directed specifically at one person, or one entity, or a small group of persons or entities, entitling the legal authority to criminalize, penalize, seize assets from, imprison, or even execute the targeted individual or group, often without trial or any right to present a legal defense. Such bills may name individuals, although more often they define the affected person or group such that the intent is very clear. These bills are at the very heart of despotic government – if they are allowed in a state or territory, no one is safe from the government. They are outlawed by the US Constitution and by the constitutions of all fifty US states. Article 8, section 2(b)(viii) of the Rome Statute creates a new standard previously unknown in international law, and is, in fact, a bill of attainder directed specifically against Israel. See "Double Standard," "*Ex Post Facto*," "Population Transfer," and "Rome Statute."

BOYCOTT, DIVESTMENT, AND SANCTIONS (BDS): A political movement to place economic pressure on Israel in order to force it to make political and territorial concessions to the Palestinians, without receiving anything in return. This is one form of "extralegal attack." Noam Chomsky has opined that there is no governmental "sanction" of Israel, neither by nations nor by international bodies, so the movement should more properly be called the BD (Boycott and Divestments) movement, or perhaps the BDI (Boycott and Divestments against Israel) movement. See "Extralegal Attacks."

C3R: An acronym for "clarity, capability, credibility, reward." See "Deterrence."

CASCADING EFFECTS/CASCADING FAILURE: When an infrastructure system or network is composed of various pieces, an attack on one piece, indeed the failure of one piece for any reason, can have cascading effects throughout the system. As one piece fails, other pieces try to pick up the work of the failed piece, but if these pieces are then overloaded, they, too, will fail. In this sense, "cascading effects" may involve not just a string of minor failures, but indeed a magnification of the effect, so that even a small failure in one piece of the entire network may snowball into catastrophic consequences. This is true, for example, of an electricity network – if any part of the network is knocked out, the entire network may fail eventually. This is true also of some transportation networks – for example, if one major airport is shut down in the United States, the effects will almost certainly spread throughout the system. In order for there to be a cascading failure of the entire network, or indeed cascading effects of any kind, the pieces of the network must be linked and working together. Cascading effects can occur for either critical or non-critical infrastructure. See "Critical Infrastructure," "Interdependent Infrastructure," and "Infrastructure."

COLLATERAL DAMAGE: Another name for "civilian harm," including harm both to civilians and to civilian assets (such as buildings, vehicles, electronics, etc.). When there is a physical attack, the resulting "collateral damage" is relatively clear in most cases. Conversely, in a cyber attack, the collateral damage is not always clear, and might include damage to civilian databases or to some kind of infrastructure. Collateral damage is part of the main legal principles of distinction (D) and proportionality (P). See "Distinction (D)," "Infrastructure," and "Proportionality (P)."

COMPLEMENTARITY PRINCIPLE: The jurisdiction of the International Criminal Court is not "primary" but rather "complementary." Primary jurisdiction resides with nation states and with international legal bodies responsible for prosecuting the various crimes set forth in the Rome Statute. The ICC will not investigate or take any other steps regarding a case that has been handled, or that is being handled, or that the ICC believes will be handled, by some body with primary jurisdiction. For that reason, countries can legitimately avoid cases before the ICC by investigating, and if necessary prosecuting, possible crimes under the Rome Statute. See "Crimes under the Rome Statute," "International Criminal Court," and "Rome Statute."

CONVENTIONAL WARFARE: See "Non-Conventional Weapons" and "Symmetric versus Asymmetric Warfare."

CRIMES UNDER THE ROME STATUTE: Article 5 of the Rome Statute lists the crimes over which the ICC may exercise jurisdiction, including "genocide" (defined further in Article 6), "crimes against humanity" (defined further in Article 7), "war crimes" (defined further in Article 8), and the "crime of aggression" (defined further in Article 8 *bis*). By Article 17 of the Rome Statute, the court's jurisdiction is further restricted by the complementarity principle, and also by a requirement that a case must be "of sufficient gravity" to be investigated and prosecuted by the court. See "Complementarity Principle," "International Criminal Court," "Rome Statute," and "War Crimes."

CRITICAL INFRASTRUCTURE: "Infrastructure" of a country that is extremely important to the functioning of that country. The exact parameters of "critical infrastructure" are not clear. At a minimum, the term includes infrastructure whose shutdown might cause widespread death or destruction – nuclear facilities, dams, hospitals, electricity networks, gas pipelines, and water networks. A broader definition would include also networks whose shutdown might not create mass killing or destruction, but that would be extremely discomforting and expensive, such as major banks and traffic systems. An even broader definition would include key cultural and historical sites, such as museums, national archives, and national monuments. The hacking of the computers of the US Democratic National Committee in July 2016 has raised the issue of whether an electoral system may also be part of a nation's critical infrastructure. Anyone who deliberately attacks critical infrastructure violates the military principles of necessity and distinction. In addition, even if an attacker focuses solely on military infrastructure, critical civilian infrastructure may also be harmed if it is linked to or interdependent with military infrastructure. See "Backbone Network," "Cascading Effects/Cascading Failure," "Collateral Damage," "Critical Infrastructure," "Cyber Shielding," "Infrastructure," and "Interdependent Infrastructure."

CULTURAL RELATIVISM: In the sense intended in this book, this is the concept that if the internal environment is introduced as one factor in judging the legality of military operations, all principles in the laws of war will be swept away by an excuse that says, in effect, "The party acted as it did because of its culture, and therefore had no choice." This is a legitimate concern against the proposition that the laws of war must be interpreted in light of each party's particular culture and understanding. The question of the degree, if any, to which national culture is relevant to the laws of war, is discussed in section III of chapter 1, and in the appendix. See "Internal Environment of Israeli Jews." Compare "Moral Relativity."

CUSTOMARY INTERNATIONAL LAW: One of the two main sources for international law generally, and for the laws of war specifically, this is the law as determined by the way nations act. In some cases, customary international law is mandatory and cannot be disavowed by any party – that is true, for example, of the Martens Clause of the Hague Conventions of 1899 and 1907. In other cases, customary international law is binding because a state, by its words or actions, has explicitly or implicitly adopted that law. For example, although almost all countries have adopted Geneva Conventions I–IV of 1949, many countries have not adopted Geneva Additional Protocols I and II of 1977. The proportionality principle, one of the four main principles of the laws of war, does not appear in the Geneva Conventions but only in Additional Protocol I. Nevertheless, the proportionality principle has been universally adopted as a matter of binding customary international law. See "Sources for the Laws of War" and "Treaties."

CYBER ATTACK: Although it is generally understood that "cyber attack" is related to the use of computer and communication systems by one party against another, there is not general agreement on what exactly constitutes a "cyber attack." There are two general theories about this, according to which a cyber attack is either (1) only an action in which there is actual, or at least reasonably expected, damage to people or physical assets (where databases and information are not "physical assets"); or (2) any cyber intrusion of any kind, whether or not there was intent to damage, or actual damage to, anyone or any asset of any kind (although cyber espionage, where there is a specific intent *to avoid* damage, might not be included under this second theory). Further, even if there is a "cyber attack" under one of these two general theories, this does not mean that any response is justified, since the proportionality principle still applies to every response. The opposite of a cyber attack is a kinetic attack. Compare "Kinetic Attack."

The process of a "cyber attack" or a "cyber operation" is generally agreed to have three stages. First, the attacker "identifies the vulnerability" by finding a flaw in a computer system. Second, the attacker "writes the exploit" by writing software code to get into the targeted computer system and achieve the goal of the operation. Third, the attacker "weaponizes the exploit" by introducing the malicious code into the target computer system. In many operations involving cyber mercenaries, the cyber mercenaries will identify the vulnerability and write the exploit, but the client will then weaponize the exploit. See "Cyber Mercenaries," and "Zero Days."

CYBER MERCENARIES: Also called "cyber soldiers of fortune," these are people who offer to create cyber attacks in exchange for money.

CYBER OPERATION: See "Cyber Attack."

CYBER SHIELDING: The design of a computer network such that military operations are interwoven with civilian operations, so that any attack on the military part of the network will automatically cause collateral damage to the civilian part. In essence, the designer is shielding the military operations with a civilian sub-network. See "Collateral Damage," "Distinction (D)," "Proportionality (P)," and "Shielding (S)."

CYBER SOLDIERS OF FORTUNE: See "Cyber Mercenaries."

CYBER SPACE: Not a physical place or location, but rather an interweaving of three layers – the physical layer (hardware), the logic layer (software), and the data layer (information). "Cyber attacks" are said to occur in or through cyber space, in which the attacker uses the physical and logic layers (hardware and software, respectively) to attack the data layer (information).

CYBER WARFARE: A military operation or conflict in which a cyber attack occurs. See "Cyber Attack."

DARK NET: This is a group of websites that have or that share privately encrypted servers and that therefore cannot be monitored by any government. Owners of dark net websites are said to use the dark net to buy and sell illegal goods (such as weapons, drugs, and identity documents) and illegal services (such as creating cyber attacks). It is believed that ISIS uses the dark net to distribute attack plans to terrorists. See "Cyber Attack," "Cyber Mercenaries."

DARPA: An acronym for the "Defense Advanced Research Projects Agency," which is an agency of the US Department of Defense responsible for the development of emerging technologies for use by the military. This is not an R&D agency, but rather a funder of specific R&D projects that are considered to have potentially high military value. One of DARPA's most notable investments, applicable to both the military and civilians sectors, was ARPANET, the precursor to the Internet. See "ARPANET."

DETERRENCE: Deterrence in general is actions that cause others to avoid or discontinue a certain activity. The political context of this term includes, as one example, Israel's successful efforts thus far to discourage attacks by ISIS, Hezbollah, and other potential enemies in the region. One theory of deterrence, pioneered by Graham T. Allison of the Kennedy School of Government at Harvard University, may be summarized by the acronym "C3R," standing for "clarity, capability, credibility, and reward." A state may implement a successful deterrence by clearly communicating activities that it will not accept, demonstrating capability to punish the deterred party, achieving credibility in the eyes of the deterred party that the state will act to prevent or punish proscribed activities, and offering some kind of reward if the deterred party abstains from these activities.

For example, Israel has clearly communicated to ISIS and other groups fighting in Syria that Israel will not accept attacks against it and will not accept such groups holding ABC (atomic, biological, chemical) weapons. The deterred groups believe Israel has the capability to harm them greatly, and in addition they believe that Israel will act if the groups violate Israel's warning. In addition, these groups benefit in that they know that if they forbear from engaging in such activities, Israel will not attack them, and in some cases Israel may provide medical care to their wounded fighters, food, medical supplies, and possibly even intelligence. The terrorist groups are deterred because they see that the forbidden activities will cause them great suffering, whereas forbearance will cause them to receive important rewards. The situation in Syria is currently chaotic, and it is extremely doubtful that Israel could eliminate all of the terrorist groups fighting there, but Israel can successfully deter such groups through a clearly communicated and believable C3R deterrence policy.

DISTINCTION (D): One of the four main principles in the laws of war. It applies to attackers (and is not relevant for defenders). This is the second legal question that must be asked by a planner of a military operation, after the first question of necessity. The question of distinction is "Are there are any civilians [that is, non-military] people or civilian assets [such as buildings] within the area of the operation?" If the answer is no, then the discussion is over. If the answer is yes, then the military planner must ask: "Is it possible to plan steps that can achieve the military objective [that is, meet the necessity], but also eliminate the threat to civilians?" If the answer is yes, then the operation may be planned, but only with those additional steps. If the answer is "No, there are civilians in the area, and some may be expected to be harmed," then according to the proportionality principle, the military necessity must be compared against the expected civilian harm. See "Collateral Damage" and "Principles in the Laws of War." Compare "Necessity (N)," "Proportionality (P)," and "Shielding (S)."

DOUBLE STANDARD: A term that is related to, but distinct from, a "bill of attainder." With a bill of attainder, a different law is created specifically against a targeted person or group. With a double standard, there is only one law applicable to all parties, but it is interpreted or enforced in a discriminatory manner. Part of the general approach of the Israel Law Center is to file complaints or other legal actions against persons under a law that is being enforced against Israel in a discriminatory manner. In response, either the legal authority will enforce the law fairly (in a non-discriminatory manner, equally against all parties), or the legal authority and the law will be seen as "shams" intended to hurt a specific party. This was the Israel Law Center's approach, for example, to Javier Solana, as discussed in chapter 2, and to Turkey's occupation of northeastern Cyprus, as discussed in chapter 3. See "Bill of Attainder," "*Ex Post Facto*," "International Criminal Court," and "Israel Law Center."

DRONE: See "Unmanned Aerial Vehicle."

DRONE SWARM: See "Unmanned Aerial Vehicle."

DUAL-USE INFRASTRUCTURE: Infrastructure that serves both military and civilian functions. The civilian part may be "critical" or non-critical. Dual-use infrastructure may be a backbone network that serves military and civilian sub-networks, or one communication network, for example a cellular telephone network, with both military and civilian customers. It is illegal to attack dual-use infrastructure with the intent of harming the civilian component, since that would violate the distinction principle. Dual-use infrastructure might be attacked in order to harm the military component, but the distinction principle would require the planner of the attack to distinguish possible civilian harm and the proportionality principle would require the planner of the attack to weigh the military objective to be achieved versus the likely civilian damage to be caused. See "Backbone Network," "Cascading Effects/ Cascading Failure," "Collateral Damage," "Cyber Shielding," "Critical Infrastructure," and "Infrastructure."

EX POST FACTO: A Latin phrase meaning, literally, "after the fact." This is a law or other legal standard that is created after some act, and is intended to criminalize the act retroactively. *Ex post facto* laws are indicative of a despotic government, since the ability of a government to retroactively outlaw or punish activity that was entirely legal when performed means that no one can know if or when a certain action may become illegal. A bill of attainder, which is directed at a certain person or group, may also be *ex post facto*, if the bill retroactively criminalizes the action of the targeted person or group. See "Bill of Attainder" and "Double Standard."

EXTRALEGAL ATTACKS: These are attacks by legal or political activists that are outside the traditional legal structure. For example, BDS is a form of extralegal attack whose sole purpose is to condemn and isolate Israel. Universal jurisdiction is also an example of an extralegal attack, but it is substantially different than BDS. Whereas BDS is an attack against the State of Israel, universal jurisdiction is an attack against individual soldiers and politicians. Further, today there is no BDS, or anything like it, against any country except Israel. In contrast, universal jurisdiction, although it has been targeted particularly against Israelis, has been used or threatened also against citizens of Argentina, the People's Republic of China, Spain, the United States, and others. See "Boycott, Divestment, and Sanctions" and "Universal Jurisdiction."

FATAH (PRONOUNCED "FA' TACH"): The largest of the armed groups that make up the PLO. See "Palestine Liberation Organization."

FIRST GAZA WAR: Used in this book to mean the first war between Hamas and Israel, which occurred in 2008–2009, and which was called "Operation Cast Lead" by the Israelis.

FLOTILLA I: Used in this book to mean the attempt by multiple ships in 2010 to break the Israeli blockade against the import of offensive weapons to Gaza. Several ships were boarded and stopped by the Israeli navy on May 31, 2010. On the largest ship, the *Mavi Marmara*, there was a physical confrontation between armed passengers and Israeli soldiers, resulting in several deaths and injuries. See "Flotilla II," "Flotilla III," and "Humanitarian Aid."

FLOTILLA II: Used in this book to mean the attempt by multiple ships in 2011 to break the Israeli blockade against the import of offensive weapons to Gaza. Ten ships intended to sail. However, due to a combination of political pressure by multiple countries and a very creative legal campaign by the Israel Law Center, only one small ship sailed; it was easily intercepted and stopped on July 19, 2011. The defeat of Flotilla II was one of the great achievements of the Israel Law Center. See "Flotilla I," "Flotilla III," and "Humanitarian Aid."

FLOTILLA III: Used in this book to mean the attempt by multiple ships in 2015 to break the Israeli blockade against the import of offensive weapons to Gaza. One Swedish fishing trawler named the *Marianne of Gothenburg* and three smaller Greek ships sailed to break the blockade, but the Greek ships quickly turned back. The Swedish ship was intercepted and stopped on June 29, 2015. Although the activists on the ship contended that they were bringing "humanitarian aid" to Gaza, including the ship itself, in fact all of the aid appeared to be contained in two shipping cartons, while the ship was purchased with borrowed money and had against it a bank lien. In comparison to Flotilla I with its tragic end, Flotilla III was a farce. See "Flotilla I," "Flotilla II," and "Humanitarian Aid."

HACK-BACK: After a cyber attack has been attributed to a particular party, the original victim hacks the aggressor in retaliation for the original attack. This is one step beyond back-hack (which only identifies the aggressor but does not take retaliatory action). However, whereas back-hack (i.e., the identification of a cyber aggressor) is clearly legal, hack-back (i.e., counter-attack against the aggressor) is possibly illegal. See "Attribution Problem." Compare "Back-hack."

HAMAS: A spin-off of Egypt's Muslim Brotherhood, this is a radical polit-ical-military organization that currently controls Gaza, that violently opposes Israel, and that has been involved in three wars against Israel since coming to control Gaza in 2007.

HANNIBAL DIRECTIVE: Sometimes called the "Hannibal Protocol" or the "Hannibal Procedure," this was a standing order of the IDF to permit actions intended to either prevent the capture of a soldier or to enable return of a soldier seized by the enemy. The order was invoked very rarely, and was allegedly applied in the Third Gaza War to return the seized soldier Lieutenant Hadar Goldin. In the case of Lieutenant Goldin, he was taken through a tunnel deep into Gaza, and the IDF allegedly bombed known outlets of that tunnel with the sole purpose of reversing the capture. The Hannibal Directive is discussed by Professors Schmitt and Merriam in their article "The Tyranny of Context: Israeli Targeting Practices in Legal Perspective," as noted in the appendix. Pursuant to a recommendation of the Israel State Comptroller, the IDF chief of staff revoked the Hannibal Directive in June 2016, but it is expected that a new directive will be issued that will clarify and possibly limit features of the old directive. See "Rules of Engagement" and "Proportionality (P)."

HUMANITARIAN AID: For each of the flotillas discussed in this book, Flo-tilla I of 2010, Flotilla II of 2011, and Flotilla III of 2015, activists stated that the purpose of the flotilla was to bring "humanitarian aid" to the people of Gaza. This was a lie in all cases, since the main intent of each flotilla, as stated by organizers of the flotillas, was to demonstrate that Israel's blockade against aggressive weapons could be breached, and in that way to break the blockade. The ships of Flotilla I did, apparently, have some humanitarian aid, but the organizers rejected Israel's proposal to transship all such aid from Ashdod harbor to Gaza. It is not clear whether Flotilla II had any such aid – the sole ship that sailed and was later intercepted had no such aid, but perhaps there was aid on the ships that did not sail. In any case, Israel, Egypt, and Greece each offered to accept the humanitarian aid of Flotilla II and transship it to Gaza, but all three offers were rejected, because the provision of aid was never a serious purpose of Flotilla II. The alleged "humanitarian aid" of Flotilla III was a farce – one (or maybe two) solar panels, one nebulizer, possibly three small containers of drugs (although that is not clear), and a fishing trawler that had been purchased with borrowed money and that was the subject of a bank lien. See "Flotilla I," "Flotilla II," and "Flotilla III."

ICC: See "International Criminal Court."

ICJ: See "International Court of Justice."

IDF: See "Israel Defense Forces."

IHL: See "International Humanitarian Law."

INFRASTRUCTURE: As used in this book, the sum of the social and economic plant of a society, including its ports, communication systems and networks, databases, utility networks (gas, water, electric), banks and financial networks, manufacturing plants, nuclear facilities, dams, transportation networks, hospitals, and the like. Also included is the social and economic plant that is not required to run the society, but is important because it creates national identity or provides for the future, such as schools, universities, monuments, museums, and national archives.

INTERDEPENDENT INFRASTRUCTURE: Multiple pieces of a particular system or pieces of infrastructure that are linked and work together. Utilities (gas, water, and electric) generally include a system in which many of the pieces are interdependent. An interdependent infrastructure is particularly vulnerable to kinetic or cyber attack. See "Cascading Effects/Cascading Failure," "Critical Infrastructure," "Cyber Attack," and "Infrastructure."

INTERNAL ENVIRONMENT OF ISRAELI JEWS: Every people has its own "internal environment," which is the way it perceives and understands reality, based on the people's character and history. The Jews of Israel also have an internal environment, which is based upon, in my opinion, the three thoughts of Judaism, the Israel Defense Forces, and the abandonment of European Jewry by the world during the time of the Holocaust. These three thoughts are ever present in the mind of Israeli Jews, even though they are not always expressed, and they affect the way Israeli Jews react to external effects of war and terrorism. See "*Actus Reus*," "Cultural Relativism," and "*Mens Rea*."

INTERNATIONAL COURT OF JUSTICE (ICJ): Also known as the World Court, the ICJ was created by the United Nations in 1945, and became active in 1946. The ICJ handles two kinds of cases: (1) disputes between member states of the United Nations; and (2) "advisory opinions," which are non-binding judicial opinions on specific questions put to the court by the UN Security Council, the UN General Assembly, or other bodies and agencies of the UN. During its history, the ICJ has handled about 161 cases, with resolutions of about 100 cases including twenty-six advisory opinions. Among the advisory opinions mentioned in this book are the *Legality of the Threat or Use of Nuclear Weapons, Advisory Opinion*, 1996 (generally called the "*Nuclear Weapons* case"), and the *Advisory Opinion Concerning Legal Consequences of the Construction of a Wall in the Occupied Palestinian Territory*, 2004 (generally known as the "*Wall* case"). Only the UN Security Council has the right to enforce an advisory opinion. See "Sources for the Laws of War" and the "*Wall* Case."

INTERNATIONAL CRIMINAL COURT (ICC): A court created in 2002 by the Rome Statute to deal with crimes that are exceptionally serious ("the most serious crimes of international concern," as stated in Article 1 of the statute) and for which there is no other adequate legal remedy. The ICC cannot possibly deal with every crime involving armed conflict, and it does not try to do so. Rather, it attempts to focus on particularly severe cases of genocide, crimes against humanity, war crimes, and crimes of aggression. The goal is not primarily to punish, but rather to deter such behavior in the future, so that potential criminals know they may be subject to liability in a court of last resort. The ICC's jurisdiction is "complementary," which means that the court will not deal with any case for which a national court has rendered, or is in the process of rendering, or is likely to render an adequate investigation and, if necessary, a prosecution.

The ICC has undoubtedly done good work in the few years of its operation, but whether it will eventually be successful is not yet clear – many countries have not adopted the Rome Statute, the number of investigations and prosecutions is considered by some observers to be very low, and thus far all the prosecutions to completion have involved African nationals. According to some commentators, the ICC's ultimate acceptance by the international community may be determined by the way it handles the Israeli-Palestinian dispute. See "Complementarity Principle," "Crimes Under the Rome Statute," and "Rome Statute."

INTERNATIONAL HUMANITARIAN LAW (IHL): A phrase that means exactly the same as "laws of war," and exactly the same as *jus in bello.*" Since this phrase includes the word "humanitarian," it tends to be used by human rights professionals and activists, as well as by people associated with the United Nations and other international bodies. Sometimes it is thought, in error, that IHL seeks to reduce suffering in war, while the "laws of war" seek means to allow attacks. This is simply untrue, since all of these concepts – IHL, laws of war, and *jus in bello* – apply the same principles, require the same decisions, and generate the same post-operation review. It is possible, even likely in some cases, that proponents of "humanitarian law" will judge a military operation more harshly, and interpret the principles in the laws of war more strictly, than would military attorneys or political officials. This difference in judgment, in cases in which it might arise, is a matter of human preference and does not reflect any split or uncertainty in the principles – in all respects, IHL, the laws of war, and *jus in bello* are the same thing. See "Laws of War," "*Jus in Bello,*" and "Principles in the Laws of War." Compare "*Jus ad Bellum.*"

INTERNET OF THINGS (IOT): A network of physical objects (for example, electronic devices, buildings, and vehicles) that have embedded electronics and that are connected to the Internet typically for purposes of measurement or control. As a result of their connectivity to the Internet, such physical objects will be subject to cyber attack, including cyber vandalism, cyber espionage, and cyber seizure of control. The IoT is just beginning now, and as it grows, so, too, will grow the threat from cyber attacks.

IOT: See "Internet of Things."

ISRAEL DEFENSE FORCES (IDF): This term encompasses all branches of Israel's military establishment, including the army, the navy, the air force, and the new cyber corps. The term includes also all military legal functions managed by the military advocate general. The term does not include the Mossad or Shin Bet, which are separate agencies. See "Military Advocate General," "Mossad," and "Shin Bet."

ISRAEL LAW CENTER: Also known as "Shurat HaDin," or "Shurat HaDin – Israel Law Center," this is the leading pro-Israel lawfare NGO active today. A number of its cases are discussed in chapters 2, 3, and 4 of this book. The Israel Law Center's basic approach to lawfare is discussed in "A Summary of Key Points," and may be characterized as (1) creative thinking about problems and potential solutions; (2) intensive research, including work with outside parties as required; (3) an interweaving of law and politics; and (4) a definition of success that recognizes achievement in both the legal and political realms. The name is taken from the Hebrew phrase *"lifnim mi'shurat hadin,"* which means "beyond the letter of the law." See *"Lifnim Mi'shurat HaDin."*

JUS AD BELLUM: Latin for "right to war," this phrase refers to the laws of determining whether a party has the right to go to war. If the party was unjustified in going to war, then by doing so the party is engaged in a "war of aggression," which is a crime. Conversely, a party acting in self-defense is acting legitimately, and is not guilty of a crime. The typical question in the concept of *jus ad bellum* is "What is a war of aggression [which is illegal] and what is an action of self-defense [which is legal]?" That question has arisen in the past, and will almost certainly become very important in the twenty-first century regarding "anticipatory self-defense," particularly in regard to cyber operations – that is, if a country knows it is to be targeted by a cyber attack, may it preempt by attacking first, possibly through a cyber operation? See also "Cyber Warfare," "Cyber Attack," "Laws of War," and "War of Aggression." Compare "*Jus in Bello.*"

JUS IN BELLO: Latin for "right in war," this is a phrase that means exactly the same as "laws of war," and exactly the same as "international humanitarian law." Academics tend to use *jus in bello* rather than the two alternatives, but there is no difference in meaning. *Jus in bello* must be contrasted with *jus ad bellum*, literally "right to war." These phrases both appear and sound similar, but they are fundamentally different: *jus ad bellum* focuses solely on the causes of war and the reasons a party goes to war, while *jus in bello* focuses solely on the way a party may conduct war regardless of the causes for the outbreak of the war or possible justifications for going to war. Two questions are asked of any party involved in armed conflict. First, under the doctrine of *jus ad bellum*: "Does the party have a right to go to war?" Second, under the doctrine of *jus in bello*: "Whether or not the party had a right to engage in war, is the party waging the war in a legal manner?" These two questions must be asked separately, and the answer to the first question must not impact the answer to the second question. By contrast, people with a predilection for one side or the other frequently confuse these two doctrines, by saying, incorrectly, "Our side had the just cause for going to war, so we may do as we wish," or, "Their side had no just reason for going to war, so everything they do in waging war is a war crime." See "Laws of War." Compare "*Jus ad Bellum.*"

KINETIC ATTACK: An attack in the real world, the non-cyber world, with physical weapons such as metal projectiles, causing physical damage to people or physical assets (such as buildings). Compare "Cyber Attack."

LAWFARE: The inventor of the word, Charles Dunlop, Jr., has defined it as "a method of warfare where the law is used as a means of realizing a military objective.... Rather than seeking battlefield victories, *per se*, challengers try to destroy the will to fight by undermining the public support that is indispensable... [to] democracies." Less formally, lawfare may be considered a tool of war, used particularly in asymmetric conflicts, in which a party seeks to embarrass a traditional army in the eyes of the world, subject the army to possible legal liability through the International Criminal Court or universal jurisdiction, and restrict the ability of the army to act or to defend its state. Similarly, the person or people exercising such a tool, frequently an NGO, are termed "lawfare activists."

LAWFARE ACTIVIST: See "Lawfare."

LAW OF ARMED CONFLICT (LOAC): See "Laws of War."

LAWS OF WAR: The laws of war are the legal rules by which war may be waged. These rules apply both to states and to non-state armed groups. All parties must obey fundamental principles, and failure to do so will constitute a "war crime." The "laws of war" are sometimes called "international humanitarian law" or "*jus in bello*," but these three concepts are exactly the same thing. (Soldiers tend to use the phrase "laws of war," human rights activists tend to use "international humanitarian law," and scholars tend to use "*jus in bello*," but in the application of these three terms, there is no difference.) Other terms sometimes used for the same concept are "law of armed conflict" (LOAC), and "rules of war." See also "International Humanitarian Law," "*Jus in Bello*," "Principles in the Laws of War," "Sources for the Laws of War," and "War Crime." Compare "*Jus ad Bellum*."

LEVEL I: See "Machine Autonomy."

LEVEL II: See "Machine Autonomy."

LEVEL III: See "Machine Autonomy."

LEVEL IV: See "Machine Autonomy."

LIFNIM MI'SHURAT HADIN: A Hebrew phrase meaning, "beyond the letter of the law," and signifying that for the sake of peace, in some cases an ethical person should be more generous than what the law requires. The leading Israeli NGO active on the lawfare front today is Shurat HaDin – Israel Law Center, which is referenced in this book as the "Israel Law Center." See "Israel Law Center."

LOAC: An acronym for "law of armed conflict." See "Laws of War."

MACHINE AUTONOMY: This is the relative degree to which machines, whether robots or cyber machines, may operate independently of human beings. This is a major issue, perhaps the single most important humanitarian and legal issue, involving robotic and cyber warfare.

There are said to be four levels of machine autonomy. In level I, the machine is essentially an extension of a person, and has no autonomy, such as a handheld gun or a scythe for reaping wheat. In level II, a human being "authorizes" action by the machine, meaning that the person must tell the machine to act. For example, in the Israeli weapon system known informally as "she sees, she shoots," a robotic sentry fires a heavy machine gun at an identified enemy, but only after a woman soldier specifically authorizes the sentry to fire. In level III, a human being "supervises" action by the machine, meaning the person observes what is happening and the machine will take the action unless the person issues an order to stand down. This is the way some remotely piloted vehicles work.

Level IV is full machine autonomy, meaning that after a person sets the initial objective, the machine then operates independently with no further human involvement. For example, the Iron Dome system, which was so effective in the Third Gaza War, may be placed in fully autonomous mode. However, autonomous anti-missile systems such as Iron Dome do not create any legal issues, because they are entirely defensive. As to offensive operations, it is not clear how extensive level IV is today, since generally there is some kind of human involvement, either in level II to authorize (that is, to validate) an attack, or in level III to supervise (that is, to cancel) an attack. In the future, however, the capability of machines will so far outstrip human capacities that any human involvement will likely degrade machine attacks, which may be fatal to the military operation. That is likely to be the case, for example, with drone swarms. If humans are no longer involved in offensive actions, that is, if level IV arises for machine attacks, have the machines become "killer robots"? The laws of war regarding level IV are not yet resolved. See "Robotic Sentry" and "Unmanned Aerial Vehicle."

MAG: See "Military Advocate General."

MARTENS CLAUSE: Named after a public declaration by Fyodor Fyodor-ovich Martens, Russian delegate to the Hague Peace Conference of 1899, this clause is part of the preamble to both the Hague Convention of 1899 and the Hague Convention of 1907. It provides that situations and acts not covered by a specific law of war are still subject to "usages established among civilized peoples," the "laws of humanity," and "dictates of public conscience." (These are the exact words used in the convention of 1907. The words in the convention of 1899 are slightly different in unimportant ways.) Although vague, nevertheless the Martens Clause supported the Nuremberg Military Trials of 1946–1949, is still valid law today, applies to the evaluation of new weapons systems, and is invoked by opponents of level IV machine autonomy. See "Customary International Law" and "Machine Autonomy."

MASKING: See "Attribution Problem."

MENS REA: Latin for "guilty mind," in common parlance "criminal intent," it is one of two requirements to define a "crime"; the other requirement is an "actus reus," or guilty act. Although a guilty act is judged according to the visible results of the action, a guilty mind is inferred from the nature of the action. See "Actus Reus" and "Internal Environment of Israeli Jews."

MILITARY ADVOCATE GENERAL (MAG): The highest legal officer in the Israel Defense Forces. The MAG guides the IDF in the laws of war, answers legal questions from the IDF and the government, helps in investigations of possible illegal activity by IDF soldiers, and manages a staff of attorneys to help in these tasks. The current MAG, Briga-dier-General Sharon Afek, is an expert in the laws of war as they apply to cyber attacks.

MORAL RELATIVITY: In the sense intended by Colonel Richard Kemp, as discussed in the afterword, this is the concept that there are no absolute rights or wrongs, that the Judeo-Christian heritage is just one set of values among many other sets, and therefore it is impossible to defend Western values such a free speech and democracy. Colonel Kemp rejects this view of morality. Compare "Cultural Relativism."

MORALITY IN WAR: A topic for moral philosophers, but of no relevance to either the laws of war or lawfare. Laws related to war deal with behavior, and with specific actions which are defined as crimes. "Morality" is a valid topic of study, and may serve as a basis for legislation against war crimes, but it is not relevant for determining whether a "war crime" has been committed. A person with a predilection for one side in a conflict might say that the other side is "immoral" and has therefore committed "war crimes," but this is not the appropriate test of legality or criminality. See "Principles in the Laws of War" and "Laws of War."

MOSSAD: The Mossad is the agency of the Israeli government responsible for the collection and interpretation of intelligence from outside of Israel. It is the Israeli equivalent of the American CIA or the British MI6. Compare "Shin Bet."

MURDER COMPENSATION: The concept that if your political cause is right, then you may reward or compensate any action for that cause, no matter how grievous the damage to non-combatants. This concept does away with the "laws of war," and focuses solely on the question whether a particular side is right in a dispute – if it is, then according to this concept, that side may do anything to advance its cause, and the side acts correctly by rewarding or compensating any such action, even the murder of innocent civilians. See "Murder Compensation Table of the Palestinian Authority."

MURDER COMPENSATION TABLE OF THE PALESTINIAN AUTHORITY: The Palestinian Authority passed a law in 2010, according to which any person who commits an act of terrorism against a Jew in any part of the land west of the Jordan River to the Mediterranean Sea is entitled to governmental compensation. The amount of compensation depends on the length of the sentence handed down by an Israeli court. For serious crimes, such as multiple murders, the level of compensation is such that after only a few years the convicted and imprisoned criminal could retire. This money is paid as the highest priority of the Palestinian Authority, before disbursements for health and welfare. The Murder Compensation Table is a monstrosity. This table, and the tens of millions of dollars paid by the PA every year to convicted terrorists as required by its terms, are the clearest evidence that the Palestinians have no interest whatever in any compromise, agreement, or accommodation of any kind with the Jews, but simply reject any presence of any Jews in the area often called the "Land of Israel." The essence of the problem is not Jewish "occupation," but rather Palestinian "rejectionism." See "Murder Compensation" and "Rejectionism."

NECESSITY (N): One of the four main principles in the laws of war. It applies to attackers (and is not relevant for defenders). An operation may be launched only if there is a "military necessity" for doing so, meaning that achievement of the objective of the operation would yield a direct military advantage to the attacker. By the definition accepted by all, targeting civilians cannot yield a "direct military advantage" regardless of any possible indirect effects, and therefore there is never any necessity to target civilians. The "necessity" of the operation, that is, whether or not the operation could reasonably be expected to achieve a military advantage, is the first legal question that must be asked by a military planner. See "Principles in the Laws of War." Compare "Distinction (D)," "Proportionality (P)," and "Shielding (S)."

NGO: See "Non-Governmental Organization."

NON-CONVENTIONAL WEAPONS: This includes the ABCs of weaponry – Atomic (or nuclear) Weapons, Biological Weapons, and Chemical Weapons. To these three must be added a new fourth weapon, Cyber, so that non-conventional weapons should now have the acronym ABCC, or perhaps ABC2.

NON-GOVERNMENTAL ORGANIZATION: Often abbreviated as "NGO," this is an organization that is neither governmental nor for-profit, and that engages in political, legal, humanitarian, charitable, or some other kind of social activity. An NGO may be formed without any formal structure and without any registration, but if legal benefits are sought (such as tax exemptions), then the organization must be both incorporated and registered as an NGO. The battles occurring in lawfare are being waged mainly by NGOs, of which the Israel Law Center is the leading pro-Israel NGO. NGOs do not replace, but rather supplement (and in the best case, complement) the activities of governmental organizations such as the Military Advocate General Corps or the attorney general. See also "Israel Law Center" and "Military Advocate General (MAG)."

NON-LETHAL FORCE: One of the alleged advantages of cyber warfare, in comparison to what is called "kinetic" or physical warfare, is that cyber warfare can often be launched without killing people. This "non-lethal force" allows cyber attackers to try to justify their action, without the public disapproval they would have faced had there been human deaths. See "Cyber Attack" and "Kinetic Attack."

OCCUPATION: The Palestinians claim that the absence of peace is due to Israel's occupation of Gaza and the area known as Judea and Samaria / the West Bank. However, Israel has had no presence in Gaza since August 2005. Further, the amount of land in Judea and Samaria / the West Bank that is owned or populated by Jews is less than 7 percent of the entire area, equal to less than one-third the size of New York City, or less than one-fourth the size of London. In addition, there have been at least five compromise offers of peace that have been accepted by Israel and rejected by the Palestinians. The real, and in fact sole, obstacle to peace is the refusal of the Palestinians to end the conflict and renounce their intention to flood Israel with Arabs through what they have called their "right of return." If and when the Palestinians renounce this right and agree to peace, there will be peace on terms that are reasonable for both parties. Until that occurs, there will not be peace. The sole problem is not "occupation" by Jews, but rather "rejectionism" by Palestinians. See "Offers of Peace," "Rejectionism," and "Sources of the Israeli-Palestinian Conflict."

OFFERS OF PEACE: Five offers of peace have been made to solve the Israeli-Palestinian dispute, all of which have been accepted by the Jews and rejected by the Palestinians. These are the Peel Commission Plan of 1937, the United Nationals Partition Plan of 1947, Israel's peace offer in

1968, Ehud Barak's offer at Camp David in 2000, and Ehud Olmert's offer in 2008. The Palestinians have rejected these offers because, in the final analysis, they simply will not accept any Jewish national presence, or any Jews for that matter, in the area between the Jordan River and the Mediterranean Sea. See "Occupation," "Sources of the Israeli-Palestinian Conflict," "Rejectionism," and most particularly, the "Murder Compensation Table of the Palestinian Authority."

PA: See "Palestinian Authority."

PALESTINIAN AUTHORITY (PA): The governmental body that has civil control over the areas of Judea and Samaria / the West Bank that are known as "Area A" and "Area B." The PA has political, welfare, and police power in these areas (but shares security control with Israel over Area B). Compare "Palestine Liberation Organization."

PALESTINE LIBERATION ORGANIZATION (PLO): A political organization dedicated to armed struggle against Israel. Unlike the Palestinian Authority, the PLO is a political party rather than a type of government, and the PLO presents itself as representing all Palestinians worldwide, rather than only the Palestinians of the area known as Judea and Samaria / the West Bank. The PLO incorporates many armed groups, including Fatah. See "Fatah." Compare "Palestinian Authority."

PLO: See "Palestine Liberation Organization."

POPULATION TRANSFER: If a territory is "occupied," then under the Fourth Geneva Convention of 1949, Article 49, paragraph 6, it is a crime for an occupier to forcibly transfer part of its population into that territory. The exact language is, "The Occupying Power shall not deport or transfer parts of its own civilian population into the territory it occupies." Israel has not "deported" or forcibly transferred Jews into Judea and Samaria / the West Bank. The Rome Statute of 1998, which created the International Criminal Court in 2002, is fundamentally different from the Geneva Conventions in that the Rome Statute defines as a crime, under Article 8, section 2(b)(viii), an action by an occupying power to transfer *directly or indirectly* its population into the territory. This new international norm was created at the explicit request of Arab states, and specifically to expand the definition of the crime to allow lawsuits against Israel. There has as yet been no such lawsuit, but the Palestinian Authority entered into the Rome Statute in 2015, and will probably file such a suit in the future.

Israel's response is likely to be: (1) The territory is not "occupied"; (2) Israel is therefore not an "occupying power"; (3) Israel is not transferring any part of its population into Judea and Samaria, although it does not prevent its population from moving there, and therefore it is not transferring its population "directly or indirectly"; (4) If "indirectly" is interpreted to include not actively stopping voluntary movements of its population, then the statute is illegitimate as a "bill of attainder" directed specifically at Israel; and (5) If "indirectly" is so interpreted, and assuming such interpretation is found to be a legitimate expansion of well-accepted international law, then the same expanded standard must be applied worldwide to Turkey in Cyprus, India and Pakistan in Kashmir, Morocco in Western Sahara, Russia in multiple territories, Spain and France in the Basque Country, and a dozen additional cases in which a country allegedly "occupies" land. On this last point, the Israel Law Center has filed a complaint with the ICC highlighting the illegal activities of Turkey in northeastern Cyprus. Either the ICC will apply the same standard to everyone, or it will be shown to be an international sham. See "Bill of Attainder," "Double Standard," "International Criminal Court," "Israel Law Center," and "Rome Statute."

PRECISION TARGETING: The ability to target and attack an objective effectively, while causing minimal or even no damage to surrounding persons or physical assets. It is generally believed that automated weapons systems, such as UAVs and robots, have a higher precision than human attackers. In cases where precision targeting systems may be used, the failure to use such systems may violate the legal principles of distinction and proportionality, and will likely lead to charges of war crimes by lawfare activists. See "Collateral Damage," "Distinction (D)," "Principles in the Laws of War," "Proportionality (P)," "Unmanned Ground Vehicle," and "Unmanned Aerial Vehicles."

PRINCIPLES IN THE LAWS OF WAR: These principles relate solely to the way a war is waged, not the reasons for going to war. There are perhaps as many as two hundred legal principles related to waging wars. There are, however, only four main principles that subsume the others, and which must be understood for any reasonable clarity or discussion related to the legality of waging war. These four main principles apply to all parties in armed combat. See the principles of "Necessity (N)," "Distinction (D)," "Proportionality (P)," and "Shielding (S)."

PROPORTIONALITY (P): One of the four main principles in the laws of war. It applies to attackers (and is not relevant for defenders). If a military operation is being planned that has both necessity (that is, successful achievement would yield a direct military advantage) and civilian harm (that is, a review of the "distinction" principle suggests that even with reasonable steps, civilians or civilian assets are likely to be harmed), then the military necessity and the civilian harm must be compared. The exact comparison is written in Article 8, section 2(b)(iv) of the Rome Statute, which says that the attack is illegal if the attacker knew in advance that the damage to civilians or civilian objects *"would be clearly excessive in relation to the concrete and direct overall military advantage anticipated"* (italics added for emphasis).

    Therefore, we might say that an attack is "proportional," and hence legal, if a reasonable argument could be made that the anticipated direct military advantage was not clearly exceeded by the anticipated civilian harm. The test of legality is *not*, "Did the anticipated civilian harm exceed in any way or at least equal the anticipated military advantage?" Rather, the correct test of legality is, "Was the anticipated civilian harm *'clearly excessive'* to the anticipated direct military advantage?" The test of legality also is *not*, "What actually happened?" but rather, "At the time the operation was planned, and given the information available, did the anticipated civilian harm clearly exceed the anticipated direct military advantage?" If, at that time and with that information, the answer is yes, then the attack was illegal. If the answer is no, then the attack was legal.

    The question of "proportionality" is almost always the main point of the argument as to whether a particular military operation was legal or not. A military planner often contends, "The operation was proportional" (or, "There was strong military necessity," or "Anticipated civilian casualties were low"), while lawfare activists typically argue, "The operation was disproportionate" (or, "The direct military advantage was nonexistent or vague or small," or "High civilian casualties should have been anticipated when the attack was being planned"). See "Rome Statute." Compare "Necessity (N)," "Proportionality (P)," and "Shielding (S)."

REJECTIONISM: Jews own or live on less than 7 percent of the land of the area variously called Judea and Samaria, or the West Bank. Jews own or live on 0 percent of Gaza. Nevertheless, the argument is made repeatedly in the media that the problem in the Israeli-Palestinian dispute is the Jewish "occupation" of Palestinian lands. The problem, however, is not "occupation" of any place, or thing, or people, but rather the complete refusal of the Palestinians to renounce their intent to destroy Israel by war or by mass immigration of Arabs from outside of the area. "Rejectionism" is the Arab refusal to accept any Jewish national presence in the area west of the Jordan River, and until that rejection changes there is no chance of peace in the area. See "Murder Compensation Table of the Palestinian Authority," "Occupation," "Offers of Peace," and "Sources of the Israeli-Palestinian Conflict."

REMOTELY PILOTED VEHICLE (RPV): Sometimes called a "remotely piloted aircraft system" (or RPAS), this is a UAV that is in communication with a human operator who gives commands regarding the activities of the UAV. In more formal terms, the RPV is operating at level II or level III of machine autonomy, but it is not fully autonomous and hence is not operating at level IV. See "Machine Autonomy" and "Unmanned Aerial Vehicles."

REVOLUTION IN MILITARY AFFAIRS (RMA): A phrase intended to capture what has been happening to modern militaries, beginning in the 1990s, continuing today, and expected to continue into about the 2030s. The phrase may have either a narrow or a broad meaning. In the narrow sense, RMA is the revolution in the provision and use in real-time of massive quantities of high-quality information about the battlefield – this would include both human and automated collection of information, real-time processing and distribution, and response by soldiers or robots. In the broad sense, RMA encompasses three mega-trends, which are the shift in warfare from symmetric to asymmetric, the massive increase and globalization of digital information, and the automation of warfare through both robots and cyber warfare. See "Cyber Attack," "Cyber Warfare," "Machine Autonomy," "Unmanned Aerial Vehicle," and "Unmanned Ground Vehicle."

RIGHT OF SELF-DEFENSE UNDER ARTICLE 51: Article 51 of the UN Charter provides that "nothing in the present Charter shall impair the inherent right of individual or collective self-defence if an armed attack occurs against a Member of the United Nations." The right of self-defense, as defined here, is also a legal defense against a charge of "war of aggression" – that is, if a state has suffered an "armed attack," it may respond in kind to defend itself. The problem is not the right to respond, but rather the prior condition. What is an "armed attack"? Is a cyber intrusion an "armed attack"? What if an attack has not yet occurred, but is clearly threatened? These issues relate solely to the question of whether a state may go to war, *jus ad bellum*, and not to any question about the means by which a war may be fought. See "Cyber Attack," "*Jus ad Bellum*," and "War of Aggression."

RMA: See "Revolution in Military Affairs."

ROBOT: See "Unmanned Ground Vehicle."

ROBOTIC SENTRY: A type of robot that stands guard at a border or other sensitive location; that senses and identifies threats; and that, typically with the consent of a human, shoots or otherwise neutralizes the threat. Today, robotic sentries stand on Israel's border with Gaza, and on the demilitarized zone between South Korea and North Korea.

ROE: See "Rules of Engagement."

ROME STATUTE: The informal name for the "Rome Statute of the International Criminal Court," this statute, which was adopted in 1998 and became effective in 2002, created the International Criminal Court (ICC). As of the beginning of 2016, approximately 60 percent of the countries of the world had adopted the Rome Statute, representing approximately 40 percent of the world's population, but with major exceptions such as Egypt, India, Iraq, Israel, the People's Republic of China, Russia, Saudi Arabia, and the United States. See "Crimes Under the Rome Statute" and "International Criminal Court."

RPV: See "Remotely Piloted Vehicle."

RULES OF ENGAGEMENT (ROE): These are the orders or directives to military forces telling them how to act, or how they may not act, in particular military circumstances. The term is somewhat flexible in that it may refer to standing, permanent orders, or to the orders and directives applicable to a particular operation. In all cases, the ROE must comply with the laws of war. See "Laws of War."

SECOND GAZA WAR: Used in this book to mean the second war between Hamas and Israel, which occurred in 2012, and which was called "Operation Pillar of Defense" by the Israelis.

SECURITY BARRIER: A wall, fence, berm, or other human-created divider between two pieces of land. There were at least sixty-five such barriers in the world as of early 2016, but many more are being created in response to large-scale international population migration and threats of international terrorism, international smuggling, or war. The security barrier between parts of Israel and parts of Judea and Samaria / the West Bank is one of these barriers. Israel's security barrier is mischaracterized as a "wall," although in fact over 90 percent of it is a fence. See the "*Wall Case.*"

SHIELDING (S): One of the four main principles in the laws of war. It applies to defenders (and is not relevant for attackers). There are three forms of "shielding," but in all its forms, shielding means that a defender hides behind or among civilians and civilian assets, and in all its forms, shielding is illegal. In one form of shielding, the defender sets up a firing position in a civilian area (such as a school, hospital, prison, house of worship) or in a location with many civilians present. In a second form of shielding, weapons and other military equipment are improperly stored in a civilian area. In a third form of shielding, symbols, vehicles, and other assets, which should be devoted to protected purposes, are instead used by combatants – for example, using a vehicle clearly marked with a Red Cross, or Red Crescent, or Red Star of David in order to transport combatants. As a result of the "Revolution in Military Affairs," terrorists or other non-state actors involved in "asymmetric war" simply cannot escape rapid identification, location, and elimination; since they cannot escape, they will increasingly rely on "shielding" among civilians, forcing an attacker either to leave them alone or to cause civilian harm which will be used to condemn the attacker in the media and in legal forums such as the ICC. See "Principles in the Laws of War," "Revolution in Military Affairs," and "International Criminal Court." Compare "Distinction (D)," "Necessity (N)," and "Proportionality (P)."

SHIN BET: Also called "Shabak," this is the agency of the Israel government responsible for internal security and for deriving intelligence from internal sources. It is the Israeli equivalent of the American FBI or the British MI5. Compare "Mossad."

SHURAT HADIN: See "Israel Law Center."

SIGINT: An abbreviation of "signals intelligence," this is one of the main ways that intelligence agencies gather information. Other ways are the gathering and analysis of publicly available information, and the running of human agents.

SINGULARITY: See "Technological Singularity."

SOURCES FOR THE LAWS OF WAR: For the International Criminal Court and international criminal law involving crimes by individuals, there are two main sources for the laws of war. These are "customary international law" (including the "Martens Clause") and "treaties." Further, as with any body of law, judicial precedent may influence the way in which rules are interpreted, and therefore such precedent could also be considered a source for the laws of war. See "Customary International Law," "International Criminal Court," the "Martens Clause," and "Treaties."

SOURCES OF THE ISRAELI-PALESTINIAN CONFLICT: The Palestinians claim that the source of their conflict with Israel is Israel's "occupation" of Palestinian lands. Israel claims that the source of the conflict with the Palestinians is Palestinian "rejectionism" of any Jewish national presence and in fact of any Jews in the area known as the Land of Israel. See "Occupation" and "Rejectionism."

SWARM (OR "DRONE SWARM"): See "Unmanned Aerial Vehicle."

SYMMETRIC VERSUS ASYMMETRIC WARFARE: "Symmetric warfare" is warfare fought between two armies, with soldiers wearing standard uniforms, using standard military weapons and tactics, and proceeding by various well-established routines with artillery, air bombardment, columns of tanks and infantry, etc. The prime examples of recent symmetric war are World Wars I and II. Conversely, in asymmetric warfare, the fighting parties are fundamentally different (usually one standard army fighting against guerillas or some other non-state armed group), in which the less organized party (that is, the non-state armed group) typically does not have uniforms, is not organized into what are considered standard army units, and does not use standard military tactics. Weapons in asymmetric war will include standard weapons such as guns and missiles, but are likely to include also non-standard weapons such as drones, robots, tunnels, cyber, international public opinion, and lawfare. The Israeli-Palestinian conflict is clearly the prime example of asymmetric war being waged today, but none of the conflicts currently raging in the Middle East (in Iraq, Libya, Syria, Yemen, and elsewhere) are symmetric and all of them have strong asymmetric characteristics.

Both symmetric and asymmetric warfare have existed for thousands of years. Moreover, even the most symmetric conflict is likely to have asymmetric elements (such as guerrilla tactics), and even asymmetric conflicts become symmetric when they transform, usually temporarily, into a set piece battle. (For example, in the First Indochina War, which was clearly an asymmetric war that was fought between the Viet Minh and France in the period 1946–1954, the climactic battle of Dien Bien Phu, in March–May 1954, was a symmetric battle with artillery bombardment, infantry assaults, and air supply.) However, warfare has undergone a massive change in that the main form of warfare in the twentieth and earlier centuries was symmetric, whereas asymmetric warfare is the main form of warfare today and will almost certainly remain the main form throughout the twenty-first century. The rise of non-standard weapons, including lawfare, is driven by this paradigm shift from symmetric to asymmetric warfare. The difference between "symmetric" and "asymmetric" is a key distinction. Lawfare, arising from and accompanying the rise of asymmetric war, is the central subject of this book. See "Lawfare."

The term "conventional war" primarily means a war using standard or conventional weapons – that is, some form of metal projectile. Thus, non-conventional weapons – atomic, biological, chemical, and now cyber – are not part of "conventional war." People sometimes use "conventional war" and "symmetric war" as synonyms, but this is inexact. The two terms indeed overlap, but they are not the same, because "conventional war" focuses on weapons and tactics, whereas "symmetric war" focuses on the nature of the fighting parties. See "Non-Conventional Weapons."

SYMMETRIC WARFARE: See "Symmetric versus Asymmetric Warfare."

T3R: See "Tooth-to-Tail Ratio."

TECHNOLOGICAL SINGULARITY: An expected event, at a presumed point of time, when machines will begin using software to improve their intelligence in an accelerating cycle of implementation and improvement. According to this concept, the cycle will become uncontrollable by people, and will lead very quickly to machines obsolescing humans in many activities. Although some futurists have predicted this may happen as early as 2030–2050, most predict it will not happen before the second half of the twenty-first century, and it may not happen at all. Whatever may be the final result of increasing machine intelligence, there is without doubt a strong trend to human-machine cooperation in weapons and tactics of warfare, and this trend will lead inevitably to new issues, arguments, and strategies on the lawfare front.

THIRD GAZA WAR: Used in this book to mean the third war between Hamas and Israel, which occurred in 2014, and which was called "Operation Protective Edge" by the Israelis.

TOOTH-TO-TAIL RATIO (T3R): A relative measure of combat soldiers in an armed force (infantry, armor, and combat aviation) to combat support (artillery, engineers, and signal corps) and other (general and administrative). The measure is a balance – either too high or too low would be sub-optimal. For example, to have a relatively high ratio would mean more combat soldiers, but may also indicate an imbalance, with inadequate support. The rise of automation and cyber will almost certainly decrease the number of combat soldiers, but is also likely to decrease the number of support soldiers (especially in general and administrative), so the ultimate effect on T3R is unclear.

TREATIES: One of the two main sources for the laws of war, treaties are formal agreements between two or more nations that have been both accepted and ratified by countries entering into the treaties. The Rome Statute created the International Criminal Court, and many nations have entered into the Rome Statute. However, as of early 2016, about 40 percent of countries, representing about 60 percent of the world's population, have not ratified the Rome Statute – these nations are not members of the Rome Statute, and therefore their citizens are subject to the jurisdiction of the International Criminal Court only in certain explicitly defined cases. See "Customary International Law," "International Criminal Court," and "Sources for the Laws of War."

UAV: See "Unmanned Aerial Vehicle."

UGV: See "Unmanned Ground Vehicle."

UNIVERSAL JURISDICTION: This is a legal concept in which individual countries use their national laws to extend their jurisdiction to individuals alleged to have committed genocide, crimes against humanity, torture, and other notorious crimes. Despite what might be implied by "universal," it is *not* jurisdiction against states, armies, or groups of people, but only against individuals. It is "universal" only in the sense that there is no national limit on the exercise of jurisdiction. For example, if one country, let's say Ecuador, feels that citizens of Russia have committed war crimes against citizens in the Ukraine, Ecuador might then exercise universal jurisdiction against the specific Russian individuals accused of the crimes. In its purest form, universal jurisdiction does not require that a defendant, or the alleged victims, have any relation to the country applying such jurisdiction. Universal jurisdiction has been asserted against citizens of many countries, including, for example, Argentina, the People's Republic of China, Spain, the US, and in particular Israel. However, through a combination of both legal and political factors, unfettered universal jurisdiction has recently been severely restricted in some of the key countries asserting such jurisdiction, including Belgium, Spain, and the UK. See "Extralegal Attacks."

UNMANNED AERIAL VEHICLE (UAV): Also called a "drone," this is essentially a flying robot. Today they are used primarily for observation, spotting attacks, and conducting precision strikes. In the future, they are likely to carry the main burden of most combat functions, with the likely exceptions of airborne command, transport of high-value cargoes, and medical evacuation of wounded soldiers. Also in the future, they are likely to appear in what has been called "drone swarms," which are fleets of tens, hundreds, or potentially thousands of UAVs, probably of different types, all operating together with real-time communication and coordination. See "Machine Autonomy" and "Remotely Piloted Vehicle."

UNMANNED GROUND VEHICLE (UGV): Another name for "robot." The formal definition of a UGV includes sensors (to input data), processors (to convert data into information), and effectors (to take some kind of action based on the information).

UNMANNED SURFACE VEHICLE (USV): A fully automated ship, in essence a naval robot. The use of such ships for military operations is only beginning, and will almost certainly intensify in the coming years.

USV: See "Unmanned Surface Vehicle."

WALL CASE (OR "WALL ADVISORY OPINION"): An informal name for a 2004 advisory opinion of the International Court of Justice ruling that Israel's security barrier was illegal in part. The formal name is *Advisory Opinion Concerning Legal Consequences of the Construction of a Wall in Occupied Palestinian Territory, 2004*. This opinion was rendered on a specific question posed by the UN General Assembly. The opinion has been severely criticized by some legal scholars due to the discriminatory nature of the question posed, the cursory way in which the court failed to deal with the arguments for the defense, and the expansive opinion of the court which went far beyond the question posed. Only the UN Security Council can enforce an advisory opinion, and in this case, neither the question nor enforcement came from the Security Council. Over the period 1989 to early 2016, the number of walls, fences, berms, or other security barriers in the world has more than quadrupled from sixteen to sixty-five, and many more are currently in construction due to fears of terrorism and mass immigration. Were the same or similar question to be posed to the International Court of Justice today, it is not clear that the opinion to be rendered would be the same as that which the court actually decided in 2004. See "International Court of Justice" and "Security Barrier."

WAR CRIMES: This term is defined in Article 8 of the Rome Statute, which lists and defines fifty specific acts, any of which may be "war crimes" in particular instances. Although it is not practicable to list all of these here, we might say that "war crimes" include (1) any attack directed at armed forces that kills or damages or creates suffering without any real need (which would be a violation of the "necessity principle"), (2) any attack directed at civilians or civilian infrastructure (which would a violation of the "distinction principle"), (3) any attack that creates damage "clearly excessive to the concrete military advantage" to be obtained (which would be a violation of the "proportionality principle"), (4) the use of civilians to protect military forces or areas (which would be a violation of the "shielding principle"), and (5) specific crimes such as torture, taking of hostages, abusing prisoners of war, using banned weapons, and others. See "Distinction (D)," "Necessity (N)," "Principles in the Laws of War," "Proportionality (P)," and "Shielding (S)."

WAR OF AGGRESSION: A party may go to war legally if it is has a legitimate reason for doing so. Although there are various possible "legitimate reasons" to justify war, the only reason that is universally accepted, and is enshrined in the United Nations Charter at Article 51, is the right of self-defense. Almost everyone would agree that coming to the aid of a third party that has a right of self-defense is also a legitimate reason. Some people (but certainly not all) feel that punishing an aggression is also a legitimate reason.

If a party engages in war without having a legitimate reason to do so, then it has engaged in a "war of aggression," which is a crime. Note that this definition is *not the same* as a layman's understanding, because this definition does not relate to the way the war is waged (that is, whether the war is waged "aggressively," or "passively," or "moderately," etc.) but only to whether the reason for going to war is legitimate or not. See "*Jus ad Bellum.*" Compare "*Jus in Bello.*"

WEAPONIZE: See "Cyber Attack."

ZERO DAYS: A potential vulnerability of a computer system that is not known to the owner or manager of the system is said to be a "zero day vulnerability," indicating that the vulnerability is known for "zero days." When a cyber attacker wants to target a computer system, the attacker looks for a "zero day vulnerability" against which malicious software could be launched. Since the owner or manager is not aware of the vulnerability, no defense is possible, and indeed the owner or manager may not even be aware when malicious code has entered the system. See "Cyber Attack."

Bibliography

ARTICLES

Abu Toameh, Khaled. "Why Palestinians Cannot Make Peace with Israel." Gatestone Institute. July 13, 2015.

Afek, Sharon. "The Cyber Attack – Legal Guidelines: Applying Principles of International Law to Warfare in Cyberspace." *Eshtonot* 5 (October 2013). Available only in Hebrew.

Ahnsaf, Zalman. "Navy Stops Vessel Bound for Gaza." *Hamodia*. October 5, 2016.

Ahren, Raphael. "Ex-ICC Prosecutor Hails Israeli Report on Settlements' Legality." *Times of Israel*. December 17, 2015.

Al Jazeera Network. "Gaza-Bound Flotilla Sails Off from Spain's Barcelona." September 15, 2016.

———. "Tensions Rise over Gaza Aid Fleet: Israeli Army Intends to Halt Humanitarian Aid Mission Head for Palestinian Territory." May 28, 2010.

Al-Hayat Al-Jadida Newspaper. "Fatah Marked the Anniversary of the Launch in Bethlehem." January 8, 2016.

Allison, Graham T. "Why ISIS Fears Israel." *National Interest Magazine.* August 8, 2016.

Almog, Doron. "Letter by Doron Almog." March 2007.

Antebi, Liran. "Changing Trends in Unmanned Aerial Vehicles: New Challenges for States, Armies and Security Industries." Institute for National Security Studies, *Journal of Military and Strategic Affairs* 6, no. 2 (August 2014).

————. "It's Not the Tool, It's the System: Use of UAVs by the United States." Institute for National Security Studies, INSS Insight no. 766. November 12, 2015.

————. "The United States: Prepared and Fit for Military Intervention in Iraq?" INSS Insight no. 567. July 1, 2014.

————. "Who Will Stop the Robots?" Institute for National Security Studies, *Journal of Military and Strategic Affairs* 5, no. 2 (September 2013).

Avni, Benny. "The Future of the Hague May Hinge on the War in Gaza." *Newsweek*. January 13, 2015.

Baram, Gil, "The Effects of Cyberwar Technologies in Force Buildup: The Israeli Case." Institute for National Security Studies, *Journal of Military and Strategic Affairs* 5, no. 1 (May 2013).

Belfer Center for Science and International Affairs, John F. Kennedy School of Government, Harvard University. "Deterring Terror: How Israel Confronts the Next Generation of Threats, English Translation of the Official Strategy of the Israel Defense Forces." Belfer Center. August 2016. This document is an English language translation of the Hebrew document "Strategy of the IDF" by Lieutenant-General Gadi Eizenkot.

Bender, Kristin J. "Activist Talks about Failed Mission to Reach the Gaza Strip." *San Jose Mercury News*. July 8, 2011.

Ben-Israel, Isaac, and Lior Tabansky. "An Interdisciplinary Look at Security Challenges in the Information Age." Institute for National Security Studies, *Journal of Military and Strategic Affairs* 3, no. 3 (December 2011).

Berman, Lazar. "Palestinian Kids Taught to Hate Israel in UN-Funded Camps, Clip Shows." *Times of Israel*. August 14, 2013.

Bernstein, Daniel. "Footage Shows Israeli Soldiers Debating Activists before Boarding Gaza-Bound Boat." *Times of Israel*. July 1, 2015.

Black, Phil. "Greeks Arrest Captain of U.S. Ship Aiming to Protest Gaza Blockade." *CNN World*. July 2, 2011.

Blair, David. "UN Commander Says Hands Are Tied in Congo." *The Telegraph*. November 17, 2008.

Blum, Ruthie, "Lawfare Group Pursuing Class-Action 'War Crimes' Suit at International Criminal Court Against Palestinian Broadcasting Chiefs (Video)." *Algemeiner*. March 2, 2016.

Bob, Yonah Jeremy. "Analysis: US Bombing of Afghan Hospital May Help Israel Face Its Own Demons." *Jerusalem Post*. November 28, 2015.

———. "Avichai Mandelblit Nominated as Next Attorney-General." *Jerusalem Post*. December 20, 2015.

———. "Exclusive: Historic Case against Bank of China for Millions in Terror Financing Dismissed." *Jerusalem Post*. August 17, 2015.

———. "Facing ICC, Ya'alon Appoints Veteran Sharon Afek as New IDF Head Lawyer." *Jerusalem Post*. November 28, 2015.

———. "Former Shin Bet Head 'Bursts Myth' on Cyber Hackers Who Attack Israel." *Jerusalem Post*. June 21, 2016,

———. "Rule of Law: Attorney-General on Deck." *Jerusalem Post*. January 11, 2016.

———. "Rule of Law: Transforming the Shin Bet." *Jerusalem Post*. June 13, 2013.

———. "The State of Cyber Warfare Law." *Jerusalem Post*. January 31, 2013.

Bronner, Ethan. "Israel Warns of Using Force If New Flotilla Heads to Gaza." *New York Times*. June 16, 2011.

Booth, William. "The 'Humanitarian Aid' Aboard a Recent Flotilla to Gaza Fit in Two Cardboard Boxes." *Washington Post*. July 1, 2015.

Brown, Larisa. "Betrayal of a Hero: Sgt. Kevin Williams Went Through 12 Years of Hell before Being Cleared of Killing an Iraqi. Now He's Jobless and Broke. . . . While the Dead Man's Family Are in Line for a Big Payout." *MailOnline*. March 26, 2015.

Brown, Larisa, Christian Gysin, Arthur Martin, and Amanda Williams. "We Were Dragged through Five Years of Hell by the Government Say British Soldiers Taken to War Crimes Inquiry by 'Shameful' Lawyers." *MailOnline*. December 19, 2014.

Buncome, Andrew. "US Forced to Import Bullets from Israel As Troops Use 250,000 Bullets for Each Rebel Killed." *Independent*. September 25, 2005.

Bussel, Ari. "Taking the Legal Rote: Suing Satellite Communication Providers." *News Blaze*. June 7, 2011.

C, Syed. "Women's Boat to Gaza: Hope Is Lost." *Middle East Monitor*. October 4, 2016.

Callimachi, Rukmini. "Kurds Team with U.S. to Combat ISIS in Syria." *New York Times*. August 10, 2015. (Available on the Internet as "Inside Syria: Kurds Roll Back ISIS, but Alliances Are Strained.")

Chomsky, Noam. "On Israel-Palestine and BDS." *The Nation*. July 2, 2014.

CNN World. "Shehade Was High on Israel Most-Wanted List." July 23, 2002.

Cohen, Amichai, and Tal Mimran. "The Palestinian Authority and the International Court." Israel Democracy Institute. February 10, 2015.

Cohen, Amichai, and Yuval Shany. "Contextuality Proportionality Analysis? A Response to Schmitt and Merriam on Israel's Targeting Practices." *Just Security* (online publication). May 7, 2015.

Cohen, Gili. "Cyberattacks Waned Amid Iran Nuclear Talks, Israeli Officer Says." *Haaretz*. February 16, 2016.

Cortés, Claudia Jiménez. "Combating Impunity for International Crimes in Spain: From the Prosecution of Pinochet to the Indictment of Garzón." *Institut Català Internacional per la Pau*. May 2011.

Darshan-Leitner, Nitsana, founder and president of the Israel Law Center, to Annika Falkengren, president and CEO of SEB. "Urgent Demand that SEB Cancel Its Mortgage of the Gaza Smuggling Ship *Marianne Av Goteborg*." Letter of June 21, 2015. Appended is the *Marianne*'s ship registration of April 27, 2015.

Dayan, Yoni, and Jeremy Sharon. "Israeli Jews Becoming More Religious, Poll Finds." *Jerusalem Post*. January 26, 2012.

Dempsey, Martin E., commanding general of the U.S. Army Training and Doctrine Command, 2008–2011 (then chief of staff of the army, and finally chairman of the joint chiefs of staff). "U.S. Army Unmanned Aircraft Systems Roadmap 2010–2035." U.S. Army Training and Doctrine Command, 2010.

Docherty, Bonnie. "Losing Humanity: The Case Against Killer Robots." *Human Rights Watch* and *International Human Rights Clinic of the Harvard Law School*. November 4, 2012.

Dörmann, Knut. "Applicability of the Additional Protocols to Computer Network Attacks." In *International Expert Conference on Computer Network Attacks and the Applicability of International Humanitarian Law:*

Proceeding of the Conference, edited by Karin Byström. Stockholm: Swedish National Defence College, 2004.

Dunlap, Charles J., Jr. "Law and Military Interventions: Preserving Humanitarian Values in 21st Century Conflicts." Prepared for the Humanitarian Challenges in Military Intervention Conference, and delivered at the Carr Center for Human Rights Policy, Kennedy School of Government, Harvard University, Washington, D.C., November 29, 2001.

Eizenkot, Gadi, lieutenant-general and chief of staff of the Israel Defense Forces. "Strategy of the IDF." Israel Defense Forces, August 23, 2015, in Hebrew. An English translation has been created by the Belfer Center for Science and International Affairs.

Elis, Niv. "Israel to Invest NIS 100m in Cyber-Security Fund Kidma." *Jerusalem Post*. December 21, 2015.

Freedom Flotilla Coalition. "New Strategic Plan Adopted by Freedom Flotilla Coalition." November 1, 2015.

———. "Strategy Plan." Facebook. November 1, 2015.

———. "A Women's Boat to Gaza Is Being Planned." Facebook. March 9, 2016.

———. "Women's Boat to Gaza" website, "Frequently Asked Questions: Why will there be only women participating on the boats?" October 1, 2016.

———. "Women's Boat to Gaza" website, "Frequently Asked Questions: Will you be bringing aid to Gaza?" October 1, 2016.

Friedman, Ron. "Lawyers, not IDF, at Forefront of Battle against Flotilla." *Jerusalem Post*. June 6, 2011.

Fulton, William. "Israel Gives U.N. Mid-East Peace Plan." *Chicago Tribune*. October 9, 1968.

Gebicke, Scott, and Samuel Magid. "Lessons from around the World: Benchmarking Performance in Defense." McKinsey and Company. 2010.

Ginsburg, Mitch. "Army to Establish Unified Cyber Corps." *Times of Israel*. June 16, 2015.

———. "The Double-Edged Sword of Cyber Warfare." *Times of Israel*. June 24, 2015.

GlobalSecurity.org. "Palestine Security and Intelligence Agencies." Last modified July 28, 2011.

Goldstein, Guy-Philippe. "Cyber Weapons and International Stability." Institute for National Security Studies, *Journal of Military and Strategic Affairs* 5, no. 2 (September 2013).

Goodman, Alana. "Meet the Legal Wonks Who Brought Down the Flotilla." *Commentary Magazine.* August 22, 2011.

Gordon, Evelyn. "Stop Subsidizing Terror Murder." *Commentary Magazine.* June 30, 2016. As an alternative source, see *Analysis from Israel,* July 2, 2016.

———. "Where Providing Water Is a Crime." *Commentary Magazine.* January 29, 2016.

Greenberg, Andy, "Hackers Remotely Kill a Jeep on the Highway – With Me In It." *Wired.* December 21, 2015.

Greenberg, Elisa. "UNRWA Summer: Camp Jihad?" *inFocus.* November 3, 2014.

Greenberg, Hanan. "Navy Gears for Turkish Flotilla." *Ynet News.* June 15, 2011.

Greenwood, Christopher. "International Law and the Pre-Emptive Use of Force: Afghanistan, Al-Qaida, and Iraq." *San Diego International Law Journal* 4 (2003): 7.

Gross, Judah Ari. "In Rare Disclosure, IDF Sets Out Its Strategy, Admits Flawed Response to Hamas, Hezbollah." *Times of Israel.* August 13, 2015.

———. "Israel Lawmakers Advance Bill to Streamline Cybersecurity." *Times of Israel.* August 1, 2016.

———. "New Military Advocate General Prepared for ICC Fight." *Times of Israel.* August 18, 2015.

———. "Yossi Cohen Has Had Iran in His Sights for Over a Year." *Times of Israel.* December 8, 2015.

Haaretz. "Israel Among the Least Religious Countries in the World." April 14, 2015.

Hamilton, Lisa Gay. "Why I Am on the Women's Boat to Gaza." *Counterpunch.* September 21, 2016.

Harel, Amos. "Israel's Military Chief Orders to Revoke Controversial 'Hannibal' Directive." *Haaretz*. June 28, 2016.

Harkov, Lahav. "Report Finds Norwegian Government Funds Organization Supporting BDS Campaigns." *Jerusalem Post*. August 29, 2016.

Hayden, Michael V. "To Keep America Safe, Embrace Drone Warfare." *New York Times*. February 19, 2016.

Herman, Arthur. "The Pentagon's 'Smart Revolution.'" *Commentary Magazine* 142, no. 1 (July/August 2016): 25–31.

Herzberg, Anne. "Lawfare Against Israel." *Wall Street Journal*. November 5, 2008.

———. "NGO 'Lawfare': Exploitation of Courts in the Arab-Israeli Conflict." 2nd ed. NGO Monitor Monograph Series. December 2010.

Higgenbotham, Stacey. "The Army Built a Wi-Fi 'Gun' That Shoots Drones from the Sky." *Fortune Magazine*. October 19, 2015.

High Level Military Group. "An Assessment of the 2014 Gaza Conflict." October 2015.

Hoffer, Eric. "Israel's Peculiar Position." *Los Angeles Times*. May 26, 1968. Reprinted in the *Wall Street Journal* on July 30, 2014.

Hsu, Jeremy. "China's Drone Swarms Rise to Challenge US Power." *TechNewsDaily*. March 13, 2013.

Independent. "Gambia Joins South Africa and Burundi in Exodus from International Criminal Court." October 22, 2016.

Israel Defense Forces. "IDF Operation in Gaza Strip Last Night." July 23, 2002.

Israel Law Center. "Defending Israeli Soldiers in the ICC." Shurat HaDin – Israel Law Center website.

———. "Shurat HaDin's Victories in the Struggle to Block the Anti-Israel Flotilla." Shurat HaDin – Israel Law Center website, June 19, 2011.

———. "Sinking the Gaza Flotilla." Shurat HaDin – Israel Law Center website.

———. "A Worldwide Campaign to Prosecute the Heads of Palestinian Television in the Hague." Shurat HaDin – Israel Law Center website.

Israel Ministry of Foreign Affairs. "Cabinet Approves Establishment of National Cyber Authority." February 15, 2015.

———. "Missile Shipment from Iran to Gaza Intercepted." March 5, 2014.

Israel Social TV. "Seven Days on the Women's Flotilla to Gaza." September 22, 2016.

Israel Today. "IDF Begins Integrating Robots into Ground Forces." May 7, 2015.

Jansen, Michael. "Greece Prohibits Gaza Boats from Leaving Its Ports." *Irish Times.* July 4, 2011.

Jerusalem Post. "Iran Helping Hamas, Hezbollah Build Fleet of Suicide Drones." April 4, 2015.

Jewish Telegraphic Agency. "Britain Freezes Aid Payments to Palestinians Over Terrorists' Salaries." *Jerusalem Post.* October 7, 2016.

———. "Spain Lifts War Crime Listing for Netanyahu, 6 Others." Reprinted in *Times of Israel.* December 27, 2015.

Jewish Virtual Library. "Latest Population Statistics for Israel (Updated January, 2016)." January 2016.

Jonas, George. "Using Lawfare to Anchor the Gaza Flotilla." *National Post.* July 6, 2011.

Kais, Roi. "Private Jets, Restaurants, Luxury Hotels: The Good Life of Senior Hamas Officials." *Ynet News.* July 22, 2014.

Kaplan, Jerry. "Robot Weapons: What's the Harm?" *New York Times.* August 17, 2015.

Katz, Yaakov. "60 Percent of Israelis Won't Serve in IDF by 2020." *Jerusalem Post.* November 18, 2011.

Kemp, Richard. "Is Britain Destroying its Military to Appease Enemies?" Gatestone Institute. October 25, 2016.

Koh, Harold Hongju. "International Law in Cyberspace." *Harvard International Law Journal* 54 (December 2012): 1–12.

Kontorovich, Eugene. "Palestinians Seek to Take Advantage of ICC's Unique 'Israel' Provision." *Washington Post.* January 5, 2015.

———. "Politicizing the International Criminal Court." Jerusalem Center for Public Affairs. April 2014.

Lapin, Yaakov. "IDF Using Relative Calm to Prepare for Future Threats." *Jerusalem Post.* August 3, 2016.

———. "Network IDF." *Jerusalem Post.* September 28, 2015.

LeClaire, Lance David. "10 Grim Separation Walls from Around the World." *Listverse*. September 27, 2014.

Levy-Weinrib, Ella. "Meet the Hamas Billionaires." *Globes*. July 24, 2014.

Lipka, Michael. "Controversy over New Israeli Law Highlights Growing Ultra-Orthodox Population." Pew Research Center. March 13, 2014.

MacFarquhar, Neil, and Ethan Bronner. "Report Finds Naval Blockade by Israel Legal but Faults Raid." *New York Times*. September 1, 2011.

Machover, Daniel, and Kate Maynard. "Prosecuting Alleged War Criminals in England and Wales." *Denning Law Journal* 18, no. 1 (2006): 95–114.

Mansour, Riyad. "15 December 2014 – Statement by Ambassador Riyad Mansour [Permanent Observer of Palestine to the United Nations] before the Assembly of States Parties to the Rome Statute of the International Criminal Court (thirteenth session), General Debate, New York." Palestine at the UN. December 16, 2014.

Marcus, Itamar. "The PA's Billion Dollar Fraud." Palestinian Media Watch. April 27, 2016.

Marcus, Itamar, and Nan Jacques Zilberdik. "Palestinian Children Wear 'Suicide Belts' to Celebrate Fatah's 51 Years of Violence." Palestinian Media Watch. January 11, 2016.

Marx, Karl. "Der achtzehnte Brumaire des Louis Bonaparte" (in English: "The Eighteenth Brumaire of Louis Bonaparte"). Essay in *Die Revolution*, a German-language monthly magazine. New York, 1852.

Matimop – Israeli Industry Center for R&D, and the executive agency of the Office of the Chief Scientist (OCS) of Israel, http://www.matimop .org.il/ocs.html.

Medzini, Ronen. "French Flotilla Ship Won't Sail." *Ynet News*. June 15, 2011.

Meir Amit Intelligence and Terrorism Information Center. "The European Campaign to End the Siege on Gaza (ECESG) Is an Anti-Israel, Pro-Hamas Umbrella Organization which Participated in the Mavi Marmara Flotilla." October 5, 2010.

Melhem, Ahmad. "Who's Going to Pay for Palestinian Budget Gap?" *Al-Monitor*. February 4, 2016.

Melman, Yossi. "The Gideon Doctrine: The Changing Middle East and IDF Strategy." *Jerusalem Post*. September 13, 2015.

————. "Netanyahu Names Nadav Argaman as the New Head of the Shin Bet." *Jerusalem Post*. February 12, 2016.

MEMRI. "Hamas Leader Khaled Mash'al: We Will Not Relinquish an Inch of Palestine, from the River to the Sea." MEMRI – The Middle East Media Research Institute. Clip no. 3761. December 7, 2012 (transcript of video clip).

Menashri, Harel, and Gil Baram. "Critical Infrastructures and Their Interdependence in a Cyber Attack – The Case of the U.S." Institute for National Security Studies, *Journal of Military and Strategic Affairs* 7, no. 1 (March 2015).

Merriam, John J., and Michael N. Schmitt. "Israeli Targeting: A Legal Appraisal." *Naval War College Review* 68, no. 4 (Autumn 2015): 15–33.

Minder, Ralph. "Argentine Judge Seeks to Put Spanish Officials on Trial," *New York Times*. September 13, 2013.

Murphy, Sean D. "Ipse Dixit at the I.C.J." Public Law and Legal Theory Working Paper no. 120, George Washington Law School. December 4, 2004.

National Post. "On Israel, Greece Gets It Right." *National Post* Full Comment editorial. July 4, 2011.

NGO Monitor. "Lawfare, International Law, and Human Rights." http://www.ngo-monitor.org/key-issues/lawfare-international-law-and-human-rights/about/.

Nunez, Michael. "DARPA's New Autonomous Submarine-Hunter Could Change Naval Combat Forever." *Gizmondo*. February 12, 2016.

Office of the Prime Minister of the State of Israel: The National Cyber Bureau. "Mission of the Bureau." 2016.

Opall-Rome, Barbara. "Interview: Eviatar Matania, Head of Israel's National Cyber Directorate." *Defense News*. July 11, 2016.

Osborn, Kris. "Future Carriers Built to Carry Drone Fleets." *Defense Tech*. July 19, 2013.

Palestinian Media Watch. "PA Salaries to Terrorists." A compendium of more than one hundred sixty articles, dated between 2000–2016, documenting payments by the Palestinian Authority to terrorists.

———. "PA to Pay Salaries to All Terrorists in Israeli Prisons." May 20, 2011.

Paltiel, Ari, Michel Sepulchre, Irene Kornilenko, and Martin Maldonado. "Long-Range Population Projections for Israel: 2009–2059." Israel Government Central Bureau of Statistics, Demography and Census Department. March 21, 2012.

Percy, Andrew. "How Not to Help the Palestinian Children." *Times of Israel*. January 7, 2016.

Perlroth, Nicole. "In a Global Market for Hacking Talent, Argentines Stand Out." *New York Times*. November 30, 2015.

Peskin, Doron. "Hamas Got Rich as Gaza Was Plunged into Poverty." *Ynet News*. July 15, 2014.

Pew Research Center. "Israel's Religiously Divided Society." Washington, D.C. March 8, 2016.

Pfeffer, Anshel. "Lethal Joysticks." *Haaretz*. July 2, 2010.

Pileggi, Tamar. "Israeli Navy Intercepts Gaza-Bound Ship, No Injuries Reported." *Times of Israel*. June 29, 2015.

Prigg, Mark. "Who Goes There? Samsung Unveils Robot Sentry That Can Kill from Two Miles Away." *MailOnline*. September 15, 2014.

Rafael Advanced Defense Systems. "Unmanned Naval Patrol Vehicle." 2010.

Ravid, Barak. "ICC Panel Orders Prosecutor to Reconsider Probe of Israel over Gaza Flotilla Raid." *Haaretz*. July 16, 2015.

———. "Netanyahu Names National Security Council Advisor Yossi Cohen as Next Mossad Chief." *Haaretz*. December 7, 2015.

Reuters. "$1 Billion Lawsuit Accuses Facebook of Enabling Palestinian Attacks." July 11, 2016.

Rohrabacher, Dana. "Threats to Israel: Terrorist Funding and Trade Boycotts." See the section "Photographs and Videos."

Ronen, Gil. "58 Percent of Jewish Israelis Are Religious or 'Traditionalists.'" *Arutz Sheva* (*Israel National News*). September 26, 2011.

———. "Maritime Lawfare Victory: Lloyd's Won't Insure Gaza Flotilla." *Arutz Sheva* (*Israel National News*). May 23, 2011.

Rosen, Lewis. "Shlomo Avineri and the Two-State Solution." *Times of Israel.* October 12, 2005.

Rosenberg, Matthew, and Eric Schmitt. "In ISIS Strategy, U.S. Weighs Risk to Civilians." *New York Times.* December 19, 2015.

Rosenzweig, Ido, and Yuval Shany. "Update on Universal Jurisdiction: Spanish Supreme Court Affirms Decision to Close Inquiry into Targeted Killing of Salah Shehade." Israel Democracy Institute. April 5, 2010.

Ross, Tim. "£150m Legal Bill for Troops Just Doing Their Duty: Ministers Draw Up Plans to Pull Out of the European Convention on Human Rights Next Time the Armed Forces Are Sent into Combat." *The Telegraph.* October 17, 2015.

Runkle, Benjamin. "The Cyber Gap: The Internet Is the Middle East's Next Battleground, But Are We Prepared?" *Tablet Magazine.* August 13, 2015.

Sanger, David E. "Nuclear Facilities in 20 Countries May Be Easy Targets for Cyberattacks." *New York Times.* January 14, 2016.

———. "U.S. Wrestles with How to Fight Back Against Cyberattacks." *New York Times.* July 30, 2016.

———. "Utilities Concerned about Potential for a Cyberattack after Ukraine's." *New York Times,* February 29, 2016.

Sayare, Scott. "Israeli Advocacy Group Helps Delay Departure of Gaza-Bound Flotilla." *New York Times.* June 28, 2011,

Scarborough, Rowan. "Iran Creates 'Suicide' Drones That Threaten Israel, U.S. Navy: Pentagon." *Washington Times.* April 8, 2015.

Schanzer, Jonathan. "The Brothers Abbas: Are the Sons of the Palestinian President Growing Rich Off Their Father's System?" Foreign Policy Group. June 5, 2012.

Scharre, Paul. "Autonomous Weapons and Operational Risk." *Center for a New American Security.* February, 2016.

Schmitt, Eric. "U.S. Caution in Strikes Gives ISIS an Edge, Many Iraqis Say." *New York Times.* May 26, 2015.

Schmitt, Michael N., "The Relationship Between Context and Proportionality: A Reply to Cohen and Shany." *Just Security* (online publication). May 11, 2015.

———. "Rewired Warfare: Rethinking the Law of Cyber Attack." *Inter-*

national *Review of the Red Cross: Scope of the Law in Armed Conflict* 96, no. 893 (2014): 189–206.

Schmitt, Michael N., and John J. Merriam. "A Legal and Operational Assessment of Israel's Targeting Practices." *Just Security* (online publication). April 24, 2015.

———. "The Tyranny of Context: Israeli Targeting Practices in Legal Perspective." *University of Pennsylvania Journal of Law* 37, no. 1 (2015): 53–139.

Schweitzer, Yoram, Gabi Siboni, and Einav Yogev. "Cyberspace and Terrorist Organizations." Institute for National Security Studies, *Journal of Military and Strategic Affairs* 3, no. 3 (December 2011).

Shenker, Jack, and Conal Urquhart. "Activists' Plan to Break Gaza Blockade with Aid Flotilla Is Sunk." *Guardian*. July 5, 2011.

Simons, Marlise. "Jean-Pierre Bemba Is Convicted of War Crimes." *New York Times*. March 21, 2016.

Socialistworld.net. "Paul Murphy Socialist Party MEP Joins 'Freedom Flotilla II.'" June 24, 2011.

Solomon, Shoshanna. "IDF Looks to a 'One-Network' Army to Fight Future Wars." *Times of Israel.* July 31, 2016.

Space Daily. "Israelis Urged to Prepare for Battlefields Dominated by Robots." February 3, 2014.

Steinberg, Gerald M. "The UN, the ICJ, and the Separation Barrier: War by Other Means." NGO Monitor, *Israel Law* Review 38 (2005): 331.

Stern, Yedidia. "A New Approach To Dealing With Israel's Ultra-Orthodox." *Jewish Week.* August 11, 2016.

Stewart, Catrina. "Israeli Campaign Stops Gaza Flotilla Leaving Port." *Independent.* June 28, 2011.

Tabansky, Lior. "Basic Concepts in Cyber Warfare." Institute for National Security Studies, *Journal of Military and Strategic Affairs* 3, no. 1 (May 2011).

———. "Critical Infrastructure Protection against Cyber Threats." Institute for National Security Studies, *Journal of Military and Strategic Affairs* 3, no. 2 (November 2011).

Tamturk, Venus. "Internet of Things Forecasts & Best Practices." *CMS Connected.* August 30, 2016.

Taylor, Guy. "U.S. Has Mapped ISIS Hiding Spots, but Won't Launch Strikes for Fear of Civilian Deaths." *Washington Times*. December 14, 2015.

Thompson, Mark. "Iranian Cyber Attack on New York Dam Shows Future of War." *TIME Magazine*. March 24, 2016.

Times of Israel. "Fatah Official: Palestine alongside Israel Is Just 'a Phase.'" January 22, 2016.

———. "IDF Appoints First Head for Unified Cyber Warfare Corps." December 1, 2015.

———. "IS Plans to Hit US Air Bases in Mideast, Warn Israelis Who Hacked into Web Group." August 3, 2016.

———. "No Violence as Israel Intercepts Women's Boat to Gaza." October 5, 2016.

———. "Spanish Judge Seeks to Prosecute PM over 2010 Flotilla Raid." November 17, 2015.

———. "UK Freezes $30M in Aid Over Salaries for Terrorists." October 7, 2016.

———. "UK to Opt Out of European Human Rights Convention in Wartime." October 4, 2016.

———. "WATCH: 'I Want to Stab a Jew,' Young Girl Tells Her Teacher Father." October 20, 2015. See also "Palestinian Preschool Girl Holds Knife, Says 'I Want to Stab a Jew,'" in the section "Photographs and Videos" below.

Tomlinson, Simon. "World of Walls: How 65 Countries Have Erected Fences on Their Borders – Four Times As Many As When the Berlin Wall Was Toppled – as Governments Try to Hold Back the Tide of Migrants." *MailOnline*. August 21, 2015.

United Nations. "Report of the [UN] Secretary-General's Panel of Inquiry on the 31st May 2010 Flotilla Incident." September 2011. Informally known as the "Palmer Report" after the name of the panel's chairman, Sir Geoffrey Palmer.

———. "The Scope and Application of the Principle of Universal Jurisdiction: Information Provided by Spain" in response to resolution 64/117 of the UN General Assembly. December 19, 2009.

United States Holocaust Museum. "The Nuremberg Race Laws" of 1935.

UPI. "Another Ship Headed to Gaza Damaged." United Press International. June 30, 2011.

Van den hole, Leo. "Anticipatory Self-Defence Under International Law." *American University International Law Review* 19, no. 1 (2003): 69–106.

Walker, Peter, and Owen Bowcott, "Plan for UK to Opt Out of European Convention on Human Rights." *Guardian*. October 4, 2016.

Washington Times. "U.S. Does Not Want to Bomb ISIS Media Headquarters." December 17, 2015.

Webster, Daniel. "Letter of July 27, 1841," from US secretary of state Daniel Webster to Lord Alexander Ashburton, including Enclosure 1 to Mr. Henry Fox, Her Britannic Majesty's Minister to the United States, regarding the seizure and destruction of the merchant vessel *Caroline* (destroyed by the British Navy on December 29, 1837).

Wilner, Michael. "Senator Questions Palestinian Aid Directed to Stipends for Convicted Murders." *Times of Israel*. June 24, 2016.

Wilner, Michael, and Ariel Ben Solomon. "Congressmen Voice Concern over Palestinian Stipend Program for Convicts." *Jerusalem Post*. July 6, 2016.

Winer, Stuart. "Israeli Envoy Calls on UN Chief to Condemn Gaza-Bound Flotilla." *Times of Israel*. June 23, 2015.

Wittes, Benjamin. "Israeli Targeting Procedures and the Concept of Proportionality." *Lawfare*. December 15, 2015

World Bank. "GDP per Capita (Current US$)." 2016.

Worldometers. "Countries in the World by Population (2016)."

Yadron, Danny. "Iranian Hackers Infiltrated Computers of Small Dam in NY." *Wall Street Journal*. December 20, 2015.

Yale Law School. "Hamas Covenant 1988." The Avalon Project: Documents in Law, History and Diplomacy. Lillian Goldman Law Library of the Yale Law School.

———. "The Palestinian National Charter: Resolutions of the Palestine National Council July 1–17, 1968," The Avalon Project: Documents in Law, History and Diplomacy. Lillian Goldman Law Library of the Yale Law School.

Zacks, Yoav, and Liran Antebi, ed. "The Use of Unmanned Military Vehicles in 2033: National Policy Recommendations Based on Technology Forecasting Expert Assessments." Institute for National Security Studies, Memorandum no. 145. December 2014. Available only in Hebrew.

Zero Anthropology. "The Political Economy of the Bullet in Afghanistan." August 18, 2009.

Ziv, Amitai. "Israeli Startups Arm World for the Online Wars to Come." Haaretz. January 14, 2016.

BOOKS, CHAPTERS, AND COMPILATIONS

Antebi, Liran. "Controlling Robots: It's Not Science Fiction." In Landau and Kurz, Arms Control and National Security, 65–80.

Baker, Alan, ed. The Palestinian Manipulation of the International Community. Jerusalem: Jerusalem Center for Public Affairs, 2014.

Ben-Ari, Raphael. "Universal Jurisdiction: Learning the Costs of Political Manipulation." In Baker, Palestinian Manipulation of the International Community, 23–45.

Bible: Deuteronomy, Esther, Isaiah, Leviticus, Psalms, and 1 Samuel.

Bolgiano, David G. and James M. Patterson. Today's Wars: How America's Leaders Have Failed Our Warriors. Mechanicsburg, PA: Stackpole Books, 2012.

Boteach, Shmuley. The Israel Warrior: Fighting Back for the Jewish State from Campus to Street Corner. Jerusalem: Gefen Publishing House, 2016.

Butler, Samuel. Erewhon. London: Trübner, 1872.

Dershowitz, Alan. Terror Tunnels: The Case for Israel's Just War Against Hamas. New York: Rosetta Books, 2014.

Dinniss, Heather Harrison. Cyber Warfare and the Laws of War. New York: Cambridge University Press, 2014.

Elon, Menachem. "Lifnim Mi-Shurat Ha-Din – Acting More Generously than the Law Requires." In Jewish Law: History, Sources, Principles, 1:154–67. Translated from the Hebrew by Bernard Auerbach and Melvin J. Sykes. Philadelphia: Jewish Publication Society, 1994.

Jerusalem Center for Public Affairs. *What Israel Has Learned about Security: Nine IDF Officers Discuss Israel's Security Challenges.* Jerusalem: Jerusalem Center for Public Affairs, 2012.

Junger, Sebastian. *War.* New York: Twelve, 2010.

Kahalani, Avigdor. *A Warrior's Way.* Bnei Brak: Steimatzky, 1999.

Kittrie, Orde F. *Lawfare: Law as a Weapon of War.* New York: Oxford University Press, 2016.

Kuhn, Thomas S. *The Structure of Scientific Revolutions.* Chicago: University of Chicago Press, 1962.

Kyle, Chris, with Jim DeFelice and Scott McEwen. *American Sniper: The Autobiography of the Most Lethal Sniper in U.S. History.* New York: Harper, 2014.

Landau, Emily B., and Anat Kurz, ed. *Arms Control and National Security: New Horizons.* Memorandum no. 135. Tel Aviv: Institute for National Security Studies, 2014.

Lein, Yehezkel, and Eyal Weizman. "Land Grab: Israel's Settlement Policy in the West Bank". B'Tselem, May, 2002.

Popkin, Ruth Shamir. *Jewish Identity: The Challenge of Peoplehood Today.* Jerusalem: Gefen Publishing House, 2015.

Roland, Charles G. *Courage Under Siege: Disease, Starvation and Death in the Warsaw Ghetto.* New York: Oxford University Press, 1992.

Sabel, Robbie. "Manipulating International Law as part of Anti-Israel 'Lawfare.'" In Baker, *Palestinian Manipulation of the International Community*, 13–21.

Schmitt, Michael N., ed. *Tallinn Manual on the International Law Applicable to Cyber Warfare.* Cambridge: Cambridge University Press, 2013.

Segev, Tom. *The Seventh Million: The Israelis and the Holocaust.* New York: Farrar, Straus and Giroux, 1993.

Senor, Dan, and Saul Singer. *Start-Up Nation: The Story of Israel's Economic Miracle.* New York: Hachette Book Group, 2009.

Shaara, Michael. *Killer Angels.* New York: Ballantine Books, 2003.

Singer, P.W. *Wired for War: The Robotics Revolution and Conflict in the 21st Century.* New York: Penguin Books, 2009.

Steinberg, Gerald B. "The Role of the NGOs in the Palestinian Political War

Against Israel." In Baker, *Palestinian Manipulation of the International Community*, 65–78.

Tenenbom, Tuvia. *Catch the Jew!* Jerusalem: Gefen Publishing House, 2015.

Tezyapar, Sinem. "The Abuse of Islam as Part of the Demonization of Israel." In Baker, *Palestinian Manipulation of the International Community*, 99–126.

van Creveld, Martin. *The Age of Airpower*. Philadelphia: Perseus Books Group, 2011.

von Clausewitz, Carl. *On War*. Translated from the German and edited by Michael Howard and Peter Parent. Princeton: Princeton University Press, 1976. Rev. ed. 1984.

Walzer, Michael. *Just and Unjust Wars: A Moral Argument With Historical Illustrations*. 5th ed. New York: Basic Books, 2015.

Yadlin, Amos. "Ethical Dilemmas in Fighting Terrorism." In Jerusalem Center for Public Affairs, *What Israel Has Learned about Security*, 127–133.

LEGAL CASES, STATUTES, AND TREATIES

Amendment to the Spanish law of universal jurisdiction, "Boletín Oficial del Estado, Núm. 63, Sec. 1, Pág. 23027, section 4(a)." https://www.boe.es/boe/dias/2014/03/14/pdfs/BOE-A-2014-2709.pdf.

Bauer v. Mavi Marmara et al. 774 F.3d 1026. (United States Court of Appeals for the District of Columbia Circuit, December 19, 2014). https://www.cadc.uscourts.gov/internet/opinions.nsf/E3AF1833D3CD749085257DB30054B6BF/$file/13-7081-1528227.pdf.

Caroline case (December 29, 1837). (Also known as the *Caroline* affair and as the *Caroline* incident.) The Avalon Project: Documents in Law, History and Diplomacy. Lillian Goldman Law Library of the Yale Law School. http://avalon.law.yale.edu/19th_century/br-1842d.asp.

Fendel v. Inmarsat Inc. et al. Case Number 11-19912CA 15, Circuit Court of the 11th Judicial District, Miami-Dade County, Florida (action filed June 27, 2011). Complaint available at http://www.investigativeproject.org/documents/case_docs/1594.pdf.

Geneva Conventions i–iv of 1949, *The Geneva Conventions of 12 August 1949*. International Committee of the Red Cross, Geneva, Switzerland, October 20, 1980. https://www.icrc.org/eng/assets/files/publications/icrc-002-0173.pdf.

Geneva Convention Additional Protocols i–iii, *Protocols Additional to the Geneva Conventions 12 August 1949*, Additional Protocol i and ii of June 8, 1977, and Additional Protocol iii of December 8, 2005. International Committee of the Red Cross, Geneva, Switzerland, February 5, 2010. https://www.icrc.org/eng/assets/files/other/icrc_002_0321.pdf.

Hague Convention of 1899, *Convention with Respect to the Laws and Customs of War on Land (Hague ii) (29 July 1899)*. http://avalon.law.yale.edu/19th_century/hague02.asp.

Hague Convention of 1907, *Convention Respecting the Laws and Customs of War on Land (Hague iv) (18 October 1907)*. http://avalon.law.yale.edu/20th_century/hague04.asp.

International Court of Justice, *Advisory Opinion Concerning Legal Consequences of the Construction of a Wall in the Occupied Palestinian Territory*, ICJ Reports 2004, p. 136, 9 July 2004 (informally known as the "*Wall* case"). http://www.icj-cij.org/docket/files/131/1671.pdf.

International Court of Justice, *Legality of the Threat or Use of Nuclear Weapons, Advisory Opinion*, ICJ Reports 1996, p. 226, 8 July 1996 (informally known as the "*Nuclear Weapons* case"). http://www.icj-cij.org/docket/index.php?p1=3&p2=4&k=e1&p3=4&case=95.

International Criminal Court, "Situations under investigation." https://www.icc-cpi.int/pages/situations.aspx.

International Criminal Court, "The States Parties to the Rome Statute." https://asp.icc-cpi.int/en_menus/asp/states%20parties/Pages/the%20states%20parties%20to%20the%20rome%20statute.aspx.

Martens Clause, Hague Convention of 1899, Preamble, ninth paragraph. https://www.icrc.org/applic/ihl/ihl.nsf/Article.xsp?action=openDocument&documentId=9FE084CDAC63D10FC12563CD00515C4D. And Hague Convention of 1907, Preamble, eighth paragraph. https://www.icrc.org/applic/ihl/ihl.nsf/Article.xsp?action=openDocument&documentId=BD48EA8AD56596A3C12563CD0051653F.

Mep Costas Mavrides & Cypriots Against Turkish War Crimes, *The complainants v. The Republic of Turkey, Accused of War Crimes*, Communication to the Prosecutor of International Criminal Court regarding the situation in Occupied Cyprus, July 14, 2014. http://israellawcenter.org/wp-content/uploads/2014/11/ICC-Turkey.pdf.

Neutrality Act of 1794, 18 United States Code sec. 962, https://www.law.cornell.edu/uscode/text/18/962.

Nuremberg Military Trials of 1946–1949, *Nazi Conspiracy and Aggression*, "International Military Tribunal at Nuremberg, Opinion and Judgment," Office of United States Chief of Counsel for Prosecution of Axis Criminality, United States Government Printing Office, Washington, D.C., 1947. https://www.loc.gov/rr/frd/Military_Law/pdf/NT_Nazi-opinion-judgment.pdf.

Nuremberg Race Laws of 1935:

Reich Citizenship Law of September 15, 1935 (defining "Reich citizenship" by blood and loyalty). Available at http://avalon.law.yale.edu/imt/1416-ps.asp.

Law for the Protection of German Blood and German Honor of September 15, 1935 (prohibiting marriage or relations between Jews and Germans). Available at https://www.ushmm.org/wlc/en/article.php?ModuleId=10007903.

Law for the Protection of the Hereditary Health of the German People of October 18, 1935 (informally known as the "Marital Health Law" of 1935, prohibiting marriage by people with infectious diseases, mental disease, or genetic defect). Available in German at http://www.verfassungen.de/de/de33-45/ehegesundheit35.htm.

The Reich Citizenship Law: First Regulation of November 14, 1935 (defining "Jew," and denying Jews rights of citizenship, of voting, and of holding public office). Available at http://avalon.law.yale.edu/imt/1417-ps.asp.

Advisory Circular of the Reich and Prussian Minister of the Interior Regarding "Gypsies, Negroes, or their bastard offspring" of November 26, 1935 (prohibiting marriages of Germans with Roma or blacks). Summary at Sybil Morton, "Holocaust: The Gypsies," 161–202, at 162. In *Century of Genocide: Critical Essays and Eyewitness Accounts*, edited by Samuel Totten, William S. Parsons, and Israel W. Charney. 2nd ed. New York: Routledge, 2004. Available at http://www.kurdipedia .org/books/67610.PDF.

Rome Statute of the International Criminal Court, adopted July 17, 1998, entered into force July 1, 2002, creating the ICC (including amendments of June 2010). https://www.icc-cpi.int/nr/rdonlyres/add16852-aee9 -4757-abe7-9cdc7cf02886/283503/romestatuteng1.pdf.

Shurat Ha-Din Israel Law Center, *The complainant v.* Khaled Mashal, *Accused of War Crimes*, Communication to the Prosecutor of the International Criminal Court regarding war crimes committed by Khaled Mashal, September 2, 2014. http://israellawcenter.org/wp-content/uploads /2014/11/ICC-Khaled-Mashal.pdf.

Shurat HaDin – Israel Law Center, *The complainant v.* Mahmoud Abbas (also known as Abu Mazen), *Accused of War Crimes*, Communication to the Prosecutor of the International Criminal Court regarding war crimes committed by Mahmoud Abbas (also known as Abu Mazen), November 11, 2014. http://israellawcenter.org/wp-content/uploads /2014/11/ICC-Complaint-Mahmoud-Abbas.pdf.

Shurat HaDin – Israel Law Center, *The complainant v.* Majid Faraj, *Accused of Crimes Against Humanity*, Communication to the Prosecutor of the International Criminal Court regarding The Crimes Against Humanity committed by Majid Faraj, January 5, 2015. http://israellawcenter.org /wp-content/uploads/2015/01/ICC-Communication-Faraj.pdf.

Spanish Judicial Power Organization Act No. 6/1985 of 1 July (Official Gazette No. 157 of 2 July). Available in Spanish at http://noticias .juridicas.com/base_datos/Admin/lo6-1985.html.

Statute of the International Court of Justice, published by the United Nations on April 16, 1946, and annexed to the Charter of the United Nations. http://www.icj-cij.org/documents/?p1=4&p2=2.

Tokyo War Crimes Trials (1946–1948), *International Military Tribunal for the Far East, Judgment of 4 November 1948*. http://werle.rewi.hu-berlin .de/tokio.pdf, uploaded by Dr. Gerhard Werle, chairman of German and International Criminal Law, Criminal Procedure Law and Criminal History, Faculty of Law, Humboldt University of Berlin, Germany.

Tokyo War Crimes Trials (1946–1948), *Notes, Selected Links, & Bibliography*,

Shira Megerman. http://law2.umkc.edu/faculty/projects/ftrials/tokyo
/tokyolinks.html.

Tribunal Supremo (Supreme Court) of Spain, Criminal Division, Appeal
No. 1979/2009, March 4, 2010 (unofficial translation from the original
Spanish into English). http://ccrjustice.org/sites/default/files/assets
/files/AlDaraj_SupremeCourt_Decision_03.04.2010_ENG.pdf.

United States Constitution, Article 1, Section 9, Clause 3, and Article 1,
Section 10, Clause 1, both references related to bills of attainder. http://
www.archives.gov/exhibits/charters/constitution_transcript.html.

United States v. Ahmad Fathi et al., Sealed Indictment by the Grand Jury of
the United States District Court, Southern District of New York, March
24, 2016. https://www.justice.gov/opa/file/834996/download.

PHOTOGRAPHS AND VIDEOS

American Sniper. Warner Bros. Pictures, 2014. Video clip from the movie,
https://www.youtube.com/watch?v=99k3u9ay1gs.

"The Amoral Revolution in Western Values, and Its Impact on Israel." Lecture by Colonel (ret.) Richard Kemp. May 21, 2015. Begin-Sadat Center
for Strategic Studies, Bar-Ilan University, Ramat Gan, Israel. https://
www.youtube.com/watch?v=IsJDbnZjQik. A transcript of the lecture
is available at http://besacenter.org/perspectives-papers/col-richard
-kemp-the-amoral-revolution-in-western-values-and-its-impact-on
-israel/.

Booth, William. "The 'Humanitarian Aid' Aboard a Recent Flotilla to Gaza
Fit in Two Cardboard Boxes." *Washington Post.* July 1, 2015. https://
www.washingtonpost.com/news/worldviews/wp/2015/07/01/did
-the-flotilla-to-gaza-have-humanitarian-aid-aboard-or-not/. Photograph
also appears in Stuart Winer. "Humanitarian Aid on Gaza Flotilla Fit in
Two Boxes." *Times of Israel.* July 2, 2015. http://www.timesofisrael.com
/humanitarian-aid-on-gaza-flotilla-fit-in-2-boxes/.

"Camp Jihad: Inside UNRWA Summer Camp, 2013." IsraelBehindThe-
News. July 22, 2013, by a television crew hired by the Nahum Bedein
Center for Near East Policy Research, Jerusalem, publisher of www

.IsraelBehindTheNews.com. Video available at https://www.youtube
.com/watch?v=aC1FR5VeuOk, and also at https://www.youtube.com
/watch?v=kbrafPTe_LQ.

"CyCon 2012 – Michael Schmitt: Tallinn Manual Part II." Lecture. NATO
Cooperative Cyber Defence Centre of Excellence, September 29, 2012.
From the Fourth Annual International Conference on Cyber Conflict
(CyCon), June 5–8, 2012, Tallinn, Estonia. https://www.youtube.com
/watch?v=f_TC3y7g4aA.

"Footage Shows Israeli Soldiers Debating Activists before Boarding Gaza-
Bound Boat." Article about the seizure of the *Marianne of Gothenburg*
with embedded video, by Daniel Bernstein. *Times of Israel.* July 1, 2015.
http://www.timesofisrael.com/footage-shows-voyage-interception-of
-gaza-bound-ship/.

"Have Palestinian Leaders Failed Their People?" Interview with chief negotiator for the Palestinians, Saeb Erekat, on the UK television program
Head to Head, Al Jazeera English, February 28, 2014. https://www
.youtube.com/watch?v=-7x0121TzKU. A transcript of the interview is
available at http://www.aljazeera.com/programmes/headtohead/2014
/03/transcript-dr-saeb-erekat-201432611433441126.html.

"Herbert Goldstein." Photograph in US army uniform. Chicago, 1943.

"Israel Law Center (Shurat HaDin) Exposes Flotilla Organizers." Lecture by
anti-Israel activist Adam Shapiro to raise money for Flotilla II, delivered
at Rutgers University during November 2010, six months after Flotilla I
and eight months before Flotilla II, uploaded on July 1, 2011. https://
www.youtube.com/watch?v=0kx5NwxAXVI.

"Israel: Military Robot Snake." June 10, 2009. https://www.youtube.com
/watch?v=8t2nFHjtIJQ

"Palestinian Preschool Girl Holds Knife, Says, 'I Want to Stab a Jew.'" A
conversation between a very young girl and her father, a Jordanian Palestinian teacher. The father posted the video to Facebook on October
16, 2015. The video was translated by the Middle East Media Research
Institute (also known as "MEMRI"), which added English subtitles
and posted the translated version on October 20, 2015. The video is
available at https://www.youtube.com/watch?v=hy-S3hcahZo. See also

"Watch: 'I Want to Stab a Jew,' Young Girl Tells Her Teacher Father," in the "Articles" section above.

"Threats to Israel: Terrorist Funding and Trade Boycotts," Hearing before the Subcommittee on Terrorism, Nonproliferation, and Trade of the Committee on Foreign Affairs House of Representatives, One Hundred Thirteenth Congress, Second Session, March 5, 2014, Serial no. 113–128, Statement by Congressman Dana Rohrabacher (US congressman for the California 48th District), at p. 4 of the transcript. Both the transcript and an audiovisual recording of the hearing are available at http://foreignaffairs.house.gov/hearing/subcommittee-hearing-threats-israel-terrorist-funding-and-trade-boycotts.

Winer, Stuart. "Humanitarian Aid on Gaza Flotilla Fit in Two Boxes." See Booth, William, above.

"Zero Days – Security Leaks for Sale." VPRO Backlight. July 14, 2015. Available at https://www.youtube.com/watch?v=4BTTiWkdT8Q.

Index

260 A Table Against Mine Enemies

About the Author

Larry M. Goldstein is a patent attorney registered with the US Patent and Trademark Office and specializing in information and communication technologies, including computers, communication systems, encryption, and weaponry. Prior to *A Table Against Mine Enemies*, he has written four books about patent quality, patent pools, and the management of patent portfolios. Mr. Goldstein holds a BA from Harvard College, an MBA from the Kellogg School of Management at Northwestern University, and a JD from the University of Chicago Law School. He is a veteran of the Israel Defense Forces and the father of four children serving in the IDF. He may be contacted at goldsteinlawfare@gmail.com.